INFLATION: The price of prosperity

Brian Griffiths

INFLATION:
The price of prosperity

Weidenfeld and Nicolson   London

012597

Weidenfeld and Nicolson
11 St John's Hill London SW11

ISBN 0 297 77028 4

Printed and bound in Great Britain by
Morrison & Gibb Ltd., London and Edinburgh

To my parents
with love and gratitude

Contents

Figures

Acknowledgements

I would like to acknowledge my indebtedness to the countless conversations and discussions on this and related subjects which I have had over the last decade with Harry Johnson and Karl Brunner. I am also grateful for various criticisms which have been made of Part One and Two of the book to Megnhad Desai, of chapter 16 to S. Markowski, and of the book as a whole to Norman Bachop. I would also like to thank Miss Kate Davies for typing an earlier version of the manuscript, and Andrew Wheatcroft and Andrew Best without whom this book would never have reached its present state. I owe a considerable debt to Benjamin Buchan not only for editing the manuscript but also for suggesting substantive improvements to the text.

Lastly I am deeply grateful to my wife Rachel and my children for allowing me the time to write this book and to my wife in particular for reading an earlier version of the manuscript and offering many helpful suggestions.

Preface

The book is the development of a paper which I gave to a conference in the summer of 1972 when inflation was approximately one-third its current rate. It is not addressed primarily to economists but to that ubiquitous breed, the responsible and intelligent layman. Economists have long been concerned with the problem of inflation at a technical level but it is surprising how little has been written for a wider audience. The purpose of this book is to present a comprehensive analysis of the problem in a way that those with interest but without any formal training in economics will hopefully find comprehensible.

In writing on inflation there are two pitfalls to be avoided – moralism and nihilism. Some writers tend to assume that inflation is of such an evil character that it will soon destroy our whole civilization. They may be perfectly right in their judgement but the case nevertheless needs to be argued rather than assumed.

Economists have a tendency to fall into the other trap; being so absorbed with the minutae of the subject, most of all the intricacies of statistical method, they sometimes appear incapable of making statements which have a direct bearing on the affairs of the world. The extent to which I have avoided or fallen into both traps is for the reader to judge.

Although the book is intended to be a comprehensive treatment of the subject, it seeks to present a distinct viewpoint. The case which I wish to argue is that an inflation of the magnitude we are now experiencing in this country is a serious economic problem which has a disquieting effect not simply on economic life but on that of the society as a whole. In suggesting that inflation can only be adequately understood in monetary terms it is a criticism of much of the conventional wisdom on this subject. I believe that in the United Kingdom we have so completely become the prisoners of the Keynesian revolution in economic thought that we still persist in analysing the central problem of our economy as if we lived at the height of the Great Depression. The paradox is that when Keynes himself analysed inflation, which he did in response to the severe inflations of continental Europe in the 1920s, he did so within a completely different context from that in which he dealt with the problem of unemployment, namely that of the quantity theory of money. In this respect therefore the book is not so much anti-Keynesian as a plea for the same intellectual flexibility and pragmatism that Keynes himself exhibited.

Part I

Preliminaries

Part 1

Preliminaries

1 The legacy of John Maynard Keynes

'I find myself moved, not for the first time, to remind contemporary economists that the classical teaching embodied some permanent truths of great significance, which we are liable today to overlook because we associate them with other doctrines which we cannot now accept without much qualification. There are in these matters deep undercurrents at work, natural forces, one can call them, or even the invisible hand, which are operating towards equilibrium. If it were not so, we could not have got on even so well as we have for many decades past.'

J. M. Keynes (1946)

Economic instability poses a grave threat to any political system. It does so because it succeeds in touching the life of the ordinary citizen – and not some, but all – in a way in which a political revolution is rarely able. Whether it is mass unemployment or hyperinflation, and the twentieth century is replete with both, the damage done to the individual and society is evident. By creating an atmosphere of insecurity and futility, by permitting wholesale economic injustice and by giving rise to abject poverty, a permanent scar is left on the social order, which makes for irrationality in politics, which deeply affects the political perspectives of subsequent generations and which, it appears, only the passage of time can change.

In this sense the most significant economic event of the past century in this country was the Great Depression. At its height in the early 1930s over twenty per cent of the labour force was unemployed and in certain parts of the country such as Wales, it rose to over thirty-five per cent.[1] The plight of the unemployed is seen in the dole queues, the soup kitchens, the Jarrow march and through the eyes of a novelist in *The Road to Wigan Pier*. The unemployment of the time was genuinely involuntary. Even if people changed jobs or moved between different regions of the country the prospects for work were just as hopeless. It was the belief that such mass unemployment was incompatible with the institutions of capitalism and democracy which ultimately prompted John Maynard Keynes to write his classic analysis of the problem, *The General Theory of Interest, Employment and Money*.[2]

By contrast with the inter-war years, those since the Second World War have been rightly hailed as a period of remarkable stability and prosperity. Something which on previous evidence seemed unimaginable is now history: since 1945 full employment has been accompanied by continued economic growth throughout the whole of the developed Western world. By contrast with the slump-and-boom business cycles of the nineteenth century which culminated in the mass unemployment of the early 1930s, the post-war years have been one long boom. Centuries of want have been replaced by decades of plenty. Living standards in Britain have doubled in less than thirty years and more rapidly in many other Western countries.

The successful record of the post-war years in providing full employment is usually credited to the ability of governments to control total spending, itself the outcome in the realm of ideas of the Keynesian revolution. In *The General Theory*, Keynes argued that unemployment was the result of a deficiency of spending. Far from being an aberration for an advanced capitalist economy, substantial unemployment could well be the norm, because a free market economy had no inherent properties which would continuously provide full employment for the labour force. As a result, the government had a responsibility to maintain total spending at a level which would provide work for all who actively sought it, something which it was in a position to do by engaging in deficit spending and fiscal policy. For example, if expenditure on private consumption fell, the government could either raise its own expenditures or cut taxes and so counteract the effect on unemployment of a fall in demand from the private sector of the economy. Since Sir Kingsley Wood's budget of 1941, which first employed a system of national income accounting based on Keynesian ideas to predict the likely deficiency between total spending and full-employment output and then offset such a deficiency by appropriate budgetary changes, successive governments have used fiscal policy to 'manage' the economy. In the United States Keynesian policy was formally adopted in the 'New Economics' of the Kennedy administration of 1960 and in Germany in the mid-1960s under the Finance minister, Professor Karl Schiller.

The post-war years have seen the high tide of Keynesianism. Throughout these years the attractiveness of fiscal policy led to the neglect of monetary policy. From the time of Dr Dalton and the 'cheap money' policy of 1946 the accepted view, developed from the Keynesian framework, has been that fiscal policy and credit controls are far more powerful than monetary policy in affecting spending, and that in any case the money supply plays a passive role in the economy, accommodating itself to the needs of business and transactions. Money adjusts to the economy, not the economy to money. This view was very clearly stated by the Radcliffe Report of 1959, the only post-war royal commission on the working of the monetary system.[3] Because money was impossible to either define or measure, in view of the proliferation of near-money substitutes, its control was both very difficult and unnecessary. The important instruments of monetary policy were the level of interest rates and direct controls on credit. This disregard of money in Keynesian economics, which developed over the 1940s and 1950s, is in sharp contrast to the view of Keynes himself. If we interpret Keynes' insights in *The General Theory* in the light of his earlier works and especially his contribution to the Macmillan Committee (1931), it becomes clear that Keynes did believe in the importance of monetary policy, though he had doubts regarding the ability of central bankers to use it properly.[4]

But as the post-war years have produced their greater affluence, a problem equally if not more intractable than unemployment has presented itself – inflation. Accelerating inflation has now become the major economic problem of every capitalist country in the world. During the 1950s and early 1960s the rate of inflation for most advanced countries was little more than two to three per cent. By the late 1960s the figure had risen to four per cent. But by 1974 inflation was raging throughout the most industrialized countries: in Britain it was over 20 per cent, in France 14 per cent, in Italy between 17 and 20 per cent, in Holland nearly 10 per cent, Belgium 13 per cent, in the United States between 10 and 12 per cent and in Japan 24 per cent.

The gravity of inflation is not its strictly economic effects but its wider social and political implications. The fact of prices rising at over 20 per cent per year has meant that hyperinflation is not a subject restricted to the reminiscences of those who lived through the history of the Weimar Republic but is being seriously and somewhat nervously debated as a possible if not probable outcome in Britain. At stake is not just the disruption of three decades of economic growth, or even the future of capitalism, but the very existence of a free society. The most gloomy prospect of all which is at present being considered is that if the inflation accelerates democracy itself could well be at stake.

Since the Keynesian revolution of the 1930s a consensus has developed in Britain with respect both to the cause of inflation and the way it should be tackled. It is a view which examines the cause of inflation in an insular rather than a global setting, which emphasizes non-monetary rather than monetary factors, which stresses the importance of the social-political rather than economic context of wage claims, and which is convinced of the necessity of prices and incomes policies as the only way of bringing inflation under control. One characteristic of this view is its emphasis on the 'newness' of the current inflation. It is held that the current inflation is different from previous inflations not only in magnitude but also in character; in particular, social and political factors rather than economic are used to explain its origin. Whereas, previously, emphasis was placed on the central banks' use of the printing presses as a means of financing government deficit spending, attention is now focussed on the conflict between labour and capital over the division of gross national product between wages and profits, and on the internecine strife of the trade-union movement. At our present stage of capitalism the traditional analysis is somehow outmoded and redundant. The unmistakable feeling we are given is that the present inflation is quite different from all others in our history. A recent book on the subject by Aubrey Jones, former chairman of the now defunct Prices and Incomes Board, was entitled, and not without significance, *The New Inflation*. And in a stimulating article with the same title, Professor E. J. Mishan, a distinguished British economist, confesses that while he would have accepted the traditional view until the mid-1960s he is unable to do so any longer.[5] One extremely undesirable consequence of the rejection of the traditional monetary explanation is that trying to discover the cause of inflation has become a sort of economic witch-hunt, in which any undesirable group is declared to be the source of inflationary pressure and the enemy of society – militant trade unions (worse still, shop stewards), property specu_ lators, asset-strippers, the banks, the City, foreigners and big business generally; something which in turn can only lead to increasing distrust and conflict between these various groups.

Not surprisingly, if the cause of inflation is held to be sociopolitical rather than economic, the remedy will be couched in similar terms. The reactions of most governments and the recommendations of most commentators have been to impose wage and price controls. Since the mid-1960s Austria, Australia, Belgium, Canada, Denmark, Finland, France, Germany, Holland, Japan, Norway, Sweden, the USA and ourselves have all resorted to controlling inflation through prices and incomes policies. Despite the increasing disillusion with these policies, mainly because of their limited success and their undesirable side-effects, they are still considered by many, especially in Britain, as essential to dealing with the problem. No discussion of the subject in *The Economist* or the National Institute of Economic and Social Research's *Review* is ever complete until traditional theory has been debunked, some reflation advocated and a return to price and wage controls encouraged.

In the context of the present consensus, the purpose of this book is to take a fresh look at the problem of inflation and to question the basis of the present crisis and of the policies advocated to remedy it. The theme of the book is that inflation is a serious problem, that the character of advanced capitalist economies is not sufficiently different from earlier stages of capitalism to jettison the importance of money in explaining the inflationary process, and that any attempt therefore to explain the current United Kingdom and world inflation in a predominantly non-monetary framework is seriously deficient. Put in a slightly different way, it is to argue that the Keynesian framework, as presented in *The General Theory*, while possibly appropriate in explaining the behaviour of an economy with mass unemployment is quite inappropriate in explaining the origins of inflation in a world of full employment. The deficiency becomes apparent when it is realized that Keynes assumed without any real explanation the prevailing level of wages and prices. But the explanation of this is the heart of the problem of inflation.

It is surely not without significance that when Keynes, earlier in his life, and before the onset of the Great Depression, sought to explain the other major kind of instability of the twentieth century –

the hyperinflations of continental Europe after the First World War – he did so within the framework of a monetary model, in which the cause of inflation was the excessive creation of money by governments. This is very clearly presented in *The Economic Consequences of the Peace* (1919) and *A Tract on Monetary Reform* (1923). The post-war years may be characterized as a period in which we have successfully applied the prescriptions of deficit spending and fiscal policy, and therefore maintained full or even over-full employment, but have in the process created for ourselves a problem which that whole way of thinking is singularly unequipped to solve.

The recognition, however, that inflation is invariably a monetary phenomenon, caused by an excessive creation of money, is an analysis of only part of the problem. In view of the fact that the money supply can be controlled by the Bank of England an equally important problem concerns the reasons *why* governments increase the money supply at the rate they do, especially if, as seems likely, they are responding to the preferences of the electorate. The fact that governments expand the money supply as a response to political pressures makes the issue of inflation highly political. A monetary explanation of the inflationary process couched only in terms of the relationship between the rate of change of the retail price index and the previous rate of change of some standard definition of the money stock, without any reference to the institutional peculiarities of a society and especially to the political factors to which governments respond, is anatomically correct, but lifeless. In the final analysis, both in origin and control, inflation is a political problem. Money is crucial to understanding the mechanism, but politics is just as crucial to grasping the motivation.

This book is divided into five Parts, each of which deals with a different aspect of the subject. After an introduction, a chapter on the problem of defining and measuring inflation and a historical discussion of inflation, Part II deals with various explanations of the cause of inflation, monetary and non-monetary, and with one of the basic techniques for analysing inflation – the Phillips curve. Next there follows a discussion of the effects of inflation. How serious a problem is it? How likely is it that the current inflation will accelerate into a runaway inflation and lead to a collapse of the currency? What is the relationship between the instability of prices and political instability? Part IV discusses the question of correcting for the effects of inflation and the net advantages to be gained from the more widespread use of cost-of-living adjustment clauses in contracts. The last Part examines the major policies which have been recommended to control inflation – reform of the labour market, prices and incomes policies and deflation. Then we consider whether the experience of the Iron Curtain countries offers an alternative. The final chapter attempts to draw the whole book together, and to argue in favour of certain policies, but is also more speculative in that it discusses the relationship between price stability and political stability.

2 Defining inflation

'A definition is either tautological and thus empty or not tautological and hence false.'

Ernest Gellner

Inflation has been variously defined. In the inflationary period following the Second World War, *The Economist* coined the expression 'too much money chasing too few goods'. Jacques Rueff relates that for him in the Ecole Nationale in the 1920s it was typically thought of as 'an increase in the amount of currency in circulation'.[1] Others have defined it as a condition of generalized excess demand for stocks of goods and flows of real income; a rise in the per capita money stock or flow of money income; a fall in the purchasing power of money and an excess of wage claims over productivity growth. Inflation is best defined, however, *as a sustained rise in the general level of prices*. Similarly, deflation is best defined as a sustained fall in the general level of prices. The prices which are typically included in this definition are those of currently produced goods and services; they do not include those of assets.

Each part of this definition is important. In the first place, inflation is a rise in the *general* price level. This does not mean that the price of all goods and services must increase by the same proportion. Some may be rising more rapidly than others – because of bad harvests, speculation, changing technology, or the imposition of subsidies, taxes, tariffs and government controls. The important fact about inflation, however, is that while relative prices may change for a variety of reasons, the average level of all prices continues to rise. A second aspect of the definition which is important is that it is a *sustained* rise in the general price level. If the price level were to rise for a few months and then remain at a higher level, such an increase would not normally be referred to as inflation. From the viewpoint of public policy, it is helpful to be able to distinguish unique adjustments in the price level resulting from, for example, a temporary reduction in output, such as the three-day working week in early 1974 in the United Kingdom, or the French occupation of the Ruhr in 1923, or a more permanent fall in output as occurred following the Black Death 1348–9, from a persistent rise in the price level which continues month after month. The main advantage of this definition over others is that it is neutral with respect to the cause of inflation and the most appropriate policy for bringing it under control. If inflation is defined as too much money chasing too few goods, or as a growth in the stock of money per unit of output, the dice is loaded in favour of a monetary theory of inflation, implying that it can be controlled only by reducing the rate of growth of the money stock. On the other hand, if the definition runs in terms of wages and productivity, the obvious implication is that the major factor causing inflation is trade-union bargaining power pushing up wages, which can only be halted by some sort of incomes policy.

Not only has inflation been variously defined, but it has also been variously categorized. Adjectives such as creeping, trotting, galloping, rapid, chronic, explosive, runaway and hyper have all been used to separate the pace of various inflations. The inflation of between two and three per cent which prevailed in the United Kingdom and the United States for most of the 1950s and early 1960s was frequently referred to as creeping inflation; the Latin American inflations of the same period and later have been described as chronic; hyperinflation is usually used to refer to periods of exceptionally rapid rising prices such as those of Continental Europe in the inter-war years. Inflations are also classed with respect to cause; wage inflation is the perverse result of trade-union activity; profit inflation, of the pricing policies of the large corporations; and imported inflation, of the fact that the rest of the world is inflating more rapidly than the domestic economy. In addition, there is the inflationary *spiral*, of wages chasing prices and prices wages, and the inflationary *gap*, which enjoyed great vogue in the immediate post-Second World War years, referring to the difference between money GNP and full-employment GNP with a constant price level. The relatively recent and uncommonly ugly sounding 'stagflation' (another innovation from *The Economist*) refers to a combination of inflation and low growth in real GNP. Yet another distinction is between *open* and *repressed* inflation. In the former, the prices which enter the price index are those resulting from the free play of market forces; while in the latter, prices and wages are determined administratively so that their increase is a distorted estimate of true inflationary pressure. An example of a repressed inflation occurred in the United Kingdom economy between 1939 and 1951. As a consequence of the war most of the prices of consumer products were officially fixed and excess demand was eliminated through queueing, the use of ration books and black market prices. The measured rate of inflation of the period was as a result, a poor guide of the true inflationary pressure.

One particularly common euphemism at present for inflation is *reflation*. Reflation is a good word in modern political economy. It is always desirable because in the short run it increases real gross national product and reduces unemployment. If, however, the reflation begins at near full capacity, and since the Great Depression no Western economies have ever been really outside this range, such a policy must invariably produce greater inflation. In most contexts in which it is used, therefore, this word should be read to mean increased real output in the short run plus a greater rate of inflation over the slightly longer run.

Exactly the same proliferation of words is used with respect to falling prices. *Disinflation* is the reduction or elimination of inflation. This is not to be confused with *deflation*, which is a reduction in the level of real economic activity in an economy. A *depression* exists when unemployment is high and capital unused for a substantial period of time, while a *recession* is a less severe form of depression. Needless to say, recession is typically used euphemistically for depression.

Measurement: the choice of index

The rate of inflation in a modern economy is measured by index numbers. In view of the fact that national economic policy is at least partly changed in response to the rate of inflation and that many wage contracts, state pensions and, in future, some part of National Savings are all adjusted in line with the rate of inflation, the choice of the index and, in particular, the fact that it should accurately reflect inflationary pressure, is important. The most common price indices are the retail price index, or, as it is usually referred to, the cost of living index; the wholesale price index and the GNP implicit deflator. All of these indices have certain biases, contain certain defects and, over short periods of time, may behave quite differently.[2]

The purpose of the retail price index is to measure the change in the cost of living to the consumer as a result of rising prices. The index is made up by observing each month the changes in the prices of those goods which are typically consumed by households. The items are chosen on the basis of a government family expenditure survey, and the weights given to various items are a reflection of their importance in the household budget; for example, food, which forms an important part of the family budget, is given a correspondingly large weighting. The index covers services as well as goods and prices include value added tax.

Various criticisms have been made of the retail price index as a measure of inflation. One constant criticism is that it fails to reflect the quality changes which are constantly taking place in consumer goods, such as changes in style and improved technical efficiency, and that this produces a systematic upward bias in the index. The impact which such a bias may have can be judged from the fact that the Stigler Committee, which reviewed the United States price statistics in 1961, concluded that if quality changes had been correctly measured over the 1950s, there would have been no increase in the price level at all, so that the annual inflation of between one and two per cent which did take place was less a reflection of excess demand in the economy as of the continual improvement in the quality of consumer goods.[3] Another criticism of the retail price index is that it is very slow to reflect the lower prices which result from improved methods of distribution, such as the establishment of supermarkets and discount stores. The compilation of the index also tends to be sluggish in adding new products and subtracting old items from the typical basket of goods. One other factor which it is claimed tends to produce an upward bias is the use of base year weights in compiling the index. Because the weights are only adjusted infrequently, they fail to reflect the changing pattern of consumer expenditures, especially when consumers switch their expenditure to those products which are relatively cheaper. During a period of price controls, the index is likely to be further biased. As the prices which most incomes policies are interested in controlling are those which most directly affect voters, price controls are most likely to be imposed and subsidies most likely to be given to those products whose prices are most heavily weighted in the retail price index. For example, in the United Kingdom in the fiscal year 1974/5 it is estimated that the food subsidies of approximately £500 million have kept the price index down by $1\frac{1}{2}$ percentage points. Similarly, the fact that the nationalized industries are running a substantial deficit over the same period is because the prices they charge for their products and services have been held down artificially as part of government policy. The effect is once again to introduce a distortion, so that the movement of the retail price index over this period is not an accurate reflection of market condition.

The wholesale price index in the United Kingdom is made up from a set of carefully defined prices, taken to be representative of those products purchased and manufactured by United Kingdom industry. Two wholesale price indices are produced: one for output prices and the other for raw materials purchased by broad sections of industry. The use of the wholesale price index as a general measure of inflation has come under quite severe criticism. In the first place, it is claimed that its frame of reference has little economic meaning. Unlike the retail price index, the transactions which are recorded by this index do not cover either a cross-section of the economy or a particular set of producers, or even some special subsection of producers. The index also includes duplication; the same index takes into account an increase in raw material prices which are then passed on to intermediate goods, and finally to finished products. In addition to this, the prices used have various defects; for certain products which are made to order, such as ships, aircraft and heavy industrial equipment, no market price exists and for other products prices are frequently list prices rather than transaction prices, the difference depending on a variety of discounts and allowances. The true price in an economic sense is that which effectively takes place in transactions, so that list prices under these circumstances are misleading. Like the retail price index, this index also suffers from the problem of having to account for quality changes.

One advantage of the wholesale price index is that because it covers raw materials and capital goods, it is a better measure of inflation for business. Another is that because it tends to be more sensitive to economic pressures as they directly affect companies and traders, in the sense for example that the index will readily reflect a predicted bad harvest or speculation in the commodity markets, it tends to be used as an indicator of the future course of inflation for the consumer. One particular piece of evidence of the sensitivity of the wholesale price index to basic economic pressures is the way it responds to the probability of wage and price controls being introduced. If businessmen expect that the imposition of controls will tend to freeze existing profit margins, they have every reason to raise the list price of the product but continue trading at the existing transactions price. The wholesale price index shows an increase but the true transactions price is unchanged. If a freeze is subsequently introduced but costs continue to rise, the firm retains the option of being able to increase the price at which it does business. There is some evidence that this happened to a certain extent in the United States in 1973 when there was considerable speculation about the reimposition of a price freeze by President Nixon.

The third most commonly used index is the GNP implicit deflator. This index is a measure of the price level of all final goods and services which enter the gross national product including those of the government sector. Because of this, its coverage is much greater than either of the other indices. The index is in fact the ratio between the current money value of GNP and the current real value of GNP. The current real value of GNP is derived by weighting the quantities of goods and services in the current year by base-year prices. The index is used much more in the United States than in the United Kingdom and because of its broad coverage it tends to be a favourite of economists. As with the other indices, it too is open to criticism. One weakness is that because it is difficult to construct any price series for the output of government and the construction industry (new buildings tend to be heterogenous and have changing quality) it is difficult to allow for increases in output per man hour, which means that the index tends to overestimate inflation. The most difficult item of all to deal with is the wage and salary bill of the government. For any given annual increase, it becomes extremely difficult to impute some figure for the increase in output to this sector; yet this is important in arriving at the measure of inflation.

By far the most accurate and meaningful measure for general use is the retail price index. It relates to a well-defined group within the economy (households) and is a reasonably accurate index of the true prices at which transactions take place. Despite the various biases to which it is subject it is the most reliable index of all. The wholesale price index is a useful complement in that it acts as a sort of 'bell weather'. While the GNP implicit deflator has a much broader coverage, this is unfortunately at the cost of accuracy.

3 Inflation through history

'Those who cannot remember the past are condemned to repeat it.'
George Santayana

Inflation is not a new problem.[1] One of the earliest recorded periods of a rapid rise in the price level was in ancient Greece around 330 BC, following Alexander the Great's conquest of Persia and his transference of the newly acquired gold to Greece. Gold replaced silver as money, and prices and wages rose throughout the whole of the Hellenic empire. Despite this example, the Greek city states, even when they were close to bankruptcy, did not have a history of coinage debasement. The Roman experience, by contrast, was quite different. In the two hundred years before the Punic Wars the copper coinage of the empire was debased. Then for the next two hundred years after this during which silver was introduced, both copper and silver were debased by minting coins with an increasing proportion of alloys. Gold was first introduced as a part of the coinage by Augustus in about 30 BC and from then on until the decline of the empire there was a succession of debasement and inflation. For example, in AD 214 the denarius had approximately a forty per cent silver content. In that year, however, Emperor Caracella replaced it as the standard means of payment by a double denarius which was only one and a half times the value of a single denarius. Over the next fifty years the double denarius degenerated into a copper coin with just a wash of silver. The most serious debasement of all was in Gallienus's reign (AD 253–68), which one numismatic authority J. R. Porteous has described as 'almost as intense as that of Germany in 1923 and far more widespread'.[2] Even after this period inflation raged and was one of the main factors leading to Diocletian's reform of the currency. One other indicator of the different rates of inflation in Greece and Rome is the different levels of interest on 'normal loans'. In Greece the interest rate fell from about 16 per cent in 550 BC to 6 per cent in 250 BC and then remained virtually constant until 50 BC, while in the Roman empire it rose from a level of 4 per cent in AD 50 to over 12 per cent in AD 250. Even though interest rates are affected by many factors other than inflation, nevertheless one cannot help feeling that the fact that rates were falling in Greece but rising in Rome was not unconnected with the quite different underlying trends in the rates of inflation.

Following the decline of Rome, Europe sank into the Dark Ages. The empire disintegrated into a set of barbarian kingdoms which invaded and plundered each other. International trade declined and from the fifth to the thirteenth century we know very little of the behaviour of wages, prices or interest rates. For the Mediaeval and subsequent periods, however, we have much better information. The behaviour of prices in Britain from the mid-thirteenth century to the present day is shown in Figure 1. The price index relates to a composite commodity, made up of the main elements of a typical consumer's budget – bread, meat, butter, drink, fuel, cloth and so on in southern England. Although this index is subject to a number of limitations – the prices are mainly wholesale not retail, there are certain gaps of a year or two at a time which are filled by inter-polation and no allowance is made for quality changes – it never-theless gives a reliable indication of the major periods of inflation, deflation and price stability over seven centuries.

A number of features of British inflation, which can be seen from Figure 1, stand out as being important. Over two long periods, each of approximately a hundred and thirty years, 1380–1510 and 1630–1760, there is a remarkable stability of the price level. Throughout these periods however the price level did not remain the same from year to year. Over a period of a few years prices tended to move according to whether harvests were good or bad. But over the periods as a whole the average level of prices from decade to decade was remarkably constant. There are also two other periods, 1270–1380 and 1815–1914, when the price level prevailing at the end of

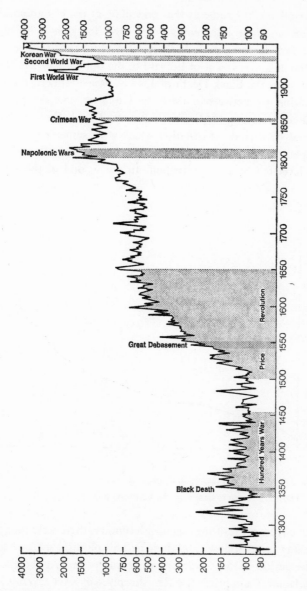

Figure 1. **Inflation since Simon de Montfort**
(a) The price of a composite unit of consumables in Southern England, 1264–1950
Source: E.H. Phelps Brown and Sheila V. Hopkins, 'Seven Centuries of the Price of Consumables compared with Builders' Wage Rates', *Economica*, November 1956.

the period was the same as that prevailing at the beginning, though in these cases the intervening years show far greater fluctuations. In the first of these periods there were rapid inflations associated with the misgovernment of Edward II, the outbreak of the Hundred Years' War, the Black Death of 1348–9, which reduced the English population by between a third or a quarter and the period immediately preceding the Peasants' Revolt of 1381. Each of these was followed by periods of deflation which were sometimes severe. For example, between 1284 and 1289 and between 1370 and 1379 the price level fell by nearly one-half. In the second of these periods,

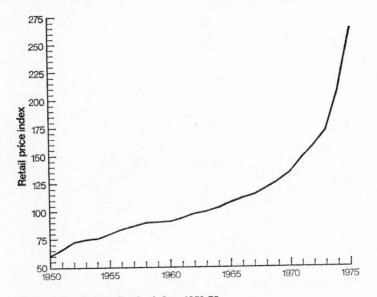

Figure 1 (b). **The retail price index, 1950-75**
Note: The 1975 figure is based on the first nine months of the year.

which covers most of the nineteenth century, there were long periods of falling prices followed by short periods of fairly sharp rises. Most of the period 1815–50 was one of falling prices. At the end of the Napoleonic Wars prices fell very sharply – by over seventy per cent in ten years – while for the remainder of the period the fall was much more gentle. The period 1875–1900 was also one of gently falling prices.

Another feature which can be seen very clearly from Figure 1 is the Price Revolution of the Tudor and early Stuart period (1500–1650). By modern standards the inflation of this period was fairly small, averaging no more than two per cent per annum. But against the background of the price stability of the fourteenth and fifteenth centuries it was substantial, and it included periods of fairly rapid inflation. By the 1550s the average level of agricultural prices was about two and a half times the level of forty years previously. Even industrial prices, which rose less rapidly than agricultural prices, were in the 1550s ninety-five per cent above their level of twenty years earlier. The most rapid and notorious inflation of this period was the Great Debasement of 1542–51, during which prices rose by sixty-five per cent. Between May 1542 and mid-1551 Henry VIII and his son by Jane Seymour, Edward VI, carried out a substantial debasement of the gold and silver coinage, largely because of the fiscal pressures to which they were subject. Over these nine years the money supply more than doubled. This was achieved by the Mint reducing the weight of re-minted coins, lowering their gold and silver content, and increasing the nominal value of existing coins by assigning them higher value, as well as melting down plate and ornament taken from the ransacked monasteries and priories.

The Price Revolution of the sixteenth and early seventeenth centuries was not confined to England. It was a noticeable trend in most other European countries. Throughout the sixteenth century prices in terms of silver (which tend to slightly underestimate prices in terms of the money of account)* rose by about 1·0 per cent per annum in England and France, 1·2 per cent in Spain and 0·8 per cent in Saxony. The origin of the Price Revolution has been a matter of considerable controversy among economic historians. One theory holds that the basic cause was the increase in the supply of gold and silver from the Spanish colonies of the New World, which led by 1660 to a doubling of the European stock of gold and a tripling of the stock of silver (initially the precious metals would reach Spain, leading to a rise in Spanish imports and an outflow of specie to other trading nations). The other major theory asserts that the inflation was caused by non-monetary factors, and in particular by an

---

* Prices expressed in terms of money of account refer to the accounting units in which prices were typically expressed, e.g. pounds, shillings and pence in England, *livres, sols* or *sous*, and *deviers* in France.

increased demand for Spanish exports, especially wool, the result of increases in population growth.

Many of the periods of sharply rising prices have been connected with the increased demand for resources resulting from wars; the beginning of the Hundred Years' War (1327), the English civil war (1642–8), the war with France (1689–97), the War of Spanish Succession (1701–13), the Seven Years' War (1756–63), the war with France and the Napoleonic Wars (1793–1815), the Crimean War (1854–6), the Boer War (1899–1902), the First World War (1914–18), the Second World War (1939–45), the Korean War (1950–53) and the Vietnam War. During the Napoleonic Wars prices rose very sharply. Between 1793 and 1813 they more than doubled and over the two years 1799–1801 they rose by more than fifty per cent. It should be remembered that the Bank of England went off the gold standard in 1797 and returned to it again in 1821 at the pre-war parity. Between 1914 and 1918 prices more than doubled and between 1914 and 1920 they tripled. At the beginning of the Second World War there was a further bout of rapid inflation. Between 1939 and 1941 the price level nearly doubled. After that the statistics have little meaning because of the controls. The other interesting feature of Figure 1 is that it shows clearly the inflationary character of the period since the beginning of the Second World War. Never in the previous three centuries has there been such a rapid and sustained rise in the price level. As we shall see later, the world inflation of the late 1960s and early 1970s has been associated with the financing by the United States of the Vietnam War. Another fact which emerges from examining the behaviour of prices over such a long period of time is the magnitude of the present inflation by contrast with earlier periods of inflation. The three most severe inflations in the past were the Great Debasement, the period of the war with France (1798–1801) and the First World War. But at the height of Henry VIII's debasement (1548–51) the rate of inflation was only 16 per cent per annum and during the war with France (1798–1801) only 23 per cent. During the First World War the rate of inflation averaged nearly 30 per cent. We can certainly conclude that the present inflation is the greatest peace-time inflation in our history and that there is only one period in our history of more rapid inflation.

One of the most interesting features of price rises in European countries up to the nineteenth century and of Europe and America since then has been the way in which major periods of rising prices have taken place at approximately the same time in all countries. In the half century before the Napoleonic Wars, prices rose gradually (around one per cent per year) in most countries for which there is reliable evidence – Spain, Valencia, New Castile, England, France and the American Colonies. The period of the French Revolution and the Napoleonic Wars was inflationary, with inflation averaging nearly three per cent in Great Britain and just over three per cent in the United States and Germany. The first half of the nineteenth century was a general period of deflation, with prices falling in Britain between 1815 and 1850, and in the United States by an average of just over two per cent, in Germany by nearly two per cent and in France by one per cent. The period 1850–73 was again a period of rising prices followed, till the end of the century, by falling prices. The inflation before and during the Great War was quite general, though the experience immediately following when there was a return to floating exchange rates was not. Some countries, most notably Austria, Germany, Hungary, Poland and Russia, experienced hyperinflation while others such as Britain experienced a sharp deflation. Between 1920 and 1922 prices fell by a total of fifty-five per cent. The deflation accompanying the Great Depression was, however, general and since the end of the Second World War all Western countries have experienced continuous inflation. Again, following the Vietnam War inflation has accelerated in all countries.

Various explanations have been put forward to explain this coincidence in timing. The monetary explanation emphasizes the creation of world money with fixed exchange rates, in particular the role of gold under the gold standard and the redistribution of gold between countries whose price levels are different. Inflation in the world as a whole is explained on the basis of the discovery of new gold, for example as in the New World in the sixteenth century and in the United States and South America in the mid-nineteenth century. Periods of more rapid inflation tend to occur when the gold standard has been suspended, for example during major international wars. Other explanations of secular inflation emphasize non-monetary factors such as bad harvests, technological improvements and more rapid rates of economic growth.

Hyperinflations afford some of the most fascinating episodes in the history of prices – for example during the French Revolution, Weimar Germany and the immediate post-Second World War in Hungary. Details of these, however, are left until chapter 9.

Part II

Causes

4 Money and monetarism

'It seems a maxim almost self-evident that the price of everything depends on the proportion between commodities and money.'

David Hume, Of Money (*1752*)

Until the Great Depression of the inter-war years and the publication in 1936 by Keynes of his classic analysis of the problem of mass unemployment in advanced capitalist economies, the accepted explanation of inflation was the quantity theory of money. According to the quantity theory, inflation could be explained only in monetary terms; too much money chasing too few goods. Changes in the prices of individual products might change for a host of reasons; changing technology, changing consumer preference, the imposition of government taxes and subsidies, a change in external tariffs and the extent of protection from foreign competitors. But all these were unconnected with changes in the stock of money. Persistently rising prices could only result from continuous and excessive increases in the stock of money, and, as typically happens during hyperinflation, by a flight from money as well. Similarly persistent deflation could only be explained in terms of a falling money stock and, if the process is sufficiently rapid, by individuals hoarding money.

The quantity theory has a long and distinguished history. It was the theory of Hume, Smith, Ricardo, Jevons, Marshall, Wicksell and Fisher.[1] In the Mercantilist writings of the late sixteenth century the analysis of inflation was closely related to a country's stock of gold and its balance of payments. A discovery of gold in one country would lead to an increase in income and the domestic price level, which in turn, by stimulating the growth of real national income and reducing the price of imports relative to domestically produced goods, would produce a surplus of imports over exports, which could be financed by a bullion outflow. The country receiving the new gold would then find that its prices were rising and in turn that its balance of payments was moving into deficit. The process would be complete only when the prices of commodities had risen proportionately to the newly mined gold. Many elements of the modern quantity theory were set out a little later by David Hume in his essay 'Of Money', published in 1752, in which he observed that 'the price of commodities are always proportioned to the plenty of money' and that 'the high price of commodities be a necessary consequence of the increase of gold and silver'.[2] One of the most interesting aspects of Hume's analysis was the way in which an increased stock of money had an initial impact on production and trade.

> Accordingly we find, that, in every kingdom, into which money begins to flow in greater abundance than formerly, every thing takes a new face: labour and industry gain life; the merchant becomes more enterprising, the manufacturer more diligent and skilful, and even the farmer follows his plough with greater alacrity and attention. This is not easily to be accounted for, if we consider only, the influence which a greater abundance of coin has in the kingdom itself, by heightening the prices of commodities, and obliging every one to pay a greater number of these little yellow or little white pieces for every thing he purchases. And as to foreign trade, it appears, that great plenty of money is rather disadvantageous, by raising the price of every kind of labour.[2]

The dilemma was to be explained by the fact that it takes time before increased money circulates throughout the whole economy. 'At first no alteration is perceived; by degrees the price rises, first of one commodity, then of another; till the whole at last reaches a just proportion with the new quantity of specie which is in the kingdom. In my opinion it is only in this interest or intermediate situation, between the acquisition of money and the rise of prices, that the increasing quantity of gold and silver is favourable to the industry'.[2]

In the late eighteenth and early nineteenth centuries David Ricardo restated the theory again in the context of an international economy, noting, as previous writers had done, the difference between the initial and ultimate effects of an increase in the money supply. 'If by the discovery of a new mine, by the abuse of banking, or by any other cause, the quantity of money be greatly increased, its ultimate effect is always to raise the prices of commodities in proportion to the increased quantity of money; but there is probably always an interval during which some effect is always produced on the rate of interest'.[3]

The most important formulations of the modern quantity theory were written in the late nineteenth and early twentieth centuries; the main contributions being by Knut Wicksell in Sweden, Irving Fisher in America and Alfred Marshall in England. In *Interest and Prices* (1898) and *Lectures* (1906), Wicksell shows the way in which money affects expenditure and in turn prices under two extreme kinds of monetary systems; a pure cash system in which money is either metal or else bank deposits backed by hundred per cent reserves and a pure credit system in which money is bank deposits backed by hundred per cent credit. The distinctive feature of Wicksell's contribution is to show how in a world of credit and interest rates, a change in the stock of money affects prices indirectly by its effect on market rates of interest. Irving Fisher, in the *Purchasing Power of Money* (1911), laid out the quantity theory in terms of the now famous quantity equation $MV = PT$, in which M is the stock of money, V is the transactions velocity of circulation of money, P is an index of the aggregate price level and T is the total number of transactions. This simple formulation has proved a remarkably useful way of looking at the aggregate impact which money has on the economy. In the next section we shall explore it in more detail. The third major contribution was that of Marshall and the Cambridge School, including such names as Lavington, Pigou, Robertson and pre-Depression Keynes.[4] They explained the influence of money in terms of the principles of supply and demand. Money is valuable not because of its intrinsic value (in the case of paper money this may be very small) but because it can be used to buy products and services which are valuable in themselves. For a given state of technology and habits it can be assumed that society wishes to hold a certain proportion of its income in the form of wealth or, in other words, that a demand for money exists which depends on wealth or income. The supply of money is assumed to be under the control of the central bank. When people find that they are holding a greater amount of money than they require they will dispose of it and so raise the level of spending, either directly by consumption and investment spending or indirectly via the capital market. Similarly when people find that they do not have enough money, they restrict their spending in order to augment their money holdings. But because in the aggregate the economy by itself can neither get rid of nor increase the stock of money, it is the price level which will change in response to changes in expenditure. One of the clearest statements of this version of the quantity theory is contained in Keynes' classic work *A Tract on Monetary Reform*.

As a consequence of the Great Depression and the successful revolution brought about by Keynesian ideas, the quantity theory fell into general disrepute and disuse, especially in the 1940s and 1950s. Its gradual rehabilitation under the label of 'monetarism' is largely associated with the work of Professor Milton Friedman at the University of Chicago; though it is only fair to mention the important work which has also been contributed by Professors Brunner and Meltzer and the research department of the Federal Reserve Bank of St Louis.[5] In his classic restatement of the quantity theory (1956) Friedman claimed that Chicago was one of the few universities which throughout the nineteen-thirties and forties did not succumb to Keynesianism but continued, through an oral tradition associated with Henry Simon and Lloyd Mints directly and Frank Knight and Jacob Viner indirectly, to expound and apply an adapted version of the traditional quantity theory. In the nineteen-fifties and sixties this was strengthened by the numerous research publications of the University of Chicago and the National Bureau of Economic Research and in particular by the publication of Friedman and Schwartz's classic monetary history of the United States – which showed money performing a crucial role in the business cycle, especially in perpetuating the Great Depression and in determining the rate of secular inflation – and Cagan's equally scholarly and pioneering volume covering the determination of the money supply over the same time period, showing in particular that the money supply was determined independently of the demand for it. It is surely no accident that the monetary approach to explaining inflation and the

balance of payments should be revived and increasingly gain acceptance, at a time when the central problem of the world economy is
inflation, something which the Keynesian model was not designed to
explain.

The quantity equation

The quantity theory can be usefully understood in terms of Irving
Fisher's famous equation of exchange,

$$MV = PT \qquad (1)$$

in which M is the stock of money, V is the (transactions) velocity of
circulation of money, P is the general price level and T is the total
number of transactions taking place in an economy over a certain
period of time. By the nominal stock of money is meant the stock
measured in whatever units are used to denote money in a particular
country or society – pounds, dollars, francs, marks, escudos and so
on. The term on the right-hand side of equation 1, PT, is the total
value of all transactions which occur in an economy over a given
period of time, i.e. it is the total number of transactions which take
place multiplied by their average price. The term on the left-hand side
of the equation is also the total value of transactions, but seen from
a rather different point of view. Because every transaction involves
the use of money, the total value of transactions is the product of the
stock of money, M, and the average number of times which each unit
of money is employed to effect a transaction, V, that is, the transactions velocity of money. It is important to stress that because there
is no unique definition of money, the magnitude which we choose to
label money in equation 1 is to some extent a matter of judgement.
Two definitions of money are commonly employed. One includes
the currency held by the private non-bank sector of the economy
including current account deposits at banks, and is derived from the
idea that money is primarily a medium of exchange which is indis-
pensable for making transactions. The other definition includes, in
addition to these terms, certain savings accounts and deposit
accounts at banks and/or savings institutions.* Corresponding to

* In the United Kingdom at present the two common definitions of the money
supply are *M1* and *M3*. *M1* is defined as notes and coins in circulation with the public

these two definitions of money are also two definitions of its velocity of circulation. The narrower the definition of money, the greater will be its velocity of circulation. Similarly the more extensive the definition of money, the smaller will be its velocity of circulation.

So far equation (1) is simply a tautology, something which must be true because of the way in which each of the four terms in the equation have been defined. In order for it to be a theory rather than an identity, two conditions must be satisfied. In the first place the velocity of circulation of money must be determined by the behaviour of firms and households rather than the structure of the economy. In this sense velocity is a behavioural relationship reflecting economic choice rather than a mechanical or engineering relationship. As a result we should not expect that velocity will be a constant number but that it will vary in a systematic way with those factors which influence the behaviour of firms and companies. The nature of this choice can be better understood by considering not velocity but its reciprocal $\left(\dfrac{1}{V}\right)$. Earlier we defined the velocity of circulation of money as the average number of times a unit of money is used to carry out a transaction $\left(V=\dfrac{PT}{M}\right)$. Alternatively, it is the ratio of a money flow during a certain time period to the average money stock. The reciprocal of this $\left(\dfrac{1}{V}=\dfrac{M}{PT}\right)$ is the proportion of the total value of transactions held in the form of money, or, in other words, the demand for money relative to total monetary transactions. For households and firms money is one way of holding wealth. There are many others. Households could choose to put their wealth in building society deposits, national savings bonds, debentures, unit trusts, equity shares, clothes, housing, consumer durables and so on. Firms could also choose to hold alternative financial or physical assets. We can assume that the choice of how much money society wishes to hold relative to, let us say, its annual income is determined by the

---

and the net sterling current account deposits of residents with the banks (clearing banks, other deposit banks, accepting houses, British overseas and commonwealth banks and foreign banks), while $M3$ is defined as $M1$ plus residents' deposit accounts at banks and discount houses in sterling and other currencies and public sector deposits with the banks.

same factors which affect its choice of holding any other asset, namely, the rate of interest which money earns (whether it be positive or negative), the yield on alternative assets, the expected rate of inflation, the wealth of the society and individuals' preferences for holding a highly liquid asset such as money to relatively liquid and more risky assets, such as long-term government bonds. The crucial assumption which is made in the quantity theory is that the demand for money, or, looked at alternatively, its transactions velocity of circulation, is a stable behavioural relationship; although it changes, it does so predictably and not capriciously.

The second important assumption which is made is that the factors affecting M are independent of those affecting V. Or, put another way, that the demand for money is independent of its supply. The supply of money, under a fiduciary standard such as we have at present, is determined primarily by the monetary authorities (namely the Treasury and the Bank of England in the United Kingdom and by the US Treasury and the Federal Reserve in the United States) because they have complete control over the creation of base or 'high-powered' money. This concept is defined as the monetary liabilities of the monetary authorities and includes notes and coin in circulation and bankers' deposits at the Bank of England.[6] The importance of this magnitude is that it is a constraint on the amount of money which the banking system is able to create. Although the money supply is not exclusively determined by the amount of high-powered money – the final outcome depends on the preferences of the public and the banking system as to how much they wish to hold as well as on its stock – it is by far the most important determinant. From the point of view of the quantity theory the important point about high-powered money is that it is under the sole control of the monetary authorities. They have a monopoly over its production. The supply of coin is determined by the Treasury and the total of notes and bankers' deposits at the Bank of England is determined by the Bank of England. Although over short periods of time the monetary authorities may relinquish their control over the growth of high-powered money – by pursuing objectives such as supporting interest rates in the gilt-edged market or the dollar price of sterling in the foreign exchange market – over longer periods of time they have no such choice. Because they have a monopoly over the circulation of high-powered money they are therefore able to exercise such control.

The consequence of making these two assumptions can be seen immediately. The stock of money is determined by the central bank. Its velocity of circulation, although determined by the private sector of the economy, is nevertheless assumed to be a stable, functional relationship. If both the stock of money and its velocity of circulation are assumed given, then from equation (1) the total value of all transactions taking place in an economy over a period of time is determined, and if we assume a close correlation between the total of transactions and income, this gives us a theory of nominal income that is the value of PT, the right-hand side of equation (1). Put in a slightly different way, we can say that the level of money income is determined by the demand and supply for money. *Ceteris paribus*, an increase in the stock of money will lead to an increase in the nominal income and the money value of transactions, and similarly a decrease in the stock of money will produce a fall in nominal income and the money value of transactions.

In the first instance therefore the quantity theory of money is not a theory of inflation but a theory of nominal income, and as such is relevant to an economy suffering from depression or inflation. To make it a theory of inflation one further assumption is necessary, namely that the total number of transactions or, alternatively, the total real output, in the economy is fixed. If T is fixed in equation (1) along with V, then an increase in the stock of money will lead to a proportional increase in the price level. Although over short periods of time the total number of transactions and the amount of real output can be increased fairly rapidly, the longer-term possibilities are restricted by the long-term rate of growth of the economy which depends on the available supply of real resources such as labour, capital, land and entrepreneurial ability, as well as the efficiency with which they are used in the production of goods and services.

In order to understand the way in which an increase in money produces inflation, imagine that the government decides to increase the money supply and that it does so by instructing the Bank of England – in this country, or the Federal Reserve in the United States – to buy long-term government debt from the market. In order to carry out such a policy, the Bank would have to bid up the price of long-term bonds, that is, force down the market rate of interest in order to induce individuals to sell their holdings of stock. As a result of such sales, individuals would increase the size of their deposit accounts at banks and the banks would find themselves with an excess holding of reserve assets, which they in turn could lend out at reduced interest rates. The result of the operation is that interest rates on government bonds, bank deposits and bank loans have all fallen and that the money supply has increased by a multiple of the increase in high-powered money.

But this is clearly not going to be the end of the process. While interest rates on certain categories of government debt and bank deposits have fallen, those on physical assets have remained unchanged, so that consumers have an incentive to use their increased money holdings to purchase additional consumer durables including houses, and companies have an incentive to use their extra cash balances to buy more plant and machinery as well as increase their holding of inventories. But if the supplies of these goods are relatively unresponsive to increased demand, owing to the limited availability of capital and labour, the effect of increased demand will manifest itself in higher prices rather than higher real transactions. In other words, an increased quantity of money results in a higher price level.

The effect therefore of the two key assumptions we have made is that they enable us to argue that an increase in the stock of money leads to a proportional increase in money income. If we further assume that an economy is operating at full capacity, a proportional rise in the stock of money will lead to a proportional rise in the price level. If we assume a growing economy instead of a static economy, as we have done till now, the rate of inflation will be equal to the difference between the growth rate of the nominal stock of money and the growth of its transactions velocity less the growth in the volume of real transactions. If we use the Cambridge form of the basic quantity theory, the rate of inflation will be equal to the growth in the money supply less the growth in money demand, which in turn is equal to the growth in real income and the proportion of income which society wishes to hold in the form of money balances.[7]

A number of points about the quantity theory are worth emphasizing. In the first place the connection between money and prices is *indirect.* The usual caricature of the quantity theory, which is still regrettably passed on in ignorance in lecture theatres and classrooms, is that the theory is based on a direct and mechanical link between money and prices. If the money supply rises by ten per cent, then prices must rise by ten per cent, no more and no less; and the process by which an increased money supply leads to higher prices is presented as if it were an engineering relationship, quite unrelated to the behaviour of either consumers or companies. Both ideas are false. The notion that there must be strict proportionality assumes that the velocity of circulation of money remains constant, which certainly need not be true. Similarly a change in the stock of money results in higher prices only because it first leads to a changed level of expenditure either by consumers or companies. The relationship between money and prices is therefore an indirect relationship based on assumptions about the behaviour of the private sector of the economy.

In the second place the time period over which the effects of changes in the stock of money are observed is extremely important. Whether the increased expenditure resulting from an increased money stock leads to increased prices or increased real output, or to some combination of the two, depends crucially on the length of time over which we observe the change. A distinction must be drawn between the initial, the short-run and the long-run effects of changing the money stock. The initial effect of increasing money is seen in the market for assets. Newly-created money leads banks and other institutions to buy equities and gilt-edge stock, so that equity prices soar and interest rates fall. Via building societies and property companies there is also an increased demand for property. Over the short run, by which is meant a period of time which is sufficiently short and during which neither consumers nor companies correctly guess the future rate of inflation, there is an expansion of real output. As a consequence, wages are not fully adjusted to take account of inflation, labour is prepared to work more hours than if it knew the true purchasing power of take-home pay, and the short-term growth rate of the economy will be greater than its long-term trend rate of growth. Over a longer time-period (the long run), real output growth is forced to fall into line with the longer-term growth path of the economy (which is determined by such factors as the extent and kind of capital investment, the size and skills of the labour force and the geographical and sectoral mobility of labour and capital), so that as a consequence the increased expenditure will result in higher prices. This distinction is precisely that which was made very forcibly by Hume and Ricardo, which we quoted earlier.

In the third place the process by which money affects expenditure in the quantity theory is sometimes referred to as a 'black box' and it is held that the theory fails to explain, by comparison with Keynes, the detailed channels by which an increase in the supply of money leads to an increase in expenditure. In the Keynesian analysis of the role of money in the economy, an increase in the stock of money leads to lower interest rates, which in turn provides an incentive for firms to increase their capital expenditure.[8] It must be emphasized, however, that according to this analysis an increased supply of money affects expenditure *only* through its impact on the flow of private sector investment. By comparison, the quantity theory permits an increase in the money supply to affect the demand for consumer goods including durables, houses and inventories, as well as the capital expenditure of companies. A change in interest rates provides an incentive to increased expenditure not just by the corporate, but also by the household, sector. Again, to the extent that a change in the money stock raises the net wealth of the private sector, this will tend to raise all kinds of expenditure and not just that of corporations expanding their capital investment. Because of the endless channels by which an increase in the money stock leads to an increase in expenditure, the measurement of certain particular effects is in some cases impossible because the relevant statistics are simply not published. But what can be observed is the overall effect of changes in the supply of money on broad categories of expenditure such as private consumption, house purchase, fixed and inventory investment and imports.

Fourthly, nothing has been said so far of deficit spending by the government and of its relationship to the money supply. Sometimes the monetary approach to inflation is presented as if the true cause of inflation were the size of the government deficit. In principle (though not necessarily in practice) the size of the government deficit is quite unconnected with the stock of money. If a government is running a deficit, which is defined as the difference between current expenditure and current receipts (mainly taxation), this must be financed by it increasing its debt. The effect on the money supply of the government increasing the size of the National Debt depends on the kind of debt which is issued and the extent to which this debt is taken up by the central bank or the private (including banking) sector of the economy. The government could increase its debt by issuing more notes and coin and using them to finance deficits which would directly increase the money supply. Although setting the printing presses to work is not a common method of financing deficit spending at present, it has been used, as we shall see later, very effectively by countries in the past. Secondly the government could issue market-able debt, such as short, medium and long-term or gilt-edged secur-ities, which would be taken up by the private sector. The immediate effect would be to decrease deposits at private banks and banks' reserves at the Bank of England and increase the Treasury's deposits at the Bank. As a result the money supply would contract. But when the Treasury spent the extra funds the process would be reversed. Therefore the net effect on the money supply of a bond issue used to finance increased government expenditure is nil.* Thirdly the government could sell bonds to the Bank of England (an internal operation between the Bank of England and the Treasury) so increasing its account at the Bank by the amount of the bond issue. As the government spends the money, so private deposits and banks' reserves rise, leading to a multiple increase in the money supply. This is the modern equivalent of putting the printing presses to work. If a government is prepared to let interest rates be determined by market forces, so that all of its deficit can be financed by the market, then the fact it is in deficit will not in itself be inflationary. (Although we have traced this example in terms of UK institutions, the principle holds for all Western countries.)

Lastly, the monetarist theory of inflation does not depend in any important way on the degree of competition in the labour market. The relationship between changes in the stock of money and the rate of inflation hold whether the labour market is competitive or com-prised of powerful trade unions who are able to restrict entry in their particular sub-markets. The main effect of restrictive practices, as

* The sequence of events should be carefully distinguished from an open-market sale of existing stock, which would lead to a contraction of the money supply.

we shall see later, is to change the wage structure, rather than to produce continuous inflation. If groups of workers are able to restrict entry to their particular skill they are thereby enabled to raise their wages relative to other groups unable to do so. This may have a once-for-all effect on the price level but is not a source of continuing inflation. The rate of increase of wages in the economy as a whole will therefore be determined by the rate of growth of aggregate demand and the productivity of labour, even though within a particular occupation wages may also be determined by the monopoly power possessed by a trade union, professional association or that of an employer.

Inflation in a world context

The present inflation is a world phenomenon. The pace of inflation more than trebled in all Western countries between 1960 and 1974. Price inflation averaged only 2·6 per cent in OECD countries from 1960 to 1965. By 1965–8 it had risen to 3·4 per cent. In 1969 it was 4·7 per cent and by 1974 it was over 10 per cent. In the light of this development there are two approaches which can be taken in attempting to explain it. Either it can be argued that inflation can only be examined in the light of the particular characteristics of individual countries and that it is simply an accident that inflation accelerated in nearly all developed countries in the second half of the last decade or else it can be viewed as a global problem and explained by some mechanism which transmits it throughout the international economy. The latter is in my judgement a far more satisfactory approach. This is not to say that the particular institutional features of countries have no impact at all on the inflationary process. They most certainly do. But such features affect the process and timing of price rises rather than their initial cause or their ultimate extent.

Until now the relationship between money and inflation has been examined in the context of an economy isolated from the rest of the world. There were no exports, imports, capital flows or foreign currency dealings. But the world in which we live is one in which countries are free to trade with each other and in which capital is permitted to flow relatively freely between countries. In this respect the post-war world is in marked contrast to that of the nineteen thirties. As a result of the Great Depression countries were eager to try and solve their employment problems at other countries' expense. The result was tariff barriers, import quotas, restrictions on capital movements and competitive devaluations. The post-war years have seen a gradual liberalization of tariffs between industrialized countries, largely the result of successive rounds of negotiations of the General Agreement on Tariffs and Trade, so that the market for manufactured goods has become a single world market. For example, British Leyland is in competition not only with British Ford and Vauxhall but with Fiat, Volkswagen, Renault, Volvo, Datsun and Toyota. A bad grain harvest in America is immediately reflected on the European market and, in a fairly short space of time, in the price of bread to the British housewife. Over the same period barriers to capital movements have either been removed or circumvented, so that a single world capital market has developed. The introduction of currency convertibility by many developed countries in 1958 and the OECD Code of Liberalization of Capital Movements were significant steps in this development. At present the Euro-currency markets, dominated in the 1960s by the Euro-dollar market, are a highly competitive international network of short-term capital markets and the Euro-bond markets a highly competitive network of longer-term capital markets, so that it makes sense to think of interest rates being determined in a global rather than insular setting.

The second important feature of the international economy since the end of the Second World War (at least until its breakdown in the early years of this decade) has been the fact of fixed exchange rates. As part of the Bretton Woods Agreement the United States agreed to fix the price of the dollar in terms of gold, and all other countries which were signatories to the International Monetary Fund agreed to peg their currencies to the dollar. Exchange-rate changes were permitted only in conditions of 'fundamental disequilibrium' and they have in fact occurred infrequently. Under the original Bretton Woods Agreement the international monetary system was therefore to be a gold exchange standard, the two main currencies being the dollar and the pound. Since that time, however, we have witnessed the demise of gold and sterling and the emergence of the dollar as the medium in which the greater part of international transactions take place.

The existence of fixed exchange rates in a world in which the markets for the products of industrialized countries have become increasingly integrated has one extremely important implication. For it means that the network of trading nations is a unified entity in which individual countries within a world economy are comparable to regions within a single country. Much as within a country there is one ruling market price, so after taking transport costs into account, there is one effective price in the world as a whole, to which individual countries' prices must adjust. The same holds for capital markets and interest rates. If capital is free to flow between countries this will lead to the development of world capital markets and world interest rates, to which individual countries' interest rates will have to adjust. If one country did maintain interest rates higher than the rest of the world, there would be an outflow of capital leading to higher rates in the capital-exporting countries and lower rates in the importing country which would restore equilibrium in the market. The workings of such an international economy as this can be analysed in precisely the same terms in which an isolated economy was analysed in the preceding section. The pace of world inflation can be explained by an expansion of the world money supply at a more rapid rate than the growth of real income in the world as a whole.

If individual countries maintain fixed exchange rates, the rate of inflation in different countries may deviate from the world rate only to the extent that those countries are prepared to accumulate or lose foreign exchange reserves (the extent of the accumulation or loss of reserves depending on the extent to which the country's money supply growth differs from that of the world as a whole). Where the balance of payments is in deficit, and the country is losing reserves, its rate of inflation will be above average, so that it has an incentive to reduce its money supply growth, devalue its currency and ultimately reduce its rate of inflation. In the opposite case, where the balance of payments is in surplus and the country is gaining reserves, its rate of inflation will be lower than that of the world as a whole and so it will be under pressure to revalue its currency, increase the rate of growth of its money supply and so bring its rate of inflation in line with that of the world as a whole.

Numerous mechanisms may exist by which inflation is transmitted throughout the international economy. The process which was tradi-

tionally emphasized in the world of the nineteenth-century gold standard deficits and surpluses was the balance of payments. If a country
increased its money supply at a slower rate than that of the world
as a whole, its rate of inflation would tend to be less than the global
rate, and it would accumulate foreign exchange reserves as a result
of a balance of payments surplus. If, on the other hand, a country
increased its rate of monetary expansion above that of the world as a
whole, the result would be a balance of payments deficit and a loss of
foreign exchange. In the first case the country concerned would have
an incentive either to increase its money supply growth more in line
with that of the rest of the world and so increase its domestic rate
of inflation, or else revalue its currency, which would raise the real
purchasing power of its currency abroad. Both measures would
reduce the country's stock of foreign exchange reserves.

On the other hand, this mechanism need not involve imbalances
in external payments. In a unified system of markets for goods and
services, prices would be fairly rapidly established throughout the
market. Hence prices in individual countries would quickly adjust to
the world price level without the need for previous changes in the
reserves through surpluses or deficits on the balance of payments.
Similarly wage levels could adjust without excess demand or supply
in the labour market. If prices and wages did adjust in this manner
there would clearly need to be a change in the money stock to enable
the new value of transactions to be carried out. Otherwise there
would in the short run be a temporary rise or fall in unemployment,
depending on whether prices had risen or fallen. Imagine, for example, a situation in which the world price level was rising fairly
rapidly. In a single market, prices of traded goods would also rise
fairly rapidly, as would the level of wages paid in those industries.
But if the money stock were not adjusted, and if the velocity of
circulation of money did not rise to offset the increased price level,
the volume of real transactions would fall (see equation 1), with a
corresponding rise in unemployment. To counter this the government
would have to increase the domestic money stock, so that the same
volume of real transactions could take place, but at a higher price
level.

One of the implications of both these developments is that it is
impossible for a country to pursue a monetary policy independent

of the rest of the world. In economic terms the world is indeed a global village. The International Monetary Fund in particular has been at pains to point out the loss of economic sovereignty for individual countries which this process involves. In its 1970 Annual Report, the International Monetary Fund stated that:

> Perhaps the most important implications of the increased mobility of capital permitted and facilitated by the Euro-currency market and the international bond market are to be found in the challenges that they present to both the effectiveness and the independence of national monetary policies, except perhaps in the United States, where resort to the Euro-dollar market by the domestic banking system or other domestic borrowers does not ordinarily expand the monetary base.[9]

Domestic monetary policy by countries other than the United States tends in practice to be countered by private borrowing and lending in the Euro-currency markets which is then converted into domestic currency. If, for example, the central bank is attempting to reduce the domestic money supply, with the inevitable short-run effect of higher interest rates, domestic companies and banks will tend to borrow abroad at the lower interest rates, convert their foreign currency into domestic currency, increase the stock of high-powered money and so check the extent to which money supply growth will be reduced.

Objections to a monetary theory of inflation

(1) *'The concept of the money supply is an elusive one. What matters from the point of view of the firm or the individual is the ability to command credit.'*

The fact that there is no single asset or set of assets which can be identified and defined as money has been and still is a source of confusion in understanding the impact money has on the economy. Put very simply, this objection to the quantity theory is that what determines expenditure is not an existing stock of money but the amount of credit which people think they can get hold of. Even if the existing stock of money was to contract but households and companies still had access to an increasing quantity of credit, there is no reason to expect a reduction in their expenditure. Consequently it is the amount of credit or the 'liquidity' of the economy which is important in determining total expenditure. The Radcliffe Report on the working of the UK monetary system which was published in 1959 put the matter quite explicitly:

> The factor which monetary policy should seek to influence or control is something that reaches beyond what is known as 'the supply of money'. It is nothing less than the state of liquidity of the whole economy. The behaviour of our economy – in particular the moderation of pressure of demand from time to time – is influenced by the relative liquidity of potential spenders at any time, and thus, at one remove, by the liquidity of those who might act as lenders to them or subscribers to their funds.[10]

This particular objection can be stated even more precisely in terms of Fisher's equation of exchange. Total expenditure is determined by the stock of money *and* its velocity of circulation. If the stock of money is reduced but the velocity of circulation increases, then total expenditure will remain unchanged. In other words, if the velocity of circulation of money is unstable, rising when the stock of money contracts and falling when the stock of money expands, and so in both cases neutralizing the effect on expenditure, changes in the stock of money will be unconnected with changes in nominal income and ultimately the rate of inflation.

A number of points need to be made about this thesis. In the first place the quantity theory of money places emphasis not only on the stock of money but also on its velocity of circulation. Changes in the velocity of circulation are just as important as changes in the stock of money in influencing expenditure. But changes in the income velocity of circulation of money are just another way of describing changes in the demand for money. As we have already seen, however, a key assumption of the quantity theory is that changes in the velocity of circulation of money, or, put in another way, changes in the demand for money, are not capricious but a response to changing economic conditions. When money supply growth is restricted (increased), interest rates rise (fall) and so the velocity of circulation of money increases (decreases), a change which offsets the impact of money supply changes. The quantity theory asserts however that such changes can be explained in terms of a stable functional relationship, so that the behaviour of the velocity of circulation can be reasonably well predicted from the movement of the variables which make up the relationship, such as interest rates etc. The stability of the velocity relationship is the main difference between those who emphasise money and those who emphasize credit. The view of the Radcliffe Report was that 'We cannot find any reason for supporting any experiences in monetary history indicating that there is any limit to the velocity of circulation'.[11] As we shall see in the next section, this is a view which is simply not borne out by the facts.

An equally serious objection to the 'credit' view is that although money may be an elusive concept, with no exact empirical measure,[9] a concept such as liquidity is more elusive to define and more difficult to measure. If liquidity is defined as 'the amount of money people think they can get hold of', then its measurement is dependent on the psychology of individuals, something which is virtually impossible to quantify.

(2) *'Changes in money result from changes in income'*

The causal sequence posited by the quantity theory of money is from money to income; more precisely, from the stock of nominal money balances to the flow of nominal income. Some, however, have interpreted the connection between money and income from the opposite point of view, namely as a causal relationship running from income to money. In the nineteenth century this particular fallacy became known as the 'real-bills' doctrine and was associated with the anti-Bullionist school who opposed the 'Bullion Report' of 1810.[12] More recently the idea has been taken up by Professor Nicholas Kaldor in the context of the post-war UK economy. The crux of Kaldor's argument is that the money supply is not exogenous but endogenous to the economic system.

What then governs, at least in the U.K., the changes in the 'money supply'? For my view it's largely a reflection of the rate of change of money incomes and, therefore, is dependent on, and varies with, all the forces or factors which determine this magnitude, the change in the pressure of demand, domestic investment, exports and fiscal policy, on the one hand, and the rate of wage-inflation (which may also be partly influenced by the pressure of demand), on the other hand.[13]

The central idea here is that money plays a purely passive role in the economy; in particular that its nominal stock adjusts to the real 'needs of trade'. Transactions are constantly taking place in the real sector of the economy which need to be financed. In the nineteenth century the extra money could be obtained by the discounting of bills issued against the security of the particular transactions which they have used to finance. In the post-war years in the United Kingdom, certainly up to the change in the Bank of England's operating tactics in the gilt-edge market in May 1971, a common assumption has been that the extra cash can be obtained through the sale of gilt-edged stock by the public to the Bank of England. Whatever the particular mechanism postulated the conclusion is that extra money is supplied to meet an increased demand. As a result a change in income is the cause, and not the result, of a change in the money supply.

The only difficulty with this idea is that it runs counter to one of the best established facts in monetary economics, drawn from the evidence of a variety of countries, namely, the existence of a time-lag between the rate of change of the money supply and the subsequent change in income. If an increase in money supply growth today leads to an increase in real output growth in approximately nine months' time and an acceleration of prices eighteen months later, it is difficult to see how current money supply growth is determined by current income. For example, how could it be said that a money supply growth of between twenty-five and thirty per cent, which was the UK experience in 1972 and 1973, was in any way related to the growth of money income in that year, which was only thirteen per cent. The authorities deliberately expanded the money supply at a much more rapid pace than the growth of money incomes precisely in order to reduce unemployment. Kaldor's only real defence of his position is to argue that such an established correlation does not conclusively prove causality; something which no one would dispute. But nowhere does he offer any systematic evidence which would explain the behaviour of the money stock in the UK over the post-war years in accordance with the predictions of his theory.

The evidence on money, income and inflation

The evidence for the United Kingdom on the inter-relationship between the stock of money, money income, real income and the price level over a period covering nearly one hundred years can be seen in Figure 2.[14] The most notable feature of the evidence is the high correlation between money income and money stock and between the price level and the money stock. Part of the high correlation is due to the fact that all the magnitudes show a secular growth pattern. Figure 3, which shows the rates of change of the same variables, does away with this bias. Yet the results are just as significant; once again there is a high correlation between the rates of growth of the money stock, money income and the price level.

If the period is subdivided into three separate periods – pre-First World War, inter-war and post-Second World War – and the evidence examined in greater detail, which has been done by a number of scholars, certain interesting conclusions emerge. For the first two periods money indeed has a significant relationship to money income; in the period before the First World War a ten per cent rise in the money stock in a given year produces a four to five per cent rise in money income in the same year and approximately the same percentage increase in the following year; in the inter-war years a ten per cent rise in the money stock tends to lead to an eight per cent rise in the current year, a six per cent rise in the following year and a four per cent fall in the year after that. Two further interesting results also emerge from examining the evidence of this period. If a test is conducted to try and distinguish the relevance of the simple Keynesian approach from that of the monetarist, then money is far more important than autonomous expenditure. This is not to say that fiscal policy has no effect on income but that its impact, although in the same direction, is less important than that of money. Secondly, in the period before 1914 a change in the real money supply (i.e. the money stock deflated by the price level) had a significant effect on the change in real output, but this relationship did not hold during the Great Depression. But, remarkably, during

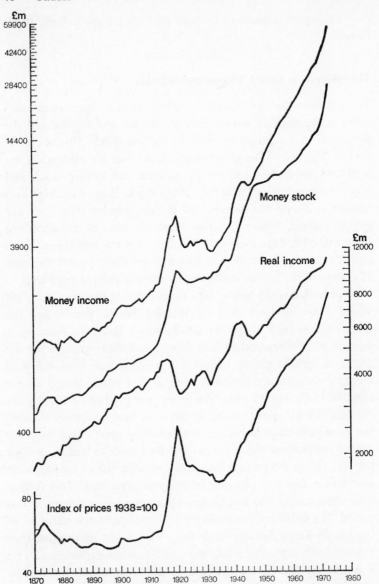

Figure 2. **Incomes, prices and the money supply in the United Kingdom, 1870-1972**
Sources (to Figures 2 and 3): National Bureau of Economic Research; money stock based on Nishimura estimates 1870–80, Sheppard 1880–1962, and Bank of England 1963–73; money income, implicit price deflator and real income using Feinstein's estimates of national income, expenditure and output of the UK 1855–1965 and from 1952–73 Blue Book estimates.

the twenties and thirties the rate of inflation could be significantly explained by changes in the money supply and real income.

The most paradoxical results are those for the period after 1945. Unlike the previous sixty years there is no significant direct relationship between the stock of money and nominal money income, but there is a highly significant relationship between changes in the real money stock and in real output. Part of the explanation may be in

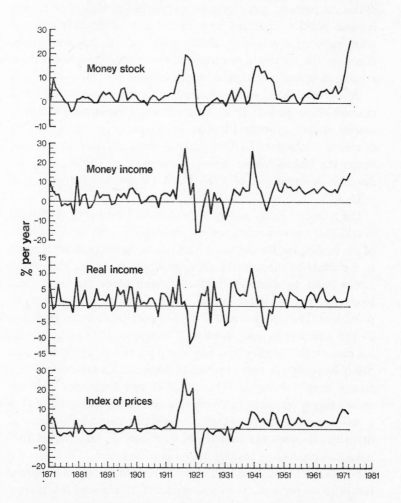

Figure 3. **Rates of change in income, prices and money supply in the United Kingdom, 1871-1973**

certain characteristics of the post-war years by contrast to the earlier periods. In the period 1850–1938 there were substantial movements in the absolute levels of prices, real output and money income not just in an upward but also in a downward direction. By contrast, in the post-war years there has been no period of falling prices or falling real output, so that most of the variation has been in rates of change and not the levels of these magnitudes. In addition to this the post-war years have seen numerous periods of prices and incomes policies, price and wage freezes and, in the early post-war years, substantial rationing. Unlike earlier periods this must throw doubt on the reliability of certain of the statistics, especially those relating to prices and nominal money income.

On the other hand what is interesting for the post-war years is to examine those periods in which there was a rapid acceleration in money supply growth. (Periods of monetary tightness will be examined in chapter 15.) Three periods stand out over the post-war years: the Dalton 'cheap money' experiment of 1945–7, the post-devaluation expansion of 1967–8 and the gamble for growth in 1972–4.

The policy of 'cheap money' which followed the end of the Second World War has very much come to be identified with the Chancellor of the Exchequer, Dr Dalton. In fact it became not so much a policy as a crusade to support 'the active producer as against the passive rentier' and to demonstrate that interest rates are determined largely by psychological factors which could be manipulated by politicians. The policy was to drive down the interest rate from 3 to $2\frac{1}{2}$ per cent and to keep it there. Throughout 1945 and 1946 the interest rate fell steadily from just over 3 per cent to $2\frac{1}{2}$ per cent. The policy however was only achieved through a rapid expansion of the money supply. Between February 1945 and December 1946 the money supply increased by 25 per cent and throughout most of 1946 it was increasing at 17 per cent. The effect on industrial output was dramatic. Between the summer of 1946 and the autumn of 1947 industrial production rose by more than 10 per cent. Then between September 1947 and June 1948 the retail price index rose at an annual rate of 13–14 per cent. As a consequence of the expected inflationary implications of this monetary policy in 1946 the Chancellor was forced to abandon his cheap money policy – and interest rates rose sharply in the first half of 1947 from 2½ to 3 per cent and then continued rising until mid-1948, even though in 1947 money supply growth was very small. This episode is particularly interesting because despite the existence of price controls and rationing, the effects of rapid money supply growth are clearly evident and very similar to other periods in which price controls were inoperative.

The second episode of monetary acceleration was in the years 1967–8 during the first Wilson government. During 1966 the money supply hardly grew at all. Then after the first quarter of 1967 it expanded rapidly; in the fiscal year 1967–8 it rose at an annual rate of 11 per cent and in the last three-quarters of 1968 reached an annual growth rate of 12 per cent. Throughout 1969 the money supply growth was again very small. The period of spring 1967 to winter 1968 therefore was a period of rapid money supply growth which was in sharp contrast to both the preceding and succeeding twelve-month periods. The episode is even more than usually interesting because it was also a period in which fiscal policy was contractionary. A special budget was introduced to accompany the devaluation of November 1967 and in the annual spring budget of 1968 taxes were raised. Despite the fiscal contraction the two effects which the monetary approach would predict do seem to have taken place. Towards the end of 1967 and continuing into 1968 there was a dramatic rise in the index of industrial production. Between January and September 1967 it increased by less than one per cent. But in the last quarter of 1967 it rose at an annual rate of fourteen per cent! Throughout the next year the boom continued, so that from the last quarter of 1967 and throughout 1968 industrial production was rising at annual rate of about five per cent. Because of a fairly substantial time lag the effect on prices would not be expected until some time later. In this particular period an additional problem is that wages and prices were subject to controls which were not finally lifted until the end of 1969. There can be little doubt that expansionary monetary policy was an important factor undermining the price and wage controls of the whole period. In any case in 1970 the retail price index rose by 8½ per cent and in 1971 by 9 per cent, both consistent with the previous behaviour of the money stock.

The third episode is the most dramatic of all. The monetary

permissiveness of 1968 was finally brought to a halt by the International Monetary Fund – to whom we owe an enormous debt – who insisted that the rate of growth of the money supply should be brought under control. Throughout most of 1969 it grew between 2 and 3 per cent. From the last quarter of 1969 to the first quarter of 1971, it jumped up to an annual growth rate of 10 per cent (even though in real terms, that is the growth in the money stock deflated by the price level, it was still not more than one or two per cent). Then in the first half of 1971, and largely as a response to enormous pressure by the media, the CBI, the TUC and above all by the rising unemployment statistics (there were three-quarters of a million registered unemployed in mid-1971 and predictions that this figure could reach over a million), the government decided to cut loose from stagnation and caution, and boldly set out on a gamble for 5 per cent growth. The money supply started growing at a frighteningly rapid rate. By the autumn of 1971 it reached 15 per cent, by the end of the year 22 per cent, by mid-1972 it was between 28 and 30 per cent and it averaged just over 25 per cent for the next twelve months. To all intents and purposes it was out of control, in the sense that it hardly seems possible that either the Bank of England, the Treasury or the Cabinet consciously planned such a phenomenal rate of growth. Once again the monetarist predictions have been dramatically confirmed by the evidence. The immediate effect of flooding the economy with money was a stock market boom and an all-time high in the equity market, falling interest rates, and a surge of funds into the property market, with house prices rising so rapidly that they precipitated a crisis with respect to home ownership. After this there was a dramatic growth of real output. Industrial production had remained roughly constant between the second quarter of 1970 and the end of 1971. But in 1972 it rose by no less than 10 per cent, and over the same period real gross national product grew by nearly 8 per cent. Despite the effect of price and wage controls introduced in 1972, which were still in force until the February 1974 general election, price indices have shown a dramatic inflation, but, as always, after a considerable time lag. In 1972 the rate of inflation measured by the retail price index was only 7·7 per cent, in 1973 10·6 per cent and in 1974 nearly 20 per cent. Because of the existence of price controls and food subsidies this last figure is an underestimate of the true rate of inflation and must go some way to explaining the discrepancy between the retail and wholesale indices for this period – judged by the behaviour of the wholesale prices the rate of inflation in 1974 was 28 per cent.

The basic thesis of this chapter has been that inflation is a monetary phenomenon and that in an international economy with fixed exchange rates it is also a global phenomenon. The evidence on inflation in the 'world' economy is given in Table 1. The data used is a weighted average of the data from the major industrialized countries – France, Germany, Japan, the UK, Italy, Belgium, Netherlands, Switzerland, Canada and the US, and is the series

Table 1. **World* Inflation, GNP and the Money Supply, 1960–75 (annual percentage changes)**

	Money	*GNP*	*Consumer Prices*
1960	4.9	8.6	1.9
1961	7.8	7.5	2.0
1962	7.1	8.5	2.7
1963	8.3	7.9	2.9
1964	6.7	9.5	2.4
1965	7.7	8.6	3.0
1966	6.6	9.5	3.4
1967	6.3	7.2	3.0
1968	8.1	9.8	3.9
1969	8.1	10.0	4.5
1970	7.1	8.8	6.2
1971	12.2	9.3	5.1
1972	11.9	10.2	4.5
1973	10.2	13.9	7.3
1974	7.3	−0.6	13.0
1975	9.9	0.4	10.0

* The countries included are the Group of Ten: Belgium, Canada, France, Germany, Italy, Japan, Netherlands, Switzerland, UK and US.

Source: First National City Bank.

employed by the First National City Bank. In the first half of the 1960s inflation averaged between 2 and 3 per cent for these countries, while for the 'world' less the US it was between 3 and 4 per cent. Over the same years for the US, however, it ranged from 1 per cent to 1·7 per cent. During the present decade the rate for the 'world' as a whole has averaged nearly 8 per cent and in 1974 reached 13 per cent. These statistics suggest a broad monetarist explanation. The cause of an accelerated inflation in the US in the late 1960s was the more rapid money supply growth of 1967–8, itself the result of a decision about how to finance the Vietnam War. For the world as a whole the more rapid money supply growth did not get under way until the last quarter of 1970. Taking quarterly figures adjusted to an annual rate, the increase in the world money stock outside the US increased by 9 per cent between the first quarter of 1966 and the third quarter of 1970; between the third quarter of 1970 and the third quarter of 1972 it averaged over 18 per cent. The consequence of this doubling in the growth of world money has not surprisingly been a doubling in the world rate of inflation.

5 Trade unions and social conflict

'The rules of economics are not working in quite the way they used to.'
Arthur Burns, Chairman of Governors, United States Federal Reserve (1971)

The overwhelming consensus among economic writers and decision-makers, whether in business or government, is that the predominant cause of the post-war British inflation lies not in the excessive creation of money but in the monopoly power of trade unions, and their attempt to raise their share of wages in the gross national product. Rising prices are thus the result of rising costs and not of increasing demand. (This is sometimes put in elementary textbooks as inflation being the result of 'cost-push', rather than 'demand-pull', factors.) Aubrey Jones, for example, argues in *The New Inflation* that:

> there is now a 'new inflation', resulting from the response of contemporary social forces to economic growth, in contrast to past inflations, which were due to sporadic, temporary and essentially economic influences. This 'new inflation' started on the morrow of the Second World War and has persisted. What is also 'new' about the new inflation is the increased public awareness of, and alarm over, the problem of persistently rising prices caused by the recent acceleration of inflation.[1]

Reginald Maudling, a former Chancellor of the Exchequer, in a celebrated article in *The Times* in 1972, put it that 'The last two decades have seen profound changes, both economic and political, in the whole capitalist system. All Western countries have been affected in varying degree'.[2] The major change has been 'an arising consciousness of the power of organized labour' which in a complex modern economy possesses the power to bring any modern capitalist economy to a halt. He then goes on, 'we see the result of all this in the problem of cost inflation which has bedevilled the country for many years, and is now infecting the whole Western world. This is a new problem; it is a political problem. The old traditional economics cannot begin to cope with it.' This is a sentiment which echoes the views of Arthur Burns, Governor of the US Federal Reserve System, in a comment on the combination of rising prices and high unemployment in the US in 1970-1: 'The rules of economics are not working in quite the way they used to. Despite extensive unemployment in our country, wage rate increases have not moderated. Despite much idle industrial capacity, commodity prices continue to rise rapidly.'[3]

The idea that inflation is the result of non-monetary forces is not something new. Although the monetary view of inflation predominated until the Great Depression there have always been certain thinkers holding dissident opinions. It was not until the 1930s, however, and Keynes' analysis of the problem of mass unemployment, that the quantity theory became generally discredited. The main reason for this was Keynes' observation that wages were determined independently of the monetary characteristics of an economy. Although Keynes did not attempt to show in any detailed way the factors which did determine wages, he left a sufficiently serious *lacuna* in his analysis of the macro-economic process of a modern economy to enable subsequent writers to explain wage determination either partially or totally in terms of non-economic factors and to explain inflation without reference to the pressure of demand. And, in the vast literature of post-Keynesian economics, this is precisely what has happened. Various factors, all allegedly exogenous to the internal pressure of demand, have been put forward as 'the' cause of inflation; the monopoly power of trade unions, high interest rates, indirect taxation, direct taxation, rising import prices, floating exchange rates, high rents, wars, inelasticity of agricultural supply, persistent balance of payments deficits, economic growth, the communications revolution, immigration, increased permissiveness, the class structure, even national character.

The dynamics of cost-inflation

Unlike the quantity theory of money, there is no generally accepted process by which rising costs create persistent inflation. Some of the mechanisms are highly impressionistic and ill-thought out, while others are much more sophisticated and offer a real challenge to monetary orthodoxy. Any comprehensive theory of cost inflation must attempt to explain at least five aspects of the inflationary process. First, it must provide a reason for the size of trade-union wage demands and, in particular, for differences between industries and through time. Why is it that demands for wage increases are running forty per cent at present, whereas ten years ago they were only for ten per cent. Next, it must explain why higher wage demands result in higher settlements. Why is it that firms are disposed to pay higher wages? After that it must explain the process by which wage awards in some sectors are transmitted to other sectors, so that the increase in wages is an increase in the absolute and general level of rates of pay and not just a change in the structure of wages, with those in some sectors rising relative to others. Fourthly, it has to produce a rationale of why such wage rises produce *continuous* and not *once-for-all* price rises. And lastly, it must explain the process in a monetary context, in which any extended period of inflation must be accompanied by a continuous rise in the money supply. Unfortunately many, but not all, explanations of cost inflation fall down because they fail to explain one or more of these steps. Usually they either put forward reasons for a unique adjustment in wages and prices, or else they explain the process as if we lived in a cashless society in which any total volume of real transactions could be readily financed, regardless of the absolute prices at which those transactions took place. What follows is an attempt to draw on various explanations of the role of cost factors in producing inflation, and to put them together to form a coherent explanation of the process.

Underlying the non-monetary theory of inflation is a quite distinctive interpretation of modern capitalist society; a world of powerful trade unions, of industries dominated by a few very large firms, of continued economic growth expected by all sectors of the economy and of 'full employment' defined in terms of the percentage of the labour force unemployed. In such a context the starting point for analysing inflation is a wage increase in a particular sector. It might be the result of a productivity gain in the export sector, or the effect of a new union leader attempting to establish his reputation among his members by successfully negotiating a very high wage award, or of low-paid employees in the public sector demanding and being awarded higher wages for social reasons. The immediate effect of such a wage rise is to change the pattern of wage differentials. If we lived in the nineteenth-century world of *laissez-faire*, we would expect a movement of labour to the particular sector whose wages had risen and in turn to the emergence of a new equilibrium structure of wages.

But in the New Industrial State the process is different. Wage rises in one sector are transmitted to another sector for *social* reasons. If society has certain norms in respect of distribution of income then it will not be able to tolerate the divergence between the standards of living of various sectors of the economy, which certain wage awards would imply. So, for example, if an industry producing goods for the export market experiences a price rise for external reasons and grants a wage increase as a result, this will set up social pressure to raise wages in those sectors with a slower growth rate, the major reason usually being the genuine hardship of the lower-paid worker. As a result of 'wage leadership', a change in wage differentials immediately sets up forces to re-establish the initial differentials and as a result raises the general level of wages.

If the markets in which companies sold their products approximated at all closely to the economists' ideal of competition, increased labour costs would lead to reduced profits on the part of firms, a stimulus to increased productivity and a small rise in price. But because the typical market in which large corporations sell their products is dominated by a few firms, price competition tends to be severely restricted. The leading firms in a market tend to have relatively stable shares of the market so that increased labour costs will be passed on to the consumer in the form of higher prices. Each company realizes that the worst possible outcome would be a price war, in which ultimately its ability to survive may be at stake. Within such an oligopolistic market structure, competition tends to focus on the quality of the product, the terms on which it is sold and the after-sales service, rather than on the price. The conclusion is, therefore, that the non-competitive structure of markets ensure that wage rises are rapidly transmitted into price rises. Another factor which tends to reinforce this process is the cost to a company of allowing a strike to take place. Because of the capital intensity of contemporary production methods, a strike by a handful of workers could lead to the shut down of a highly automated production plant, and as a result be very expensive for the company. In order to avoid such an outcome the firm is prepared to grant the higher wage award and offset some of the higher costs by raising prices.

At the beginning of the last chapter we saw that for a given volume of transactions to be financed in a modern economy at the prevailing price level, it was necessary to have a certain stock of money. This, it was argued, was a tautology, which held true regardless of whether inflation was caused by monetary or non-monetary factors. In the case of cost inflation, unless we are prepared to argue (and in fact very few are) that the velocity of circulation of money can easily increase or decrease to offset the fall or rise in the money stock, a rise in prices caused by a rise in wages, with no offsetting change in the stock of money, would lead to higher unemployment. But if the government has a target level of unemployment, above which it is not prepared to see unemployment rise, then, in order to avoid the increased unemployment resulting from cost inflation, it will increase the money stock. As a result the inflationary process is complete – the arbitrary wage rise; a transmission of wage increases for socio-political reasons to other sectors, leading in turn to higher prices and, lastly, the central bank being forced to increase the money supply.

A number of aspects of this process are worth noting carefully. In the first place we can see that there is no necessary and inevitable connection between inflation and the monopoly power of trade unions. If a trade union decides to use its potential monopoly power to restrict entry into a particular trade or profession, it thereby raises the wage of its members relative to other occupations. As a result of the higher wages, less are employed and prices are higher in that sector and more will be employed and prices will be lower elsewhere in the economy. In this case there is no effect on the general wage level nor on the general price level. The use of monopoly power in the labour market has affected *relative* wages but not the general wage level, and *relative* prices but not the general price level.

It may be argued, however, that such an adjustment process is too simple in that it assumes a degree of wage and price flexibility and labour mobility which is uncharacteristic of the imperfect world in which we live. Providing the increase in wages in one sector were not offset by a fall in wages somewhere else in the labour market this would lead to an increase in the general level of wages and in turn to an increase in unemployment. If the government responded to the increase in unemployment by increasing the money supply, the increase in the general level of wages would result in a permanently higher price level. But such a price increase would be a once-for-all adjustment in the price level as a response to the increased use of monopoly power in the labour market. It would not be in itself the trigger to release a process of continuous inflation. This would only occur if the monopoly power of unions was constantly growing. If the government increases the money supply to reduce the level of unemployment, it is this, rather than the monopoly power of trade unions, which imparts continuity to the inflationary process, because in the absence of such monetary action the price level would not be rising continuously.

But if a government is intent on selecting an arbitrary level of unemployment, defining that as 'full-employment', and declaring its commitment never to let unemployment rise above that level, then, regardless of whether the labour market is competitive or not, the result will be inflation, providing only that its target level of un-employment is below that which would result from the free interplay of the labour market. The real cause of inflation in this case is the government's commitment to maintain unemployment at or below an arbitrarily selected figure, even though such a figure may make no economic sense at all. The fact of whether the labour market is highly unionized or not may clearly affect the way in which inflation proceeds, but it is irrelevant as regards its cause. In this respect the term 'cost-inflation' is a *description* of the mechanism of wage and price rises in a typical modern capitalist economy, even though the real *cause* is the government's commitment to over-full employment or to a set of wage differentials. Some may object that such a distinction is semantic and serves no useful purpose. When, however, we come to a discussion of the ways in which inflation may be brought under control, such a distinction, as we shall see later, is absolutely crucial. Similarly if the government is intent on maintaining the existing system of wage differentials, then it must respond to a wage increase in any one sector by increasing the money supply and so maintaining the same set of differentials but at a higher absolute level of wages and prices.

Cost inflation and monetarism

One problem raised by the attempt to outline the process of cost inflation is its relationship to a monetary theory of inflation. In particular, if the arguments for cost inflation are interpreted within the kind of monetary context outlined in the last chapter, what precisely do they mean? It turns out that examining a non-monetary theory of inflation in the context of a monetary framework for the economy adds clarity to the analysis. Using this approach three different interpretations of cost inflation can be distinguished.

In the first place, cost inflation may be taken to mean that the velocity of circulation of money, even if viewed as a functional relationship rather than simply a constant, is unstable. In Fisher's famous equation, it will be recalled that the two key assumptions were that the real volume of transactions was determined by the underlying characteristics of the economy and that the velocity of circulation, though by no means a constant magnitude, behaved in a stable and reasonably predictable manner. On this basis we could then go on to assert that over a reasonable length of time there was a relationship between the growth of the money supply and the rate of inflation. If, on the other hand, the velocity of circulation of money or, to put it in a slightly different way, the demand of money, was unstable, no such relationship need hold. It was precisely this argument, incidentally, which Keynes used in his *General Theory* to discredit the quantity theory of money in the context of an economy suffering from depression. In such an economy, where interest rates on financial assets had fallen to their very lowest possible levels (the yield on UK Treasury bills in 1932 was one quarter of one per cent), investors would be indifferent as to whether they held a portfolio consisting of money or fixed interest securities. If, in this 'liquidity trap', the central bank increased the supply of money, it could be achieved at existing market rates of interest and so would have no impact on expenditure. In other words, an increase in the stock of money would merely be offset by a decline in the velocity of circulation.

A similar sort of argument can be used in the present context. If prices rise because of cost factors, and if neither the stock of money nor its velocity of circulation changes, the volume of real transactions which could be financed would fall. But if the velocity of circulation rose, the same volume of real transactions could be financed despite the higher prices. The basis for the change in the income velocity of circulation of money is the high degree of innovation which exists in the financial sector. If companies and financial institutions find themselves short of cash on a more or less permanent basis, they can economize on their cash holdings by developing markets for short-term credit. For example in the credit squeeze of 1969–71 large corporations in the United Kingdom developed the inter-company loan market in which large firms lent to each other on a very short-term basis. In this situation therefore a continuous rise in the price level due to cost factors can be financed by a continuous rise in the velocity of circulation of money. Even though the money supply remains constant, prices can continue to rise.

Secondly, cost inflation could be taken to mean that the supply of money is not fixed by the central bank but is determined by the transactions 'needs' of the economy. If, for a given set of retail and wholesale prices, the economy 'needs' more money in order to finance transactions, it will be produced and by just the necessary amount. This is the distinguished fallacy – the real-bills doctrine – which we encountered in the last chapter.

The idea that the money supply is somehow mysteriously adjusted to meet the needs of trade needs to be carefully distinguished from the situation in which the central bank purposely restricts its ability to control the money supply by pegging either interest rates or the exchange rate. If the Bank of England decides to peg interest rates on government stock it immediately loses control over the money supply. If, for example, it fixed rates at eight per cent and at that rate holders of government stock wish to exchange government bonds for cash, then, in order to stabilize the rate, the Bank is obliged to buy the stock. But, as a result, the banking system's deposits at the Bank rise, followed by even larger rises in the money supply. *We can say as a general rule that the Bank of England can choose either to control interest rates or the stock of money but not both.* All governments can put forward powerful reasons why interest rates need to be controlled. For example, interest rates affect the cost of financing the national debt, the cost of mortgages for house purchase and, with a fixed exchange rate, the net flow of short-term capital.

The government also loses control of the money supply if it decides to fix the foreign exchange rate but maintain convertibility of the currency and few controls over trade. If the government increases the money supply in an open economy so that companies and consumers find themselves holding an excess of cash, expenditure will rise and goods, services and financial assets will be sucked in from abroad. Similarly, a shortage of cash can be corrected by investors selling more assets abroad or corporations raising their exports of services and products. If, on the other hand, the exchange rate is floating, in order to purchase foreign goods or assets it first becomes necessary to find some existing domestic holder of foreign currency who is prepared to sell. At the right price this transaction takes place and the purchase can be carried out. But the domestic money stock remains unchanged. Similarly, a foreign sale results in the acquisition of foreign exchange. But to convert the foreign exchange into domestic currency requires some purchaser. With a suitable adjustment of the exchange rate, this once again becomes possible. This leads us to put forward another general principle. *In an open economy the central bank can either control the money supply or the exchange rate but not both.*

As can be now seen, both of these cases have in fact nothing to do with cost inflation. But cost inflation may, thirdly, be an attempt to analyse the particular reasons why the central bank restricts its freedom to control the money supply. It might be argued that if there were a large public sector deficit which could only be financed in a non-inflationary way at an unacceptably high level of interest rate the central bank might be forced to increase the money stock. Or if with a given target level of unemployment, trade unions were awarded an exceptionally high wage demand, there would be a sharp rise in unemployment unless there was a correspondingly large increase in the money supply. In such examples as these it could be argued that inflation is determined by the structure of the financial system or the wage demands of trade unions. But if this is what is meant by cost inflation, it is certainly compatible with the explanation of inflation being essentially a monetary phenomenon. In neither case was the central bank forced to increase the money supply by a given amount. If the government was prepared to pay a market rate of interest on its debt, deficits could most certainly be financed without inflation. Similarly, if the government was prepared to tolerate a higher level of unemployment, wage awards would not lead to a process of continuous inflation.

Structuralism and inflation in the Third World

So far our discussion has been confined to the debate which has taken place in developed countries. But since the Keynesian revolution a parallel debate has taken place in the Third World, and particularly Latin America, which in the post-war years has had an enormously varied experience of inflation. For example, during the period 1940–69 the annual rate of increase in the cost of living index of Mexico averaged only 4 per cent and of Venezuela just over 1 per cent, whereas Peru has averaged 9 per cent, Colombia 11 per cent, Chile 37 per cent, Argentina 65 per cent and Brazil 193 per cent. The controversy in developing countries has centred on whether inflation can be best explained in terms of monetary or structural factors. On the one hand, central bankers and the International Monetary Fund have emphasized the importance of money and the necessity of monetary control in stabilizing inflation. On the other hand, those economists usually associated with the Economic Commission for Latin America have emphasized the importance of 'structural' factors as the basic cause of inflation and of credit as a propagating mechanism.

The context of the structuralist-monetarist debate has been the attempt of developing countries to raise their rates of economic growth. One of the most influential of structuralist writers, Joseph Grunwald, put it that the essence of the structuralist argument is that price stability can be attained only through economic growth. The basic forces of inflation are structural in nature. Financial factors might be important but only as forces propagating inflation and not originating it. It is admitted that monetary policy can be easily managed and has relatively quick effects, but it attacks only symptoms and therefore cannot cure.[4]

Structuralism as an analysis of inflation distinguishes two sets of factors – the basic inflationary pressures and the mechanisms of propagation. The basic inflationary pressures are factors which lead to initial disturbances in the economy and which in turn cause the inflation, whereas the mechanisms of propagation are various institutional and structural features of the economy which help propagate the inflation once it is under way but are not its cause. Numerous structural factors have been alleged to be important, but all emphasize the rigidity of the economic system and its failure to respond to economic incentives.

One basic factor making for inflationary pressure is failure of the agricultural sector to meet the Third World's demand for food. As a result of rapid population growth and the steady migration from the land to the cities, demand for food has grown enormously. Supply has failed to keep pace with demand, largely because of outmoded and inefficient systems of land tenure which exist in these countries, such as the *latifundis* system in Latin America. Another causal factor is the seeming inability of most of these countries to extricate themselves from balance of payments difficulties. The demand for their exports grows neither proportionately with the growth of world trade nor with the income of the developed world and seems almost unaffected by a devaluation of the domestic currency. Typically exports are primary products and their composition is such that a significant proportion of total export earnings comes from only one or two products. For example, in 1969 over 48 per cent of Bolivia's exports came from tin, 62 per cent of Colombia's from coffee, 73 per cent of Chile's from copper, 92 per cent of Venezuela's from oil, 71 per cent of Uruguay's from wool and meat, 34 per cent of Brazil's from coffee and iron ore and 46 per cent of Paraguay's from meat and timber. On the other hand, these

countries have a great need for imports because of the need to purchase investment goods from abroad as part of the necessary input
for an increased rate of growth. A third area structuralists pinpoint
is the rigidity of the public finances. Because of the urgent need to
develop transport systems and public utilities and to provide better
health facilities, government expenditure on public investment projects and its salaries to staff tend to be high and predictable. But the
government's tax revenues depend heavily on export prices, over
which the government has no control because they are determined
on world markets. If taxes happen to fall and the government faces a
prospective deficit it can respond in one of two ways. Either it can
cut back on its investment programme, which is likely to retard the
rate of growth of the economy and, because of the nature of the
expenditure, socially undesirable, or else it can finance the deficit by
a monetary expansion, which in turn is inflationary.

In contrast, the importance of the propagation mechanisms is that
they spread the inflation throughout the economy and determine
both its total impact as well as its effect on relative prices and the
incomes of various groups in the economy. The two most discussed
mechanisms are the banking system and the supply of credit, and
the wage-price mechanism. As we have already noticed, because of
the periodic inevitability of government deficits the government is
forced to expand the banking system, thereby creating extra money.
The wage-price mechanism is allegedly due to the existence of
powerful trade unions and private sector monopolies.

The typical inflationary process which repeats itself in one
developing country after another can now be readily understood.
Due to the pressures created by the movement to the cities, rapid
population growth and the necessity of buying vital capital equipment from the developed world in the quest for higher growth, there
will be a growing demand for imports and also food. Because of
the failure of food supply to respond to the increased demand, prices
will rise. Increasing food and import prices will produce an increase
in the cost of living, which, because of the existence of powerful
trade unions, will readily be translated into demands for higher
wages. And so the wage-price spiral is triggered off. But as the
inflation gets under way, the expenditure of the public sector rises
more rapidly than their receipts, producing in turn a deficit which

has to be financed. Interest rates cannot be allowed to rise to finance the deficit in a non-inflationary way because of their inequitable impact on the distribution of income – those with savings gain at the expense of those without – and because of the increased interest repayments which will be needed in the future. Resort to external financing must also be restricted because of its implications for the balance of payments in the future. And so the only course for the government is to borrow from the central bank and the domestic banking system, thereby increasing the domestic money supply. Similar action has also to be taken to finance wage and price rises and thereby avoid unemployment.

The Latin-American experience of inflation in the post-war years has been subjected to a good deal of analysis; notably by Harberger, Diz and Diaz-Alejhandrino.[5] Although the expression 'Latin-American-style inflation' has become synonymous with rapid if not hyper-inflation, Latin-American countries in the post-war years have had an extremely diverse experience of inflation, as can be seen from Table 2. Despite such different rates of inflation and other structural characteristics of their economies, most of the statistical studies which have seriously examined the cause of inflation find that the rate of growth of the money supply is one of the most significant determinants of the rate of inflation. In a statistical test which pools the data from all sixteen countries, the current and lagged rate of growth of the money supply is an important factor in explaining inflation; an increase in the rate of growth of the money supply leads to a proportionate increase in the level of prices within a period of two years, though the greater part of the adjustment takes place within twelve months. In contrast, other variables which were introduced to pinpoint structural changes, such as wage and exchange rate changes, while in certain cases significant could not be used as the basis for a general explanation of inflation. This evidence does not imply that a monetarist model can adequately explain all the variations in the rate of inflation of Latin-American countries. It cannot; and in some cases it does fall down rather badly. But the main conclusion which emerges is that monetary factors are in general far more convincing in explaining inflation than structural factors. Even this fairly strong conclusion, however, is not sufficient to finally resolve the structural-monetarist debate in the context of certain countries. For example, in his study of Argentina, Diaz-Alejhandrino claims that money supply growth, which is a proxy for bank credit, is simply an accommodating rather than

Table 2. **Inflation in Latin America, 1950–69**

	Rate of Inflation*	Money Supply Growth*	Real Income Growth*	Velocity
Uruguay	43.0	40.1	0.7	5.96
Bolivia	41.3	41.6	3.0	11.77
Brazil	35.1	38.2	3.9	4.17
Chile	28.2	35.2	4.6	11.35
Argentina	26.4	24.6	2.4	4.14
Paraguay	12.5	15.4	5.5	11.27
Colombia	9.2	16.5	5.4	6.56
Peru	8.5	13.4	5.7	8.38
Mexico	5.3	11.3	6.9	8.22
Nicaragua	3.4	8.6	3.7	8.85
Ecuador	3.0	8.8	4.7	8.00
Honduras	2.1	8.0	4.0	10.21
Costa Rica	1.9	9.0	5.7	6.16
Guatemala	1.1	5.9	3.9	9.47
Venezuela	1.1	7.9	6.8	6.70
El Salvador	0.3	3.5	4.6	7.58

* Per cent per year, averaged over 1950–69.

Note: S.D. is the standard deviation. Inflation is measured by the consumer price index; money supply is currency plus demand deposits; real income is nominal GNP deflated by the consumer price index.

Source: R. C. Vogel, 'The Dynamics of Inflation in Latin America, 1950–69', *American Economic Review*, March 1974.

an initiating factor in the inflationary process and, in particular, that the Argentinian government increased bank credit in response to the increased wage demands of the labour market.

The evidence for cost-inflation

The kind of evidence which is put forward to show that post-war British inflation or, for that matter, the inflation of other industrialized countries, is cost inflation is especially varied. It ranges from news-paper comments about the aggressive personalities of trade-union leaders or shop stewards to highly mathematical and statistical models of the wage-price process buried away in learned academic journals. In the UK the evidence falls into three main categories:

the perverse behaviour of the Phillips curve and the wage explosion of 1970–1; the increasing share of wages in the GNP and the declining share and rate of profit since the early 1950s; and econometric evidence of the impact of trade-union militancy.

The perverse behaviour of the Phillips curve and the wage explosion of 1970 can be seen from Figure 6 in chapter 5. The rate of wage increases in 1970 was almost double that of the previous year, despite a slight *increase* in unemployment. Professor Paish who throughout the post-war period and on the basis of the evidence had argued that the Phillips curve for the UK was stable and evidence of demand inflation, is convinced that the 1970–1 explosion could only be explained as cost-inflation.[6] On the basis of the behaviour of the economy between 1952 and 1966, the annual increase in income from employment in 1970 should have been four per cent, whereas it turned out to be nearly fourteen per cent. Two major reasons were discussed by Paish to explain this enormous ten per cent discrepancy. One was that the unemployment statistics required a different interpretation after 1965–6 because of the introduction of redundancy payments and higher unemployment benefits. As a result of these new measures the cost of remaining unemployed while searching for a job was reduced, so that those unemployed would be expected to use greater discretion before deciding their choice of a new form of employment and, as a consequence, remain unemployed that much longer. Because of this the number of unfilled vacancies has been suggested as a far better indicator of the demand for labour rather than the number unemployed. Professor Paish however estimates that this change in social security only accounts for approximately two per cent of the discrepancy. The other eight per cent is allegedly due to the use of monopoly power by trade unions and shop stewards. Up until 1969 labour made very little attempt to use its monopoly power but after that time it did so in order to raise its real income. As a result of the devaluation of sterling in November 1967 and the higher indirect taxes which accompanied it, real personal disposable income and real personal consumption hardly rose at all between the first quarter of 1968 and the third quarter of 1969. According to Paish it was this which triggered off high wage demands. Professor Phelps-Brown also explains the wage explosion as a phenomenon of 'cost-push' inflation but places more emphasis on the way in which a large settlement in a particular sector is transmitted to other sectors for social reasons. The dustmen's settlement of seventeen per cent which was won after a successful strike in 1970 had 'a symbolic and emotional impact'[7] which led to inordinately large rises in other sectors.

The major points to note about 'cost-push' explanations of the 1970 wages explosion are, firstly, that they are ad hoc and specifically restricted to socio-economic features of the period 1968–70 and, secondly, that they assume that the phenomenon of the 1970 wages explosion is inexplicable in any form other than trade-union militancy. The problem with any ad hoc explanation of wage behaviour is that it is extremely difficult to refute. But if union militancy is allegedly the cause of the 1970 wages explosion, then surely union militancy as an explanation of the United Kingdom inflation in the post-war period cannot be restricted simply to this particular episode. The only attempt, as we shall see later, to test the importance of trade-union militancy as a cause of inflation in any sort of systematic way is unsuccessful in explaining inflation in these terms.

But there are in fact, as we have already seen, alternative explanations of the behaviour of wages and prices in the United Kingdom in 1970–1. In the last chapter we argued that the timing of the price inflation was the result of the more rapid money supply growth of 1968. If we put this particular episode in a longer-term perspective, it can also be viewed as the adjustment of the United Kingdom price level to that of the world as a whole. A particular country in a world economy with fixed exchange rates will find that, after taking into account the effect of exchange rate changes, it's rate of inflation will tend to be the same as that of the world as a whole.

To be precise, in equilibrium the percentage growth of the United Kingdom price level would be related to the percentage growth of the world price level and the percentage change in the exchange rate. Between 1966 and 1971 the world price rose by approximately twenty-four per cent. If we add to this the effect of the fourteen per cent devaluation in November 1967 then we would expect to find that over the period as a whole, during which time we would have adjusted to the effects of the devaluation, the United Kingdom price level rose by about forty per cent, which is roughly speaking what happened.

The fact that it happened after the White Paper on *Productivity, Prices and Incomes Policy after 1969* had laid down a higher norm for wages in 1970 than in 1969 and also after the failure of the government's policy in passing legislation on industrial relations, and that it was accompanied by strikes in various public sector disputes, is merely the precise form it took. But these particular circumstances should not mislead us into thinking that they were important causal events. The adjustment was certain to take place with a fixed exchange rate whatever government happened to be in power and whatever the degree of monopoly possessed by the trade-union movement. Both these factors may influence the particular way in which the domestic economy adjusts and the speed with which it takes place. But the ultimate necessity for such an adjustment does not depend in any essential way on domestic institutions or politics.

In *The New Inflation* Aubrey Jones argues that the evidence for cost-inflation over the post-war years is the behaviour of the share of wages in the gross national product and the pre-tax rate of return on capital. 'The fact that over a long span of years the share of labour in the national income has increased while the pre-tax rate of profit has somewhat declined suggests that the main cause of persistently rising prices is to be found in rising wage costs per unit of output.'[8]

On the basis of economic theory two things need to be said about this argument. Even if it is true, as Aubrey Jones suggests, that the United Kingdom has in fact suffered from cost inflation since the end of the Second World War, cost inflation as such has no particular relationship with the distribution of income. 'Wage-push' inflation is equally compatible with a rising, falling or constant rate of profit or with a rise or fall in the share of wages in national income. Similarly an upward or downward movement in the rate of profit or share of wages is equally compatible with demand or cost inflation.

The idea that cost inflation is either the cause or the consequence of a rise in the share of wages in gross national product is usually made from two kinds of argument. In the first place cost inflation is often thought of as implying that price rises must follow wage rises in time. Thus, if this happens continuously, then in the aggregate this must result in a rise in the share of wages in the GNP and a fall in the share of profits. Such a simple view implies, however, a very rigid behaviour of price-setting on the part of companies and is derived from the notion that firms set prices by calculating unit cost and then adding a mark-up for overheads and profit. It is true that if a company finds either that the market price of its product has risen or that due to market conditions it can increase its profits by raising prices it is clearly in the best interests of its shareholders to follow such a policy. But such a price rise may either coincide with, follow or lead a wage settlement.

A second and separate notion is that because trade unions exist to raise the standard of living of the working class, their success should be marked by a rise in the share of wages in gross national product. The assumption here is open to serious question. A trade union has no way of directly raising the standard of living of the working class as a whole. It can use its monopoly power in its own occupation and raise wages by restricting entry. But this leads to an increase in the standard of living of the members of trade unions at the expense of other members of the working class who are not members of trade unions, rather than a rise in the standard of living of the working class as a whole. Trade unions therefore can get a bigger slice of the wages cake but they cannot raise the size of the cake itself.

The most sophisticated attempt to argue the case for cost-push inflation and, in particular, to relate it to the empirical evidence of the USA in the present century, especially over the post-war period, is to be found in the work of A. G. Hines.[9] He finds that changes in the proportion of the labour force which is unionized is a statistically significant and important variable in explaining the rate of change of wages in the post-war period in the United Kingdom. He interprets this as evidence for the fact that when trade unions flex their muscles and reveal their power in the labour market they not only drive up wages but also increase their membership. The proportion of the total labour force which is unionized is therefore an index of trade-union militancy.

The apparent success of trade-union membership, along with unemployment and the rate of change of prices, in explaining UK inflation, has been subjected to a systematic and vigorous analysis by D. L. Purdy and G. Zis.[10] Using slightly different methods of measuring the variables, which Hines used in his estimating equations, such as estimating the proportion of the labour force unionized with respect that potentially unionizable (i.e. excluding members of the armed forces and the self-employed) rather than the total labour force, using annual rather than quarterly observations, and using similar methods of comparing the rates of change of the basic variables, they find that the significance of the trade-union militancy as a determinant of inflation is dramatically reduced. Whereas Hines found that a one per cent change in the proportionate rate of change of the labour force which is unionized resulted in an eight per cent change in wages, they find such a change would only produce a change in wages of a little over one-half of one per cent. Their general conclusion therefore is that Hines' results lack robustness and that they seem to be especially dependent on the particular way the variables are measured and computed.

In a separate study they went further and examined the extent to which the proportion of the labour force which was unionized was an independent cause of wage inflation or to what extent it reflected the relocation of the labour market and was therefore a passive element in the inflationary process. In order to analyse this they divided the change in the proportion of the labour force which is unionized into two separate elements; that arising from a reallocation of labour between unionized and non-unionized industries and sectors and the remainder which is a measure of militancy. They found that the latter might have had a very small impact in influencing wages in the inter-war years but that it had no effect whatever in the post-war period. They also went on to criticize the choice of the proportion of the labour force unionized as an index of militancy on the ground that it bore no relation to any underlying theory regarding the behaviour and objectives of trade unions. The conclusion therefore which we are forced to draw from their studies is that while trade-union militancy may in principle be a cause of inflation, the evidence which we have suggests it to be of negligible importance.

Cost inflation and market power

Unlike the debate over the causes of inflation in the UK – which has tended to focus on the militancy of trade unions – that in the US has been more concerned with the market power of large firms. The point of departure, which derives from the work of Gardiner Means in analysing the behaviour of industrial prices in the United States during the Great Depression, is the observation that in an advanced industrial economy very few markets are characterized by the kind of price flexibility which is assumed in neo-classical economic theory. Prices tend to be rigid, 'sticky', inflexible; in general unresponsive to changing demand and, in certain cases, remaining unchanged or even rising in a recession. The stock market, the commodities market and the foreign exchange market, in which prices change daily and even hourly, are the exception; the markets for steel, cars and manufactured goods, in which prices change infrequently and rise even when demand is falling, are the norm. The major reason which is put forward to explain this phenomenon, with its inflationary bias, is the highly concentrated industrial structure of modern economies. Most industries are dominated by a few large firms which have discretion over the prices they can fix and who realize that it is not in their own joint interest to engage in price wars. In other words, unlike the competitive ideal of traditional economics most industrial firms are 'price setters' rather than 'price takers'. Somehow – and regrettably it is rarely if ever well explained – the existence of discretionary pricing power imparts an upward bias not only to the price level but also to the rate of inflation. This is a thesis which has had powerful support in certain Congressional and Presidential committees and forms the background to the Kennedy wage-price guideposts of 1962 and the Nixon price freeze of 1971. Needless to say, it easily fits into the Galbraithian schema of the workings of contemporary capitalism.

A classic example of the 'perverse' behaviour of prices and one which has been used extensively in support of the present thesis is that of the United States steel industry in the fifties and early sixties. Between 1955 and 1960 the wholesale price index of iron and steel rose by 21 per cent whereas the wholesale price index of all commodities rose by 8 per cent. Over the same period the steel industry output fell by 22 per cent despite the fact that capacity utilization was no greater than 80 per cent, and was less during strikes and recessions. Higher prices meant that profit margins remained high despite the fall in output and that the rate of return on capital fell by less than in other industries. Because increased steel prices accounted for 52 per cent of the rise in the general wholesale price index from 1953 to 1958, the steel industry was accused of using its market power to raise profits and create inflation. It was against this background that the confrontation between the industry and President Kennedy took place in 1962. In the previous year Kennedy had written to the steel companies and the unions concerned urging them to forego price and wage rises. When US Steel responded with an across-the-board price rise the President threatened anti-trust action, the use of the FBI and created considerable bitterness between the business community and the administration. Although such Presidential intervention has made the pricing policy of the steel industry notorious, the 'administered price' thesis would claim that such behaviour is not untypical of a large number of industries.

A number of comments need to be made about this view. In the first place because the effective price at which transactions take place can change even though the list price remains unchanged, the official price index tends to distort the extent of price flexibility in the economy. The quality of the product, lot size, location, the credit-worthiness of the buyer, 'trade relations', tie-in sales, introductory offers, speed of delivery and the guarantee of being supplied in times of 'shortage' are all factors which can and do vary, thereby effectively changing the price at which transactions take place. In order to take account of the effect of these factors on price, Stigler and Kindahl, in an important study, collected data from buyers of actual prices paid over the period 1958–63 and then used this data to construct price indices. These indices behaved differently from those of the Bureau of Labor Statistics, which were compiled from returns by sellers, and in particular revealed much greater downward flexibility of prices – the result of a widespread practice of sellers offering discounts from list prices. For example, in a comparison of price changes between sixty-two different industries, the official statistics showed no change in prices in 31 per cent of the indices during the 1958 recession, whereas the Stigler and Kindahl index showed no change in only 3 per cent; in the 1961 recession the respective figures were 39 and 5 per cent. Individual price indices also show much greater variation than official indices, especially during periods of slack in the economy. Even though the evidence does not refute the general asymmetry in price movements nor the fact that price changes are less volatile and sensitive to recession than they used to be, it does suggest that there is much greater flexibility, especially downward, in prices than appears from the official index.

In the second place the inertia of the price system – namely the fact that over the short run many prices are unresponsive to changing demand, as well as their failure to fall significantly in the face of a recession – is only tentatively linked to industrial concentration and oligopolies. In fact there are many reasons why prices do not adjust instantaneously to changing demand. Changing prices is a costly business for a company even if it operates in a competitive market; not only are there administrative costs involved to the sellers but constantly changing prices also impose an inconvenience on buyers who are forced to devote more time to finding out about prices. As a result we tend to observe stable prices even in certain markets which are reasonably competitive, such as restaurants and entertainment. Moreover, in markets for durable products changes in demand are reflected in the first instance in changed inventories and only later in changed prices. In many markets (not least labour markets and sources of supplies of raw materials for companies) contracts tend to be fixed for a certain length of time so that if demand changes the terms of the contract and especially the price are not easily affected. In nearly all industrial economies many services whose prices are included in the official price index (such as transport, housing and public utilities) are either provided by the public sector or else by the private sector but subject to public regulation; in either case the timing of price changes depends on many factors other than the state of the markets. Lastly price changes tend to be infrequent during periods of price and wage controls and when firms do raise prices they are typically 'justified' by reference to a previous cost increase. Even if, therefore, there was little concentration in the industrial structure of modern economies we would still expect considerable inertia in price changes. But if there are only a few firms in an industry it will of course be advantageous for them to co-ordinate price changes in order to avoid price wars and earn the reputation of charging more than their competitors – one more factor making for sluggishness in the price mechanism.

The evidence from studies of price behaviour in manufacturing industry in the United States suggests that concentration is a factor which does affect price behaviour. In highly concentrated industries firms tend to delay price rises during periods of accelerating inflation and to catch up by raising prices later in the cycle – typically during a period of slack demand. Because price rises in such industries tend to follow cost increases and especially because of their timing, the operation of a lag between changing demand and price can easily be mistaken as evidence for a cost-push theory of inflation. The evidence from the US manufacturing industry over the period 1954–73 suggests that prices both rise *less* and fall *less* over the business cycle in concentrated industries than in other industries making it very difficult to conclude that such industries are using their market power to promote inflation.

The greatest weakness of the administered price thesis, however, is that like many versions of the wage push theory it is seriously incomplete as an explanation of inflation, largely because it confuses a theory of relative prices and of industry pricing with a theory of the general price level. If a small number of firms which control the output of an industry collude to increase profits, the effect is to raise the price at which they sell their output relative to that of other industries. Even if the government pursued a passive monetary policy, for market power to be the cause of inflation it would be necessary to show that the extent of market power itself had been increasing over the last decade. If we approximate market power to the average market concentration in manufacturing industries in the United States, this does not hold. In addition, the average rate of price increase for high concentration groups in the US manufacturing industry between 1954 and 1973 was substantially less than for low concentration groups, which is very powerful evidence against the former being a cause of inflation. The reason for this, incidentally, is that these industries have shown greater productivity gains, largely as a result of management introducing cost-saving methods of production. The conclusion to which we are drawn therefore is that while firms which are price-setters behave differently to those in an atomistic market, and that while this is of considerable significance for the transmission of monetary impulses throughout the economy, they are not themselves an autonomous factor in creating inflation.

6 Inflation or unemployment – the false dilemma

'To be able to pay off the national debt, defray the expenses of government without taxation, and in fine, to make the fortunes of the whole community is a brilliant prospect, when once a man is capable of believing that printing a few characters on bits of paper will do it. The philosopher's stone could not be expected to do more.'

J. S. Mill, Principles of Political Economy

No discussion of the causes of inflation would be complete without reference to the relationship between inflation and unemployment referred to as the 'Phillips Curve'. Over the last decade a good deal of debate has centred on this concept not only within the economics profession but also in political debate. The term itself originates from a celebrated paper by A. W. Phillips of the London School of Economics and Political Science, in which, on the basis of evidence drawn from the United Kingdom between 1861 and 1957, he showed the existence of a negative but non-linear relationship between the percentage increases in wages and the percentage of the labour force unemployed.[1] Figure 4 shows the annual plots from 1861 to 1913 of the percentage rates of change of money wage rates and the average rate of unemployment.

The basic idea behind Phillips' original work was a fairly straightforward application of the principle of supply and demand to the labour market. One of the cornerstones of economic theory is the notion that the price of any product or service is determined by supply and demand. If the demand for a product or a service is greater at the prevailing price than the supply coming on the market, the theory predicts that in ordinary circumstances the price will rise to clear the market. Similarly if the demand for a product or service falls short of the quantity coming on the market, the price will fall. In both cases we can also assume that the rate at which the price rises or falls is related to the discrepancy between demand and supply. As the wage rate is the price of labour services and as these services are exchanged in a market, it seems reasonable to assume that the price in this market can be explained on the same grounds as prices in other markets. When the demand for labour is high, we would expect unemployment to be relatively low and employers to be bidding against each other to attract existing labour to their particular companies. In the process, therefore, wage rates would be rising fairly rapidly. On the other hand, when the demand for

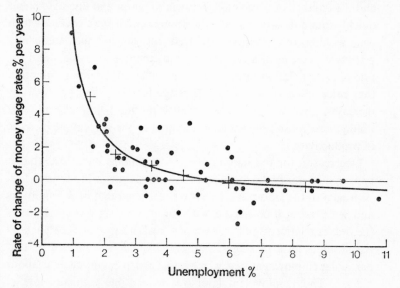

Figure 4. **The original Phillips curve, 1861-1913**
Source: A. W. Phillips, 'The Reation between Unemployment and the Rate of Change of Money Wages in the United Kingdom 1861–1957', *Economica*, November 1958.

labour is low, unemployment would be relatively higher and firms would not have to compete so aggressively against each other to attract additional workers. As a result wages would not be rising rapidly. Apart from the level of unemployment, Phillips also argued that wages would be affected by the rate at which the demand for labour was changing and the rate of change of retail prices. If we imagine two years in which the average level of unemployment is the same but in one of which the demand for labour is rising rapidly while in the other it is rising slowly, we would expect that wages would rise more rapidly in the former situation than the latter. Similarly if retail prices are rising rapidly because of, for example, sharp increases in import prices, we expect cost-of-living considerations to appear in wage bargaining.

In the decade following Phillips' contribution in 1958, the Phillips curve was hailed by the majority of economists and policy-makers as one of the great empirical laws of economics.

Phillips' curves were constructed for most developed countries, and the concept of a trade-off between inflation and unemployment quickly found its way into most textbooks and lecture courses which dealt with macro-economics. The trade-off was, however, frequently presented in terms of a relationship between unemployment and the rate of *price* inflation rather than wage inflation. On the assumption that price increases are equal to wage increases less productivity increases, such a curve was parallel to but below the original Phillips relationship by an amount equal to the percentage increase in productivity.

One reason for the importance of the Phillips curve was that it appeared to clarify the meaning of 'full employment'. In the classical approach to the labour market, it was assumed that both employers and workers were concerned with the purchasing power of wages (i.e. wages relative to prices, so-called 'real' wages), rather than with the absolute level of wages. Full employment was defined as that particular employment level which happened to equilibrate the labour market. This employment level was compatible with any rate of inflation. The labour market as Keynes saw it at the height of the Great Depression was far removed from such a delicate equilibrating system. Workers were concerned not with the real purchasing power of wages but with their absolute level. They were resistant against any attempts to reduce nominal wages but at this wage level there were enormous numbers who found themselves involuntarily unemployed and who at the going rate would certainly accept work if it could be found. If the demand for labour rose more workers could be hired at prevailing rates. But a point would come when all those who were involuntarily unemployed had found work, so that if the demand for labour kept rising beyond this point wages would rise. This point was full employment. In both the classical and the Keynesian approaches the concept of full employment was thought of in terms of a definite total of workers or, put in a slightly different way, as a percentage of the labour force which was unemployed. The Phillips curve, however, denied that full employment could be thought of in this black and white way and seemed to offer an explanation of the co-existence of some unemployment and some inflation in a capitalist economy working at or near full capacity. Full employment was to be thought of as a region or zone in which there could be varying combinations of inflation and unemployment.

Another reason for the popularity of the Phillips curve was that it appeared to offer society a definite set of choices. It was impossible to achieve both full employment and price stability, because the region to the left of the Phillips curve was unobtainable. The region to the right of the Phillips curve was undesirable because that meant a higher rate of inflation and a higher level of unemployment. The best that society could do was move along the Phillips curve. Here the choice was between less inflation at the cost of higher unemployment or less unemployment but at the cost of more inflation. However unpalatable the menu might seem – in that both inflation and unemployment were in themselves undesirable – the trade-off was assumed to be a stable relationship which forced policy-makers to choose. The exact point a country chose would depend very much on its previous history of inflation and unemployment. A country like the US which had suffered severe unemployment in the inter-war years but had not experienced the holocaust of hyperinflation, would in all probability be prepared to tolerate more inflation in order that unemployment might be reduced. On the other hand, a country such as Germany which had experienced a near-total collapse from a runaway inflation would be much more cautious and would insist on a relatively low rate of inflation.

The Phillips curve could also be used to show the impact of different types of economic policy. Through the use of monetary and fiscal policy the government could change aggregate expenditure, and move along the Phillips curve. A reduction in the rate of growth of the money supply, higher taxes and reduced public expenditure would produce a deflationary policy, but at the expense of increased unemployment. An increase in the money supply and a public sector deficit would produce an expansionary policy, with less unemployment but higher inflation. The more attractive economic policies were not those which moved along the curve but those which could shift the curve so that a given rate of inflation would be accompanied by less unemployment, or a given level of unemployment associated with a lower rate of inflation. An incomes policy has been presented as something which could do just this. Either through a voluntary policy, by which the government can 'lean' on wage and price agreements to make them conform with guidelines, or a statutory policy of wage and price controls, the Phillips relationship is changed (moved to the left) and the menu of choice for society improved. Similar results could be achieved through a whole range of policies which tried to improve the efficiency and mobility of the labour market – job-retraining programmes, the dissemination of information, manpower planning, the abolition of minimum wage laws, restrictive practices, subsidies, tariffs and quotas.

The collapse of the Phillips curve

The experience of nearly all developed capitalist economies in the late 1960s and early 1970s presented the Phillips curve with a major challenge. In one country after another a higher rate of inflation was accompanied by a higher level of unemployment. The evidence for the UK shown in Figure 5, which is fairly representative of the experience of all developed countries, shows that over the post-war period until the mid-1960s the Phillips curve seemed to have had a certain empirical validity: periods of relatively rapid wage rises were accompanied by low levels of unemployment, while periods of fairly small wage increases were associated with higher levels of unemployment. But between 1968 and 1972 an explosion in wages and prices was accompanied by a higher level of unemployment than at any time in the post-war period. This experience, which was totally unpredicted, led economists to question not only the *stability* of the Phillips relationship but also its very *existence*. And in the spate of literature which has attempted to come to grips with this problem, three major strands of thinking stand out.

In the first place there are those to whom inflation is synonymous with cost inflation and who find any relationship between inflation and unemployment to be utterly spurious. Because wage inflation and unemployment are supposedly determined by separate factors, any empirical connection there may be between the two is explained entirely by random factors. Wage inflation is the result of the conflict between labour and capital over the size of their respective shares in

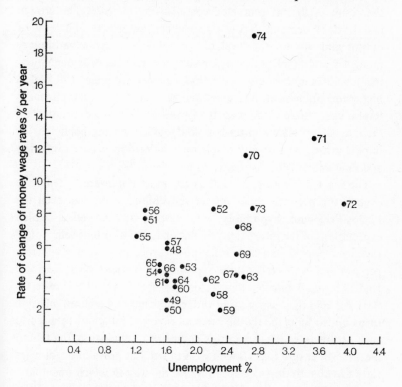

Figure 5. **Unemployment and the rate of change of wages in the United Kingdom, 1948-74**

the gross national product, and of the attempt by trade unions to change wage differentials to their own advantage; and price inflation depends on wage increases, direct and indirect tax rises and upward movements in import prices. The important point about this thesis is that neither wage nor price inflation have anything to do with either the level, or the rate of change of the level, of aggregate demand, and therefore by implication with the size of the public sector budgetary surplus or deficit, or the rate of growth of the money supply. In fact, according to this hypothesis, a reduction in aggregate demand by, for example, an increase in indirect taxation will be inflationary in that it will lead directly and indirectly to higher prices: directly through the increased mark-up in the shops as a result of the tax rise and indirectly through higher wage demands, the result of the tax-generated cost-of-living increase. The growth and level of demand, however, do affect the growth and level of output and in turn the level of unemployment. An expansionary monetary and fiscal policy will result in a reduction in unemployment, while a more cautious demand management policy will lead to higher unemployment. As a consequence a particular unemployment level is compatible with a variety of rates of inflation depending on the intensity of class and trade-union conflict and the behaviour of import prices, so that any empirical relationship between inflation and unemployment must be spurious.

The most interesting, as well as the most important, attempt to explain the perverse behaviour of the Phillips curve has been the Phelps-Friedman hypothesis with respect to the effect which expectations of the future rate of inflation have on current behaviour.[2] Imagine a world in which inflation is proceeding at a given rate per year and in which consumers, producers, workers, borrowers and lenders have all adjusted their behaviour in the light of this expectation. All hold their expectation with confidence and realized inflation turns out to be precisely the same as expected inflation. In a world such as this in which inflation is completely anticipated, the labour market will ensure that all who wish to work at prevailing real wage rates are able to do so. Depending on the way in which unemployment is defined and the method by which unemployment statistics are collected, the published labour market statistics still record a certain percentage of the labour force as unemployed. This we define as the 'natural' rate of unemployment.[3] It is not 'natural' in the sense that it cannot change or be changed through time. It clearly can. It can be influenced by restrictive practices in the labour market, minimum wage laws, manpower policies, the availability of information about job vacancies, the efficiency of employment exchanges and so on. But this state of unemployment is 'natural' in the sense that if all of these features of the economy are taken as given, it is the one rate of unemployment compatible with price stability or a *stable* rate of inflation – regardless of the magnitude of that particular *rate* of inflation. In other words, in an economy in which the behaviour of individuals is fully adjusted to future price changes, the Phillips curve is a vertical line which cuts the ordinate at the natural rate of unemployment, so that the natural rate is invariant to the rate of inflation.

The situation is very different, however, over a short period of time in which individuals guess future prices incorrectly. Imagine a situation in which prices have been rising steadily at 3 per cent per year, wages at 5 per cent per year, labour productivity at 2 per cent per year, in which the real economy is growing at 4 per cent per year, the central bank has been increasing the money supply at 7 per cent per year and the 'natural' rate of unemployment is $2\frac{1}{2}$ per cent. In addition, let us assume that individuals have come to adjust their behaviour to a 3 per cent annual rate of inflation, so that all kinds of economic contracts reflect this fact. Now suppose in this situation that the central bank raises the rate of growth of the money supply to, let us say, 10 per cent a year. The increased expenditure which results from the process will mean that companies find their sales have risen and their inventories are being depleted so that they can raise their prices and as a consequence they will wish to produce more to meet the extra demand. As a result they will in time try to hire more labour. But this will just not be true for one company but for all. As a result companies will start bidding-up wage rates in order to attract more labour. But the individuals who either supply or potentially supply labour services still continue to assume that prices will carry on rising at only 3 per cent a year. The fact therefore that wages are rising more rapidly than 5 per cent but that prices are expected to rise by only 3 per cent means that more workers are attracted into employment and that un-employment falls below the 'natural' rate of 2·5 per cent. Put in a more familiar way, the economy is moving along the Phillips curve, unemployment is falling and the rate of wage increases has risen by a small amount. But at this point we reach the crux of the argument. The economy can only move from one point to another on the Phillips curve providing that people do not revise their expectations of the future rate of inflation. While this may be a sensible assumption to make about the short run it makes no sense whatever over a longer time-period, as it implies that individuals are irrational and

I—4

unconcerned with their own best economic interests, in that they do not adjust their behaviour in the light of revised estimates of the future rise in the cost of living.

As a result of the monetary expansion, prices as well as wages will begin to rise more rapidly. But as both sides of the labour market come to realize that an inflation of 5 per cent rather than 3 per cent is not temporary but permanent, wages will tend to settle down to a growth of 8 per cent a year. The more rapid rate of growth of wages will force companies to realize that they employed too much labour; and the permanently higher rate of growth of prices will force workers to realize that when they previously observed money wage rates rising, they were tricked into believing that real wages had risen, but in fact as a result of the reduced purchasing power of their pay packet they find that they are no better-off than before. The combination of employers wanting to shed themselves of some of the labour they mistakenly hired, and of labour wanting to work less because they are no better-off in real terms than before, means that unemployment will tend to rise. It may temporarily rise above its natural rate, but if the labour market is stable, and there is no good *prima facie* reason for thinking otherwise, unemployment will settle down at the natural rate of 2·5 per cent, for only at that unemployment level can wages rise at 9 per cent, prices at 6 per cent and the money supply at 9–10 per cent per year. It alone is consistent with these three magnitudes. This example has shown therefore that the Phillips curve exists only in the short run, in which individuals incorrectly forecast the future. When they adjust their behaviour in the light of new evidence, the economy returns to the natural rate of unemployment, accompanied by a rate of price inflation which is fully anticipated.

The Phillips curve, therefore, offers a temporary but not a permanent trade-off between inflation and unemployment. Over a short period of time it is certainly possible to reduce unemployment, with very little extra cost in terms of a more rapid rate of inflation, but over a longer run period such a trade-off becomes impossible as individuals adapt their behaviour to a changed economic climate. In the long run there is no trade-off between inflation and unemployment at all. If the money supply grows more rapidly the only lasting feature is a permanently higher rate of inflation.

The third major view of the Phillips curve accepts the fact that expectations of future price movements have an effect on present economic behaviour, but denies that expectations are ever fully incorporated into actual decision-making. In the long run there is still a trade-off between unemployment and inflation however perverse it may be; in other words the long-run Phillips curve may be very steep, but it is not vertical. One reason for this outcome is the view that although the participants of the labour market form expectations of future inflation, their expectations are rarely correct. During a period of accelerating inflation, the rate of future inflation tends to be underestimated and during periods of deceleration overestimated. Another reason for a long-run non-vertical Phillips curve, even when inflation is correctly anticipated, has to do with the cost of making wage changes. It is typically observed that when employers are faced with a labour shortage they tend to hire less able workers, spend more on recruitment and hire specialist contractors rather than raise wages. While these facts may be partly explained in terms of the inability of firms to discriminate in pay between new and old employees and in part by the expectation that the labour shortage is temporary, nevertheless one reason for this is that any wage rise creates problems relating to the whole wage and salary structure of the company which could be very troublesome. The effect of such behaviour is continuous disequilibrium in the labour market; because of the cost of adjusting wages, an excess demand for labour results in more workers being hired rather than increased wages. A moderate rate of inflation will therefore result in a permanently higher level of employment than for example no inflation at all. If the rate of inflation becomes sufficiently high, however, so that the cost of inflation is greater to companies than the cost of making wage changes, no such long-run trade-off exists and the Phillips curve is once again vertical. A third explanation of the same phenomenon has to do with market imperfections. Assume that prices tend to be rigid in a downward direction, and that for various reasons an adjustment of relative prices is needed. If this took place in an economy in which there was a stable overall price level it would result in considerable unemployment. But if it was accompanied by a moderate rate of inflation, the amount of unemployment that would be needed to facilitate the adjustment would be that much less. Once again the conclusion which we reach is that a moderate rate of inflation will result in a lower permanent level of unemployment than a zero rate of inflation.

Economic theory and the Phillips curve

The fact that the Phillips curve has in such a short space of time become one of the basic concepts of macro-economics should not cause us to overlook the fact that it is at variance with traditional price theory since the time of Adam Smith.[4] The theory of price determination which is based on the assumption that both consumers and producers act in their own best interests in order to maximize consumption and the net wealth of companies suggests that prices will respond fairly rapidly to changes in supply and demand. An excess demand will lead to a rise in price and an excess supply to a fall in price. This is something which is as true for the labour market as for commodity, financial or capital markets. But the Phillips curve seems to suggest that labour markets can be in permanent or quasi-permanent disequilibrium. High unemployment coexists with substantial and continued wage rises. In this sense the Phillips curve seems to depend either on irrational behaviour on the part of employers or workers or both, or on the existence of constraints which prohibit the labour market from working. It is extremely unsatisfactory that one of the cornerstones of macro-economics should be in conflict with the vast body of economic theory, which is based on the assumption of the rational behaviour of various economic units. Numerous attempts have been made in the last decade by economic theorists to resolve this paradox, and to develop a theory of the Phillips curve that assumes that consumers and producers act rationally and that markets are not constrained for institutional reasons from being allowed to work.

One such explanation is the 'search' theory of labour market behaviour, in which workers are assumed to search for jobs and employers to search for labour. The basis of the search theory is that the problem of gathering information about potential jobs, wage rates, employers' offers and employees' bids is crucial for understanding the way in which these markets work. The labour market is a heterogeneous collection of separate markets in which employers and workers have only partial information on the state of the market and in which for both groups there are real economic costs involved in obtaining more information. In this situation both employers and workers have to develop a search strategy as it would clearly not make sense for a worker to accept the first wage which was offered or for an employer to set the wage at a level so that he obtained as much labour as he needed instantly. The worker has to balance the gains from search (the discounted value of higher wages) against the cost (the loss of earnings) and the employer the gains from waiting (the discounted value of paying lower wages) against the cost of hiring more labour immediately (higher wages). From these assumptions we can argue that at least a certain amount of unemployment is voluntary, due to a perfectly rational response on the part of the labour market. Imagine a world in which prices are rising at a stable rate and in which inflation is completely anticipated, but in which changes are taking place because of changing consumer preferences, new products and technological innovation. Such changes as these would necessitate changes in the labour market and because of the necessity of search would create a certain amount of unemployment, which could be termed frictional or natural unemployment.

These assumptions also enable one to derive a Phillips curve. Imagine the economy is at a position in which a completely anticipated inflation is proceeding at a steady rate and that initial unemployment is entirely voluntary. Assume further that the central bank increases the rate of growth of the money supply. This will lead to an increase in the rate of growth of demand which will be accompanied by a rise in corporate sales, and a running-down of stocks, so providing firms with an incentive to hire more labour. As firms increase their wage offers, they will be able to hire more workers who interpret the higher wages not as part of the inflationary process but as their success in obtaining a higher wage as a result of search activity. But this process is simply a movement along a Phillips curve; the rate of inflation has increased and has been accompanied by a fall in the level of unemployment. We can imagine a similar movement in the opposite direction if the rate of growth of the money supply was reduced: corporate sales fall, stocks accumulate and rather than take a cut in wages, workers engage in search activity based on the conviction that their own experience is not representative of the market as a whole. In other words, a reduction in the growth of wages is accompanied by increased unemployment and so we have a movement along the Phillips curve.

Another new theory of the labour market which provides a rationalization for the Phillips curve is the continuous auction market theory. In this theory the labour market is treated like any other commodity market; it being assumed, in contrast to the search theory, that labour is 'homogeneous' and that the information of the state of the market is fairly readily available to all. Much as in a commodity market, where the price of commodities would be responsive to the forces of supply and demand, so in this market the wage rate is also assumed to respond to these factors. In particular we can assume an upward trend in wages which results from the trend rate of growth of real output and inflation but with deviations from this trend resulting from an excess of demand or supply. During a boom period when wages and prices are above their trend level we would expect that the number employed would rise and, during a recessionary period, the number employed would fall. The rationalization for this is very straightforward: if workers are concerned not only with their immediate wage but also with their lifetime earnings, they are clearly going to find it advantageous to work more in boom periods when wages are relatively high and less in periods of recession when wages are relatively low, invest their increased earnings at a market rate of interest and so spend them in periods when prices are relatively low. But the process by which when inflation is at a higher than average rate during boom periods, more people are drawn into employment so that unemployment falls, and when inflation is at a lower than average rate during periods of recession less people are drawn into employment so that unemployment rises, precisely fits the facts described by the Phillips curve. For people who remain in the labour force most of their working life this theory would explain the amount of overtime worked. It would also be especially pertinent in explaining the behaviour of those who enter and leave the market: married women, part-time workers, young people, the retired and semi-retired.

Yet another approach in explaining the Phillips curve which

assumes rationality on the part of labour and employers and which makes minimum concessions to institutional factors is the quasi-contract model. The basis of the model is that in general (though there are notable exceptions) workers have an aversion to exposing themselves to risk. In particular they are interested in security of employment and in the fact that wage rates should advance steadily as a result of productivity and cost-of-living changes, rather than fluctuate in the short term in response to market factors. The employ-ment of labour can therefore be thought of as a legally unenforcible contract – the quasi-contract – which guarantees that under normal conditions the employer will have a reasonable degree of security with respect to wages and employment. Employees are prepared to accept a lower wage if they have an undertaking that it will not move up and down during periods of tightness and ease in the market and if in addition they have reasonable security of tenure. This means that an employer has an incentive to maintain a fairly sticky wage or set of wage rates and to develop the reputation of being a 'good employer' by not sacking during periods of slight recession and hiring less during periods of boom. The reason this model produces a negatively sloped relation between inflation and unemployment is that during periods of continued ease or tightness in the labour market, employers will revise their long-term expectations and so change the wage rate. For example, during a period when the labour market is tight as a result of an expansion of demand and more rapid price inflation, employers will be induced to raise wages because of the expected rate of inflation being that much greater.

The evidence on the Phillips curve

Interpreting the empirical evidence on the Phillips curve is difficult for a number of reasons. In the first place existing evidence is by no means conclusive even on such basic matters as the existence of a short- or long-run trade-off between inflation and unemployment or the effects of inflationary expectations. In addition, the data on which the studies are based relate to periods in which the labour market has operated relatively freely, but also to some periods in which there has been substantial intervention by the government in order to control wages and prices. Thirdly, different studies relate to different countries over different time-periods and employ different statistical techniques. And lastly, the amount of research which has been done and is being done is formidable. Despite the heterogeneity of the studies and the nihilism in the guise of statistical refinement which underlies some studies in particular, a number of conclusions can be drawn.

In the *short run* the Phillips curve exists and is not very steep. Most studies which have examined the inflationary process have found that unemployment is a significant explanatory variable in predicting the behaviour of wages, and that in turn the rate of change of wages has a substantial and significant impact on the rate of change of prices. This is true for the UK, the US, Canada, West Germany, France, Australia and Japan. They have also found that the slope of the curve is rather small. In a study of quarterly wage determination in the UK between 1956 and 1971, Parkin, Sumner and Ward estimated the coefficient relating wage changes to un-employment as two per cent, so that if the unemployment rate increased from, for example, two per cent to three per cent, the rate of wage inflation would be reduced by two per cent.[5] The fact that the curve is fairly shallow implies that in the short run there could be a considerable increase in real output and therefore reduction in unemployment, as the result of an expansionary monetary and fiscal policy, without a notable change in the rate of inflation. On the other hand, a reduction in aggregate demand would lead to an initial reduction in unemployment and real output without a notice-able reduction in the rate of inflation.

Some studies which have been carried out on UK data also show that the slope of the curve is significantly affected by whether or not the government is operating an incomes policy. Other things being equal, the existence of an incomes policy tends to reduce the slope of the curve, so that an expansionary monetary and fiscal policy pursued during an incomes policy would result in a smaller increase in the rate of inflation than one pursued in the absence of such a policy.

Secondly, nearly all models find, and indeed Phillips' original work found, that the wage inflation-unemployment trade-off is affected by the rate of change of prices. The greater the rate of change of prices, *ceteris paribus*, the greater will be the rate of change of wages.

In other words, the Phillips curve shifts to the right, the greater the expected rate of price inflation. In particular the study mentioned previously found that it was this factor which was responsible for explaining the wages 'explosions' of 1966 and 1969. This is a very important conclusion for it implies a rationality on the part of the suppliers of labour which is absent in Keynesian analysis. Workers as well as employers are interested in the real rather than the nominal value of their wages.

The rate of wage inflation, and therefore the position of the Phillips curve, is also affected by the expected rate of income tax and social security payments. An increase in the ratio of take-home pay to gross pay, the result, for example, of a reduction in income tax or social security contributions, will result in a lower rate of wage inflation. An increase in income tax will shift the curve to the right and a lowering of tax to the left.

Fourthly, there is the question of the long-run trade-off. The study by Parkin, Sumner and Ward finds that there is no long-run trade-off between inflation and unemployment. If the long-run rate of productivity growth is $2\frac{1}{2}$ per cent per year this implies a natural rate of unemployment of 1·7 per cent. In the long run policy-makers cannot reduce unemployment below the natural rate without an accelerating rate of inflation.

7 How new is the 'New Inflation'?

It is now time to piece the jigsaw together. Over the past few years various explanations of the present inflation have been advanced: excessive growth of the money supply, trade-union militancy, higher import prices, property speculation, excessive taxation. These explanations do not fit at all easily together and in some cases are mutually exclusive. The picture which emerges, therefore, tends to be incomplete and confused. Most people intuitively feel that any explanation which ignores the power of trade unions is somehow untrue to what they judge to have been the realities in the United Kingdom over the past decade; equally any explanation which pays no regard to the creation of money and the imbalances in the national finances is also found deficient. The core of the problem is the role and importance of money in explaining the inflationary process and the way in which increases in the stock of money relate to non-monetary factors such as trade-union militancy, the quest for economic growth and the restlessness of contemporary society; more generally it is the extent to which the cause of inflation can be explained by monetary or non-monetary factors.

As a general problem this one is not new and past inflations have given rise to a remarkably similar debate. On the one hand, there have been those who have seen inflation as the result of the debasement of the coinage or the excessive issue of fiduciary paper, but there have invariably been others who have explained the same phenomena in non-monetary terms. Diocletian in the *Edict on Maximum Prices* in AD 301 cites as responsible for inflation those 'persons of unlimited and frenzied avarice', the merchants; Louis Blanc, writing on revolutionary France, evidences the monopolists; even in Germany during the hyperinflation of 1923 one school of thought held that the inflation resulted from a depreciating exchange rate itself the effect of perverse foreign influences. Despite different views of causation most are agreed on one fact: no sustained inflation has ever taken place without an accompanying rise in the stock of money. But to say that inflation is a monetary phenomenon is to say more than this. The thesis I have sought to advance in the last three chapters is that inflation is the result of an excess demand for the output of a society and that the primary cause of such excess demand is the creation of money by the government. This is not to deny the importance of non-monetary factors, but to argue that their role is in bringing pressure to bear on governments to increase the rate of growth of the money stock more rapidly than otherwise. In this sense all inflations which are either the result of coinage debasement or the growth of fiat money have a political *raison d'être*, because the creation of money by governments is invariably the result of competing and inconsistent political claims being made on an economic system.

If we use this framework to analyse British inflation we need to distinguish three particular phases over the post-war period. Firstly we have to ask why it is that we have had continually rising prices since 1945, whereas over the preceding hundred years there were periods of rising, falling and stable prices. Next we have to explain the global acceleration of inflation since the late 1960s; and thirdly we have to account for the fact that British inflation in the mid-1970s is twice that of the average for other Western countries.

In the first instance, each of these phases of post-war inflation can be associated with different rates of growth of the money supply. If we compare the creeping inflation of the last three decades with the previous century we find that with the exception of only one year, 1955, money supply has grown every year since 1945. Then if we examine its behaviour since the late 1960s we find that its annual growth rate was substantially greater – around 14 per cent. In the two years 1972–3 it was dramatically higher, averaging 25 per cent. The argument of the last few chapters has been not simply that these distinct phases of inflation have been accompanied by distinctly different growth rates of the money supply but that the monetary factor has been a causal influence.

Such is the basic anatomy of inflation in post-war Britain. But, left at that, monetarism is a valley of dry bones. The bones only acquire life when put in a political context; and it is here that non-monetary factors play an extremely important role. In this sense the unrelenting inflation of the post-war years is the result of the commitment of successive governments to the concept of full employment, which was first put forward in the employment policy White Paper of 1944. It was a concept of full employment defined in a rather special way. In *Full Employment in a Free Society* Beveridge defined full employment to mean 'having always more vacant jobs than unemployed men' so that 'the labour market should always be a sellers market than a buyers market'.[1] In such a world as this the dice are necessarily loaded. If the labour market is to be a sellers market, then regardless of the structure of the trade-union movement, the militancy of trade unions, the degree of unionization in society or the particular framework of the collective bargaining process, inflation *must* result. In fact, even if there were no trade unions at all, such a commitment would inevitably produce inflation. In fairness to Beveridge it should be said that he recognized the inflationary potential of his ideas but claimed that it could be avoided by a responsible attitude on the part of trade-union leaders.

Over the post-war years the commitment to this kind of full employment has been taken up by all political parties, and it has been extended into the overwhelming importance of prosperity and economic growth as the proper objectives of a modern economy. Economics has dominated post-war politics and as a result the political parties have vied with each other, like supermarkets engaged in a price war over breakfast cereals, to produce a more rapid growth GNP, higher consumption, better hospitals, more schools and larger motorways in the quest for the good life. By disturbing the baser passions of greed, envy and covetousness, expectations have been created which no political party is in any position to satisfy. Witness the fact that although each party has made so much of growth and has introduced a succession of policy measures to stimulate the economy, all such measures have been singularly unsuccessful. Yet the restlessness which the taste of such expected affluence produces is the political breeding-ground for inflation. It is surely no accident that the money supply explosion of 1972–3 and the price explosion of 1974–5 were the result of a calculated gamble for a more rapid rate of economic growth in this country.

The basic commitment to full employment is the explanation for the post-war inflation. But the acceleration since the mid-1960s, although linked to the commitment to full employment, was triggered off by a more specific factor. The only reasonable explanation for the *global* acceleration of inflation since the later 1960s was the particular way in which the Vietnam War was financed by the United States government. In the mid-1960s President Johnson was determined to go ahead with his welfare programmes for the Great Society. At the same time the scale of war in Vietnam escalated. While the Joint Chiefs of Staff were pressing for a more realistic assessment of the scale and costs of the war, which would almost inevitably have led to higher taxes, President Johnson adamantly refused to consider higher taxes. Worse than this, as David Halberstam shows so clearly in his book *The Best and the Brightest*, he purposely misled even his own economic advisers by concealing from them the true military effort which was being planned by the Pentagon. If the massive increase in government spending was not to be financed by higher taxes there was only one avenue left: to pump more dollars into the economy and tax the nation through inflation.

The problem for the world, however, was that it was effectively on a dollar standard: since 1945 most countries currencies had been pegged to the US dollar. Like water finding its own level, dollars pumped into the US economy soon seeped out to the rest of the world. And what started as a trickle in the mid 1960s became by the late 1960s and the early 1970s an irresistible flood. Despite the strenuous efforts by countries such as Germany and Switzerland to stem the tide, they proved ultimately to be of no avail. Surplus dollars piled up in the foreign exchange reserves of most developed countries. Not surprisingly the results of the whole process were predictable: a more rapid inflation in the US in the later 1960s followed by a more rapid world inflation in the early 1970s.

But the British inflation of the mid-1970s is twice as rapid as the average of other developed countries. Once again, the rapid money supply growth of 1972–3 was the outcome of a political situation – in this case the misguided monetary policies of the 1970–4 Conservative government. After pursuing the cautious monetary policy which had been instituted by Roy Jenkins, the Chancellor of the Exchequer in the Labour Government during 1969–70, the government, after it had been in office less than a year, suddenly decided to make its famous U-turn. Enough of stagnation and controlling inflation: the time had come for bold adventurous policies designed to finally lift Britain out of decades of gloom. The target was nothing less than five per cent growth per annum – twice the historical record; and was to be realized by our entry into Europe and the larger market. The immediate stimulus to reflation was the prospect that if policies remained unchanged, unemployment would reach over a million bringing in its wake social and industrial unrest. While there was a very strong case for arguing that monetary and fiscal policy in 1971–2 should have been expansionary there was no case for an expansion of the order of 25–30 per cent which was the cause of the subsequent inflation. In order to maintain low interest rates to stimulate invest-ment and in turn growth, the Bank of England abandoned control over the money supply; yet the government repeatedly kept insisting that money supply growth defined in the proper way (M_1) was one of the lowest in Europe, and that through a fair and comprehensive prices and incomes policy they were well on the way to beating inflation. The intellectual confusion which underlay this policy was gross: prices and wages bore no relation to the money supply; interest rates could be arbitrarily fixed by the Bank of England with seemingly no adverse consequences for the economy at all, and the long term rate of growth of the economy could apparently be raised simply by stimulating aggregate demand. The end result has been a record level of interest rates, no increase in investment, zero growth, confrontation between the government and the trade union movement and the defeat of the Conservative Party at the polls twice in one year.

This then is the valid distinction between monetary and non-monetary factors. Needless to say, over the post-war years we have been inundated by a variety of invalid distinctions, the most common of which is the power of trade unions to directly lead to wage and price rises. One of the most curious distortions which inflation produces is to reverse in the popular (and, unfortunately, the less popular) mind the process of cause and effect. Effect is so easily mistaken for cause, and nowhere is this more obvious than in the role of trade unions in the inflationary process.

Trade unions can in principle exert three kinds of influences on the rates of inflation and the growth of the money supply.[2] Certain trade unions, namely those in the public sector, may be able to exercise a direct influence over the growth of the money supply. If a trade union in a nationalized industry successfully claims higher wages unmatched by higher prices or increased productivity, the industry will move into deficit, which in turn will have to be financed by the government and one such method of finance is to expand the money supply. This is a valid inflationary influence, but it is important to notice that it works through the subsequent effect of money creation and not directly through the wage rise. The direct effect of the wage settlement is the change in the structure of wages and prices. If, to raise its revenue, higher prices in this industry result, then less will be spent elsewhere in the economy. But total income and total spending remains unchanged. Another and equally valid role by which trade unions and especially the trade-union movement and the TUC is able to influence inflation is as a political pressure group urging the government to pursue reflationary policies. To the extent that the TUC is able to threaten a general strike or serious disruption of industry unless the government embarks on an easier money supply policy, and to the extent that the government concedes to such pressure for political reasons, money supply growth will be that much more rapid. Once again this may be a perfectly valid explanation of why governments behave as they do in response to trade-unions pressure, and of the causes of a more rapid rate of inflation.

From this political point of view there is no doubt that the Heath government was under enormous pressure in 1971 to pursue a reflationary policy. But even though this would explain the necessity of a reflationary policy, it would hardly account for its magnitude.

But these two processes need to be carefully distinguished from a third which is that trade unions are able to and do raise money wages, which are then underwritten by a more rapid expansion of the money supply. The idea is sometimes put forward that wage demands are produced by powerful trade unions like random numbers from a telephone directory and are then backed up by the threat of a general strike to ensure that they are translated into settlement. As a result cost increases lead directly to price increases and a higher rate of inflation. The evidence, as we have seen, does not justify such a view. If this particular view were just another idea it would be fairly innocuous. The problem however is that as a diagnosis of inflation it has plagued British economic policy throughout the post-war years and has been used as the theoretical foundation for a prices and incomes policy. If wage demands are arbitrary numbers, then the obvious remedy is for the government to step in and in the interests of the nation as a whole replace arbitrariness by order and fairness.

It is the mistaking of effect for cause leading to the false dichotomy between monetary and non-monetary causes that is responsible for the idea of the 'new inflation'. From an economic point of view the present inflation is 'new' only in a trivial sense, and even then not in the sense in which it is used by those who believe in the idea. The ultimate cause of inflation is still the excessive creation of money by the government; but the political pressures which are brought to bear on the government to act will in all probability be different from in the past. In a fundamental sense the present British inflation is no different from the major inflations of history, such as those of ancient Rome, France during the Revolution, England during the Napoleonic wars, Weimar Germany and various Latin American countries in the post-war years (not least the final months of Allende's Chile). All are the result of excessive money creation brought about by governments determined on the pursuit of policies which are fundamentally in-consistent with the basic characteristics of their economies. Yet although each was characterized by the creation of money, there were always reasons which can explain the monetary behaviour of governments; in ancient Rome it was to meet the expenses of the army; in Revolutionary France to pay for the expenses of the Revolution; in England during the Napoleonic Wars to finance the war effort; in Weimar Germany to finance the reparation repayments and alleviate the problem of poverty during the aftermath of war; in various Latin American countries in the post-war years to pay for capital and welfare expenditures; and in Allende's Chile to finance government expenditure programmes and provide finance for state-owned companies.

Despite the institutional differences between these historic parallels the British inflation is in exactly the same tradition as them; it is caused by an excessive creation of money, which results from pressures being made on the economic system which it is incapable of sustaining.

Part III

Effects

8 The inflation tax

*'The power of taxation by currency depreciation is one which has been
inherent in the State since Rome discovered it.'*

J. M. Keynes, A Tract on Monetary Reform (*1923*)

In the world in which we live, unlike those which are created in the
minds of economists, inflation is never an isolated event. It occurs in
a concrete political situation and its various effects are apparent in
specific historical situations. The appeal of an economic model
derives from the fact that one can double the money supply, halve the
level of government expenditure, devalue the currency and, as a result
derive fairly general conclusions with respect to the rate of inflation
regardless of political and social circumstances. Any discussion of the
effects of inflation is therefore immediately presented with a problem:
to be fairly general and pay little regard to the historical detail or to
be very careful about preserving the integrity of specific historical
situations and pay less regard to general economic principles. Needless to say economists have tended to the former, historians to the
latter. This chapter is concerned with the classical economic treatment of the problem of inflation as a tax on money and its various
effects. The principles are fairly general and apply to all inflationary
situations. The next chapter deals with the breakdown of the world
dollar standard and the international monetary system devised at
Bretton Woods. Then we discuss the fascinating subject of hyperinflation, when the supply of money is hopelessly out of control, and
we conclude this section by discussing the effects of inflation on the
institutions of capitalism and democracy.

Inflation as a tax on money

The starting point for analysing inflation is as a tax on money. Anyone who holds money during a period of inflation sustains a loss in its value or purchasing power, while anyone who issues money is able to secure a greater command than otherwise over real resources. As the government is the sole issuer of fiat money in all countries, it is the government which is able to increase its control over resources as the result of rising prices. In this respect, inflation has a similar effect to the government raising the rate of explicit taxes such as income tax, value added tax, or capital gains tax. In all cases, the government would find that as a result of higher tax rates it has more resources at its disposal.

It must be made clear what is meant in this context by the government gaining from the process of inflation. Some government expenditure such as defence exists for the general benefit of all while others exist for the particular advantage of some such as higher education. In either case it is financed either through taxation or debt. For a given level of expenditure, an increase in tax revenue from one source must result in its reduction from another, or else the redemption of debt; in both cases the discounted value of future tax liabilities for tax payers are lowered. Inflation as a tax, while directly benefiting the government, is ultimately of benefit to the taxpayer in that it may reduce present, and certainly will reduce future, tax liabilities in real terms. Inflation, therefore, is a tax levied on the holders of money which provides a benefit for all those who pay other kinds of taxes.

The nature of the inflation tax can be illustrated by a simple example. Suppose that the stock of money in the UK is equal to £5,000 million, and that the value of the UK GNP, measured in terms of a currency whose value is stable, say gold francs, is Fr.25,000 million. This implies that a pound sterling can be exchanged for five gold francs, or equivalently, for five gold francs worth of the gross national product. Let us further suppose that the UK government prints and coins an extra £5,000 million, so that the UK money stock is doubled. As a result, the stock of money is £10,000 million, but the total supply of goods and services which make up the gross national product are still only valued at 25,000 million gold francs. Instead of, as before, £1 being able to purchase 5 gold francs, it is now able to buy only 2·5 gold francs, or 2·5 gold francs worth of the gross national product. Those persons who held the initial £5,000 million balances find that their total purchasing power has been halved, because their initial money holdings are now able to command only 12,500 million gold francs or the equivalent amount of gross national product. A doubling of the money stock has resulted in a halving of the value of money. While those who initially held the money have lost, it is the government which has gained, because the government has been enabled to control real resources worth 12,500 million gold francs as a result of the issue of £5,000 million of extra notes and coins. A sum equivalent to 12,500 million gold francs has therefore been transferred from the private sector to the government as a result of the inflation; this is the revenue collected by the government from the inflation tax. Such an outcome as this would be equivalent to the government passing a law demanding that each person holding money must hand over fifty per cent of their money balances as a special levy. In both cases, whether through inflation or the imposition of the levy those holding money balances would find that their real purchasing power had been halved.

The revenue which the government collects from the inflation tax, like that from any other form of taxation, is equal to the tax rate times the tax base. The rate of tax is the rate of inflation while the base of the tax is the total outstanding monetary liabilities of the government sector, namely those of the central bank and the finance ministry. The revenue which the government collects from inflation depends, therefore, on two factors: the public's demand for money and the rate of inflation. In the case of the UK, the base is equal to the total of notes and coins in circulation with the non-bank public plus the cash reserves of the banks, notes and coins in tills plus bankers' deposits at the Bank of England. In 1974 the total of these two items was approximately £5,000 million. With a rate of inflation of between 10 and 15 per cent, the tax yield from inflation was approximately between £500 million and £750 million per annum.

It may be thought that the only way by which the government can increase its revenue from inflation is by increasing the rate of growth of the money supply, and so changing the rate of tax. If, however, we examine the kinds of policies pursued by governments, particularly by some countries in the Third World whose alternative sources of tax revenue are severely restricted, which rely or have relied on inflation as an important source of revenue, we find that various controls and regulations are purposely introduced in order to increase the demand for money and so raise the tax base.[1] The demand for money will be greater the less available are those assets which are fairly close substitutes for money. If the holding of money yields certain benefits which cannot be easily got from holding the next most liquid asset, more money will be held. In many countries restrictions are placed on the capital market which prevent the development of near-money substitutes and so increases the demand for money. Another measure which has exactly the same effect is government imposition of a legal maximum on the interest rates which banks are permitted to pay on deposits. One way in which payment of the inflation tax is avoided is by the holding of a foreign currency, whose rate of depreciation is less than that of the domestic currency. If corporations and individuals were to use foreign rather than domestic money as a store of value and only purchase domestic money when they needed to carry out transactions, the revenue which the government could collect from inflation would be reduced. This is one reason why in so many countries the holding of foreign currency is severely restricted, if not prohibited.

In one important respect, however, inflation is a rather special form of taxation. Unlike all other taxes which have to be approved by Parliament, it requires no such approval. The inflation tax is never debated in a finance bill. The government increases the money supply, usually for some seemingly desirable reason – to raise the rate of growth, to reduce the number of unemployed, to lower interest rates – the result is inflation, and, in the process, the government automatically collects the extra revenue. Because the administrative costs of the tax are small and tax avoidance is unprofitable until the rate of inflation reaches fairly substantial proportions, inflation is an attractive form of taxation for many governments who find it difficult to raise taxes in other forms.

It may be objected that viewing inflation as a tax, and therefore as an alternative to an income, excise or wealth tax, while perfectly feasible in the context of developing countries is somehow wholly inappropriate in the case of the UK Treasury. To the extent that the Treasury has never, to my knowledge, made an explicit justification for using inflation as a form of taxation, this is perfectly true. On the other hand, the Treasury has shown a certain reluctance to introduce measures which would reduce any gain which it receives from this particular method of taxation, such as paying an inflation-proof rate of return on its debt, or changing the tax allowance in line with inflation.

Apart from the tax which inflation imposes on money holdings, the government also gains from inflation in other ways. To the extent that certain forms of government debt, such as gilt-edged stock, Treasury bills, tax reserve certificates, national savings and deposits at trustee savings banks, pay rates of interest which are on average lower than the rate of inflation, a wealth transfer takes place from the private sector to the government. The government also benefits from inflation by being able to collect increased taxes, something which is usually referred to as 'fiscal drag'. If income tax is progressive then taxpayers will find that the proportion of their income which they pay as tax is greater simply because of the inflation.[2]

The costs of inflation

Like any other tax, inflation imposes a cost on society, which is measured by the loss in economic welfare which occurs *solely* as a result of the inflation.[3] It is a measure of the fact that resources have been directed from more productive uses merely in order for the economy to cope with inflation. It is important to emphasize that this cost is measured simply in terms of the increased inefficiency with which resources are used by the economy. It is not an attempt to measure the injustices created by the redistribution of income; nor is it an attempt to take into account any cost which may arise in connection with increased political instability.

Before we analyse the nature of this cost an important distinction has to be made between an *anticipated* and an *unanticipated* inflation. An anticipated inflation is one in which consumers, savers, tax-payers, producers, employees, rentiers, governments, exporters and importers correctly guess the timing and extent of future price rises and are free to adjust their behaviour accordingly; while an un-anticipated inflation is one in which they do not completely estimate the pace of future inflation and consequently adjust present contracts only partially. For example, in negotiating a wage contract over a future twelve-month period, a trade union will not only want to estimate its members' increased productivity in real terms, but also the expected rise in the cost of living which should be reflected in the higher prices at which the company is able to sell its products. If it correctly forecasts the rate of inflation over the year and the company is prepared to agree with its estimate and therefore settle the particular claim, the percentage wage increase will be equal to the productivity increase plus the expected rate of inflation. This is a situation of anticipated inflation. On the other hand, if the rise in the general level of prices over the next twelve months is totally unexpected, the wage demands and the wage settlements will be that much less. The same is true for financial contracts. The rate of interest paid on a bank loan in the absence of any general rise in the level of prices would be equal to a base rate which reflected the supply and demand for loanable funds, plus an extra mark-up which depended on the credit risk of the borrower. But, if the bank as lender anticipated an inflation over the duration of the loan, then it would charge a higher rate, depending on the expected rate of inflation. If the borrower anticipated the same rate of inflation as the lender, he would be prepared to pay the higher rate, because it would just equal the fall in the real value of his liability as a result of inflation. If the course of future price rises was not foreseen, the rate charged would once again be that much less.

In a situation, therefore, in which all economic decision-makers correctly anticipate the course of future inflation, all contracts fixed in money terms will be adjusted to take account of the higher rate of inflation. Rents, pensions, wages, salaries, and interest rates will all be higher in money terms, though unchanged relative to one another and in real terms. Tenants would be prepared to pay higher rents because of the rise in the money value of their incomes and landlords would be demanding higher rents to ensure the real rate of return on their capital did not fall; firms would be prepared to pay higher wages because of the increased prices they obtained from selling their products, and employees would demand higher wages because of the rise in the cost of living; insurance companies would be prepared to pay higher pensions as a result of the capital gain derived from their investments, and pensioners would demand higher pensions as a result of the rising cost of living; borrowers of funds would be prepared to pay higher money rates of interest because of the reduction in the purchasing power of their debt, while lenders would demand a higher nominal rate of interest to protect themselves against a depreciation in the value of their savings. Although the money value of rents, wages, pensions and interest rates will be that much greater, depending on the extent of the inflation, their real value (i.e. their money value adjusted for the change in the value of money) will be unchanged; this is because their increased nominal value will be just offset by the fall in the purchasing power of money.

One cost to which inflation gives rise, irrespective of whether the inflation is anticipated or unanticipated, is as a result of attempts to economize on the holdings of real money balances. Even if inflation is completely anticipated, individuals and corporations still have an incentive to economize on their holdings of monetary assets, because they do not bear interest. In most countries their money balances would consist of coin, paper currency and the deposits of the banks at the central bank – all debt of the government. As a result of inflation, the value of money balances falls – the inflation tax. In order to avoid this, individuals economize on the amount of money they hold and so devote more resources to carrying out those tasks previously undertaken by the larger holdings of extra money; for example, by making more frequent trips between commercial banks and savings banks, and by devoting more effort to synchronizing the timing of receipts and payments.

During a hyperinflation attempts to economize on money holdings lead to very explicit and inefficient alternatives; firms pay their workers more frequently, consumers spend immediately they receive payments, retail stores tend to open and close many times a day in order to use newly acquired money to augment their stock. And in certain extreme cases of hyperinflation there is a total breakdown in the monetary system, with money being discarded as a means of payment, consumer goods being traded through barter and firms paying their employees in kind rather than cash.

In a world in which inflation is completely anticipated, the only cost of inflation, or at least the only cost that has been emphasized by economists, is that which results from economizing on the holding of money. Unless the inflation reaches quite substantial proportions this cost is likely to be quite small. Professor James Tobin, in a recent Presidential Address to the American Economic Association, expressed this view by saying that 'I suspect that intelligent laymen would be utterly astounded if they realized this is a great evil economists are talking about. They have imagined a much more devastating cataclysm, with Vesuvius vengefully punishing the sinners below. Extra trips between savings banks and commercial banks? What an anti-climax!'[4] If we measure the costs within the orbit of traditional economic analysis, Professor Tobin must surely be right. What an anti-climax indeed! If therefore we measure the effects of inflation in terms of traditional economic analysis the discussion so far must raise grave doubts about the burden it imposes on a society. In the first place we can say that in a fully anticipated inflation the costs of inflation are negligible, amounting only to the attempt by society to economize on its holdings of money balances. In a situation of hyperinflation, these same costs are substantial, resulting in the breakdown of money as the means of payments. Lastly, the costs associated with an unanticipated inflation suggest that an acceleration in the rate of inflation imposes more of a burden on society than a steady but higher rate of inflation.

These important conclusions lead us to two possibilities. One assumption we can make is that inflation becomes fairly rapidly built into the structure of an economy, that such a situation is fundamentally stable, that its costs are negligible and that the great fuss within the body politic over this subject is a temporary protest which will soon die down. The other is that this fuss is evidence of grave disquiet, that the costs are real and substantial, even if they cannot be captured within the traditional framework of economics, and that as a result its control becomes a serious problem in political economy.

The major problem in distinguishing between these approaches is that it is extremely difficult to measure much of the inefficiency created by inflation. Nevertheless, we can suggest three areas of inefficiency apart from that resulting from the non-payment of interest on money.

First, there is the real problem of adjusting individual prices to bring them into line with the rising general price level, usually referred to by economists as the 'parking meter' problem. During the process of inflation, the prices of goods and services have to be continually marked up. This requires the expenditure of capital. If the pace of inflation is being repeatedly underestimated, and producers, wholesalers and retailers find that their prices are all too soon inappropriate to the pace of inflation, this becomes a very tiresome burden.

A more serious problem is the cost of information associated with an unanticipated inflation. In assuming that households and companies have a fairly definite expectation of inflation the usual basis of such an assumption among economists seems to be that the cost of obtaining information is no greater than if there were no inflation at all. After all, even if there were no or little inflation, some resources would still have to be devoted to examining the implication of budgetary and monetary policies and the rate of inflation to which they would give rise. Yet this argument seems to fly in the face of the facts. As a result of uncertainty about the rate of inflation we observe that consumers devote extra time to shopping, because the prices of products rise differently in different shops, producers have to revise their prices more frequently and investors tend to devote more time (itself one of the most scarce of all resources) to predicting the rate of inflation and its implications for different kinds of investments.

Possibly the most serious of all effects in terms of resource efficiency but one that is exceptionally difficult to assess is that associated with increased uncertainty. A situation of accelerating inflation in which the current rate of inflation is much greater than imagined can only succeed in creating an atmosphere of uncertainty, especially in the field of corporate investment planning. Before an investment is undertaken a company must have some idea of its profitability, which in turn requires some assessment of the prices at which it will be able to sell the output. Because of the uncertainty regarding the future price level it is much easier and less costly to invest in 'hedges against inflation', and as a result those resources available for capital investment are inefficiently allocated.

The measurement of these costs is difficult. There is hardly any evidence to go on for the United Kingdom. In the United States between 1947 and 1957, when the annual average rate of inflation (measured by wholesale prices) was only 2·5 per cent, the role of the price mechanism in allocating resources in response to changes in supply and demand seems to have been undermined very little.[5] On the other hand, when inflation has accelerated rapidly, as in China between 1937 and 1949, even though the currency continued to be used as a medium of exchange and even though the inflation was partially anticipated with adjustments in prices because of the absence of price regulation, the social cost through distortions in relative prices and the holding of capital goods as reserves, increased dramatically. The experience of Chile, which has had rapid inflation for nearly a century, suggests that here inflation has not been 'institutionalized', that there are important sectional interests motivated to demand price control because it is equivalent to a subsidy, and that this makes it all the more difficult for the government to remove the price regulation, that is, to withdraw subsidies. The business sector, in particular, has objected to paying more for its loans, imports, power and transportation and has successfully demanded interest-rate regulation,[3] even though the inflation has continued to be substantial.[6]

The impact on the balance of payments is sometimes mentioned as a cost of inflation. If inflation in the United Kingdom proceeds at a faster rate than the rest of the world, and the dollar-sterling exchange rate is pegged, the United Kingdom balance of payments will move into deficit. The size of such a deficit is sometimes taken as a cost of inflation. A balance of payments deficit *per se* is hardly a cost, because, it means by definition, that we are augmenting the supply of goods and services available for domestic consumption. Removing such a deficit, however, does impose a cost, as it means that we have to reduce our consumption and increase our exports in order to pay for the deficit. In an economy in which the exchange rate was neither officially pegged nor tampered with by the central bank engaging in the 'dirty'* float, but was allowed to float freely, inflation would not impose a burden on society via the balance of payments. An inflation, for example, which doubled the price level would cut the exchange rate by half; so that in real terms the volume of exports and imports were as before.

---

* A 'dirty' float refers to a foreign exchange market in which the central bank intervenes temporarily to stabilize the exchange rate. A 'clean' float is a foreign exchange market in which the central bank does not intervene to influence the rate.

Income and wealth redistribution

Like any other form of taxation, inflation results in a redistribution of income and wealth. Much as the imposition of an excise tax transfers resources from consumers to governments, or a wealth tax transfers resources from the wealth-owners to governments, so inflation redistributes purchasing power from the holders of cash balances to the governments which issue the money.

One important distinction in analysing the redistribution effects of inflation is between those assets and liabilities which are fixed in *money* rather than in *real* terms. A monetary asset is a claim to a fixed amount of money now or at some time in the future, while a monetary liability is a payment which has to be made either now or at some time in the future, but which is fixed in money terms. Examples of monetary assets and liabilities are bank loans, bank deposits, mortgages, debentures, commercial bills, national savings, gilt-edged stock. Typically, monetary assets and liabilities pay interest, again fixed in monetary terms. A real asset, on the other hand, is a claim to a piece of property, such as a house or a car, whose price can change; while a real liability is the obligation to deliver such an asset, either now or in the future.

The importance of this distinction arises from the different effects an unanticipated inflation has on monetary, by comparison with real, assets and liabilities. By definition, real assets and liabilities will remain unchanged in real terms as a result of a price rise. A doubling of the price level will mean, for example, a doubling in the price of real assets and real liabilities, if nothing changes to affect their relative price. If I own a house, and the general price level doubles, while relative prices remain unchanged, the price of my house will double. By contrast, the real value of *monetary* assets and liabilities will change, as a result of inflation. Unanticipated inflation reduces the real value of a monetary asset, such as currency or a bank deposit, in that, as a result of the higher price level, such an asset is now able to buy less goods and services than before. It also reduces the real value of a liability, such as a mortgage on a house, in that the amount of real purchasing power which has to be repaid is lower as a result of the general price rise.

The effect of an unanticipated inflation on an individual or company's net wealth depends on the amount of net monetary assets held, i.e. the amount of monetary assets less monetary liabilities. If monetary liabilities are greater than assets, net wealth will rise. A person whose main asset is a house financed by a mortgage will gain as a result of inflation, as will a company with large outstanding debt relative to small holdings of monetary assets. On the other hand, a person whose main assets are savings invested in a bank, building society or national savings, will find that his net wealth reduced as a result of a rise in the general price level, as will a company which has large holdings of monetary assets, such as cash and government stock, relative to its debt. As a result of inflation, therefore, debtors with obligations fixed in monetary terms gain, while creditors with claims fixed in monetary terms lose.

A. Alchian and R. Kessel have produced interesting evidence on the effect of inflation by examining the market value of equity for net monetary debtor and net monetary creditor business firms.[7] Although the equity value of business firms can change for numerous reasons, such as better management, new products and a greater demand for the product, the price of an equity share will rise, *ceteris paribus*, if the firm is a net monetary debtor and fall if it is a net monetary creditor, as a result of inflation.

In view of the fact that the government is the largest debtor in society, with its debt fixed in money rather than real terms, it is the government which has the largest redistribution in its favour as a result of inflation. Although banks are commonly thought of as gaining from inflation, because they issue current accounts which are monetary debt, their monetary assets are usually greater than their debt, and so in fact they tend to lose as a result of inflation. The common idea is that those who lose most as a result of inflation are pensioners and those who have savings. To the extent that pensioners hold monetary assets such as gilt-edged stock, bank deposits or national savings, in order to finance their retirement, they do clearly lose as a result of inflation. The same applies of course to any saver who holds his savings in the form of a monetary asset. As a group, pensioners are extremely dependent upon the state and their welfare really depends on the extent to which the government raises pensions by the same percentage as the inflation.

One particular factor which increases income redistribution during inflation is price controls. The key assumption, which we made earlier regarding anticipated inflation, was not simply that households and companies correctly forecast the expected rate of inflation, but also that as a consequence they were able to adjust their behaviour. The existence of price controls – whether in the form of price ceilings for goods and services, rent controls, or restrictions on interest rates which banks and other financial institutions can pay and charge – and statutory controls of wages and salaries means that such adjustments are restricted so that the extent of income redistribution which takes place is that much greater. Tenants gain at the expense of landlords because rents do not rise to reflect inflation; companies gain at the expense of labour because product repackaging and therefore an effective price rise, is easier to achieve than job reclassification; those workers who succeeded in obtaining a wage rise immediately before controls were imposed gain at the expense of those who were just about to receive one.

The empirical evidence on the redistribution of income and wealth, though piecemeal, nevertheless offers some firm conclusions. In the first place, moderate inflation has been accompanied by a significant, though not a major, change in the distribution of current income among the major income groups in the US.[8] During the war-time and post-war US inflation of 1939–54 the share of the GNP going to labour income and corporate profits rose at the expense of interest, rental income and the profits of unincorporated businesses, but only to a limited degree. If corporate profits were evaluated to include a realistic estimate of depreciation changes, there would have been a fall not a rise in the share of profits.

A similar pattern emerged during the fifties and sixties, as can be seen from Table 3. Column 1 shows the shifts between factor shares for the whole period, while the remaining columns show the shifts during three particularly inflationary periods – the Korean War of 1950–2, the world inflation of 1955–7, and the Vietnam War of 1965–71. Throughout the whole period the share of wages and salaries in national income rose by 6·6 per cent and by nearly 8·0 per cent over the three inflationary periods. On the other hand, corporate profits fell by 6·2 per cent over the whole period and by more during the inflationary sub-periods. If corporate profits during the latter part of this period had been fully adjusted for inflation, then it is certain published profits would have shown an even greater fall.

In the second place, the redistribution of wealth from debtor to creditor as a result of inflation seems to have been quite large. It is estimated that between 1939 and 1952 in the US no less than $500 billion (in 1952 prices) was transferred from creditors to debtors as a result of the inflation. As the largest net creditor sector was households, and the largest net debtor was the government, this was primarily a transfer from householders to taxpayers. Given the substantial amount of monetary assets which now exist, it is estimated

Table 3. **Shifts in Percentage Shares of National Income in Inflation in UK, 1950–71**

	1950–71	1950–52	1955–57	1965–71
Wages and salaries	+6.6	+2.6	+1.4	+3.9
Unincorporated businesses				
Non-farm	−3.8	−0.7	−0.2	−1.4
Farm	−3.7	−0.5	−0.4	−0.7
Rents	−1.0	+0.1	−0.2	−0.5
Interest	+3.4	+0.1	+0.3	+1.0
Corporate profits*	−6.2	−2.0	−1.7	−4.0
Transfer payments†	+4.7	−1.8	+0.6	+4.7

* After inventory valuation adjustment, before payment of income taxes.

† Not a part of national income.

Source: G. L. Bach and James B. Stephenson, 'Inflation and the Redistribution of Wealth', *Review of Economics and Statistics*, February 1974.

that each one per cent of unanticipated inflation will transfer $35 billion per year in the future, and that the figure will be greater as the total of monetary assets grows. Again, this is mainly a transfer from households to the government. Within households, the evidence suggests a transfer from old people, who tend to have savings in the form of monetary assets but few monetary liabilities, to young families who tend to have substantial debt such as housing mortgages and consumer durables financed by hire purchase. Again there appears to be a transfer from the very poor and the very rich, both of whom have few debts, though for different reasons, to middle-income families who tend to be heavily in debt.

Although the evidence suggests that inflation has not dramatically affected the shares of wages, profits, rents and dividends in personal and national income, this does not exclude considerable redistribution within a particular group. For example, from the US evidence, executive salaries have tended to lag behind the general wage increase and there was substantial variation between unskilled and semi-skilled labourers. Those who lost most from inflation – pensioners, insurance recipients and college professors, for example – tended to be scattered throughout the economy rather than concentrated in any income or occupational groups. On the basis of post-war evidence Bach and Stephenson conclude that,

> Overall the redistributional effects of inflation are more complex than is often suggested, requiring analysis cutting across the broad functional income groups to individuals and smaller groups with lagging incomes and substantial net creditor positions not offset by debts or large holdings of variable price assets. Clearly simple conclusions that inflation is good for the rich and bad for the poor, or other comparable statements, need to be viewed with considerable doubt.[9]

One frequently held proposition is that during inflation money wages tend to lag behind prices, with a corresponding fall in the real wages and a rise in the real value of business profits. This has been put forward in a number of important studies of inflation, such as Earl T. Hamilton's study of inflation in Europe and the New World from 1350 to 1800, Wesley C. Mitchell's study of inflation during the American Civil War, A. H. Hansen's study of inflation in the First World War and C. Bresciani-Turroni's study of the German inflation of 1923.[10] All of these writers alleged that, as a matter of fact, real wages fall during inflation and that their fall was attributable to inflation. Numerous reasons have been put forward as to why wages should lag behind prices: the 'inertia' of the labour market because of custom; the weak bargaining power of labour; the lack of information; the fact that employees are creditors while employers are debtors, because wages are paid after they are earned, and the lack of foresight by employees regarding the true extent of inflation.

One weakness of these studies is their assertion that on the basis of evidence real wages did in fact fall during the inflations studied.[11] The evidence on this is ambiguous for Spain (1350–1800), England

(1500–1700), the United States (1820–1923) and Germany (1918–23), mainly because of the favourably chosen initial and terminal dates of the inflations and the particular choice of wage and price indices to measure real wages, such as the inclusion of turnover taxes in the price index in the North during the American Civil War, the choice by Hansen of weekly earnings rather than hourly earnings, the choice of wages in London rather than the north of England to measure wage changes in England over the sixteenth and seventeenth centuries. In those cases in which it can be shown that real wages did unambiguously fall – France (1500–1700), the North and South during the American Civil War (1861–5) and Germany (1923) – the difficult problem is to disentangle the part played by real as opposed to monetary factors in explaining real wage changes. None of the studies ever attempt to solve this problem, although all indicate that real factors did change during the period of the inflation. For example, the movement of the terms of trade against the North during the Civil War; a fall in the productivity of capital in the South which was highly specialized to the production of cotton as a result of the Northern blockade and, as in Germany in 1923, the higher cost of using money to carry out transactions. All of these changes would have produced a fall in real wages regardless of the rate of inflation and until their contribution is evaluated the wage-price lag cannot be assumed as an inevitable concomitant of inflation.

Inflation and economic growth

One of the major arguments which has been used to justify the pursuit of inflationary policies by governments is that inflation results in a more rapid rate of economic growth. Numerous mechanisms have been suggested. One is that an important condition for an efficient economy is price and wage flexibility. Only by sufficiently flexible price systems will a market economy be able to allocate scarce resources to those ends in which they have the greatest return. But there are many prices, especially those of products produced by large corporations, which tend to be rigid and strongly resistant to any absolute decline. Most of all this applies to the labour market, in which trade unions will not reduce their money wages because there happens to be an excess supply in the market. As a consequence of this, changes in relative prices resulting from changing tastes, technology, foreign prices etc, would not take place if the overall price level were to remain constant. A fall in demand for a particular product, rather than leading to a fall in the price of the product and in the wages paid in that industry, would produce unemployment instead. A zero rate of inflation, so the argument runs, is therefore a prescription for stagnation and inefficiency. On the other hand, if the price level is rising gradually from year to year, relative price adjustments can take place without any necessity for an absolute fall in any particular price or wage rate.

There is a slightly different argument, which follows on from the earlier part of this chapter. To the extent that inflation is a tax on money, expenditure in the private sector of the economy is reduced because of such a tax, releasing resources which can be used by the government. As the percentage of resources devoted to investment in many underdeveloped countries is low, inflation provides a way by which the government is able to divert resources into capital expenditure, a necessary condition for growth.

Another argument which leads to a similar result is that inflation tends to redistribute income from wages to profits. As the marginal propensity to consume out of profits is allegedly much lower than out of wages, this leads to 'forced saving' in the economy as a whole, with a corresponding increase in investment and in turn the rate of growth. Using this argument, inflation also increases the level of saving by maintaining GNP at its full capacity level.

Inflation is also alleged to increase investment because it reduces the real rate of interest, which is relevant to the investment decision. During inflations interest rates typically do not adjust fully to the expected rate of inflation, either because investors underestimate the actual rate of inflation or because they are prevented from adjusting to it because of controls in the capital market or government interest-rate policy. This means that the real rate of interest falls, and may even become negative. As a result, investment and therefore growth, is stimulated.

Before we examine the evidence on this issue, two points need to be emphasized. The argument does not assume that a higher rate of economic growth is necessarily desirable. From this point of view the argument is neutral. A more rapid rate of economic growth may be considered desirable or undesirable; the argument is simply concerned with whether or not a more rapid rate of inflation leads to a higher rate of growth. Even if it does, this does not necessarily mean that it would be desirable to implement such a policy. Secondly, it is important to distinguish between short-run economic growth, which must take as fixed a certain capacity to produce in an economy, and long-run economic growth, where the underlying productive capacity itself changes. In the short run hardly anyone would doubt that the rate of growth could be raised by rapidly expanding the money supply and so creating an inflation. The substance, however, of the present thesis is that inflation will produce an increase in the long-run rate of growth of an economy. We are concerned with the trend of economic activity rather than the upswing in the cycle.

A number of studies of the relationship between economic development and inflation have been undertaken by staff members of the International Monetary Fund.[12] In broad terms, the findings of all the studies has been the same. Rapid economic growth has taken place in countries with high rates of inflation, such as Brazil, and in countries with low rates of inflation, such as Mexico and West Germany. Similarly, low rates of economic growth have taken place with varying rates of inflation. In particular, it is not true that a more rapid rate of inflation tends to be associated with a more rapid rate of economic growth. A more recent study suggests that an inflation of between 3 and 10 per cent tends to be a positive encouragement to growth, while inflation of more than 10 per cent tends to retard growth. The mechanism by which this allegedly takes place is that such a moderate rate of inflation tends to be a stimulus to saving and investment. The evidence for this must be considered very tentative because the possibility of a third factor which may affect both the rates of inflation and the extent of total investment, such as a public sector deficit created by public sector investment, is ignored. In fact, one major criticism of all these studies is that they tend to assemble facts rather than test hypotheses.

9 The end of Bretton Woods

'No one told us we could do this.'

Sidney Webb (1931)

The announcement by President Nixon on the 15 August 1971 that the United States was no longer prepared to maintain the convertibility of the dollar marked the end of an era in international monetary relations. Even though the Smithsonian agreement of December 1971 attempted to fix rates, by 1973 the currencies of the leading Western nations were all floating against each other. After a long and painful struggle the gold-dollar exchange standard, which had been so carefully constructed by Keynes and others in 1944 at Bretton Woods, New Hampshire, was dead. One of the most important factors leading to its demise was the global acceleration of inflation since the mid-1960s, produced in the first instance by the way in which the United States financed the Vietnam War.

The 1971 international monetary crisis was above all a crisis of confidence in the dollar. With the Nixon administration intent on pursuing an inflationary domestic policy, the balance of payments at a record $29·8 billion deficit and the gold commitments of the United States to foreign central banks standing in August 1971 at about $43 billion – just over four times the value of the total gold stock of the United States – it was hardly surprising that confidence in the dollar collapsed. Instead of devaluing the dollar by raising the official price of gold and announcing counter-inflationary policies which might have restored confidence in the currency, the United States decided that it was no longer prepared to carry on playing under the existing rules of the game and that, in particular, it was no longer prepared to be the 'key currency' of the system, when the onus imposed on it as a result of such a commitment was contrary to its own best interests as a nation. In these respects the events of August 1971 were to the dollar standard what those of September 1931 had been to the gold standard. Both resulted in the collapse of key currencies because of the decision of governments to give greater priority to the internal rather than the external implications of their economic policies.

The Bretton Woods system

The 1930s were a chaotic period in international monetary affairs. Following the failure of the attempts to re-establish the gold standard, most countries pursued 'beggar-my-neighbour' policies in an endeavour to improve their balance-of-payments position and secure greater domestic employment. One country after another misguidedly embarked on a policy of deflation, which soon reverberated throughout the whole of the international economy, creating a slump in world trade which was without parallel for over a hundred years. The situation was made even more chaotic as countries engaged in a series of 'offensive devaluations', in which the external depreciation in the value of the currency bore no relation to its internal depreciation, and introduced a whole set of exchange controls, quotas, tariffs and export subsidies, which had a perverse effect on the extent and character of international trade and trade relations.

It was against this background that the Bretton Woods conference took place towards the end of the Second World War. The major concern of the conference was to restructure the international monetary system so as to avoid the two key problems of the thirties – a global recession and the disruption of trade between nations. At the time the conference took place the outlook was gloomy on both counts; the fear was that at the end of the Second World War there would be a short boom due to reconstruction and restocking, after which advanced capitalist economies faced the prospect of secular stagnation, and that this in turn would act as a stimulus to countries pursuing mercantilist trading policies. To avoid these stark possibilities, it was hoped to create a framework which would simultaneously permit countries to pursue monetary and fiscal policies resulting in full employment and trade policies which would entail as few as possible restrictions on trade and capital flows between countries. As a result of the conference three new institutions were created to deal with the problems: the International Bank for Reconstruction and Development (the World Bank), concerned with the granting of aid; the General Agreement of Tariffs and Trade (GATT), responsible for promoting freer trade arrangements; and the International Monetary Fund, which was to be at the centre of the new international monetary system.

One feature of the new monetary system was that exchange rates between currencies were fixed but adjustable from time to time. Each currency was pegged to the dollar and the dollar was linked to gold at a price of thirty-five dollars an ounce. The way in which this took place was that each central bank would deal in the foreign exchange market and be prepared to buy back its own currency if investors wished to sell, and sell it if they wished to buy. The market rate was allowed to vary within a band extending one per cent on either side of the fixed parity. Once the 'ceiling' or the 'floor' was reached the central bank was then forced to intervene to buy or sell its own currency for dollars and so stabilize the rate. The onus on the United States was slightly different. The Federal Reserve stood ready to buy and sell gold for dollars at the fixed official price of thirty-five dollars per ounce. At the end of the war, when the United States gold stock was not only high in absolute terms, $24,563 million, but also relative to the rest of the world, and the balance of payments was in substantial surplus, such a commitment seemed entirely reasonable, both from the viewpoint of the United States and the rest of the world. The purpose of having fixed rather than flexible rates was to avoid the alleged chaos which resulted from the 'dirty' floating of the 1930s, and to reap the economic benefits which accrued in a common currency area in which traders and businessmen were not inhibited from trading because of the uncertainty attaching to floating exchange rates. It was also thought that a fixed exchange rate would discourage destabilizing speculation. Although rates were to be fixed rather than flexible it was not intended that they would be rigid and unresponsive to long-term economic changes. Article IV of the Fund stated that in conditions of 'fundamental disequilibrium', exchange rates could and should be changed, though it is also fair to say that such conditions were envisaged as being exceptional rather than the rule. If a particular country, for example, pursued an inflationary policy, by permitting a public-sector deficit to be financed by money supply growth which in turn produced a chronic payments imbalance, it was expected that it would devalue. Similarly, if a country pursued a very cautious economic policy, resulting in a balance of payments surplus and an accumulation of foreign exchange reserves, it was expected that it would revalue its currency. Even in generally recognized conditions of fundamental disequilibrium, however, the Fund had no way of compelling member countries to change the dollar value of their currencies.

Because exchange rates were fixed, central banks desired to hold as assets certain key currencies which could subsequently be used in supporting their own currencies. Along with gold the dominant currencies in the system, when it was conceived, were the pound and the dollar. Most transactions were denominated in one of these currencies and along with gold they constituted the major part of most countries' foreign exchange reserves. The system still remained (at least until the setting up of the two-tier gold market in March 1968) a gold-exchange standard, in that convertibility into gold from any currency was always a possibility. In 1970 the key currencies and gold were supplemented as world money by Special Drawing Rights – a fiduciary creation of the IMF usually referred to as paper gold, because until the summer of 1974 their value was denominated in terms of gold. The supply of SDRs is controlled by the Fund.

The lynchpin of the whole system was the International Monetary Fund, of which most Western countries were members. Each country deposited certain balances with the Fund and in turn had the right to borrow from the Fund if they found themselves in balance-of-payments difficulties. In this respect the object of the Fund was to provide short- and medium-term credit to countries with balance-of-payments problems, so that they could overcome their short-term difficulties without having to engage in severely deflationary policies. For example, when Britain was in serious balance-of-payments difficulties in the late 1960s, she was borrowing at the rate of £2 billion in order to tide her over the problem of adjusting from a substantial deficit position. If this credit had not been available the adjustment problem might well have been more severe. The more a country borrows from the Fund, however, the greater are the conditions the Fund is able to impose on the way in which it conducts its monetary and fiscal policies.

Judged by the fact that since the end of the Second World War there has been a continuous growth in international trade, that barriers to trade have gradually been removed and that, by historic standards, all Western countries have experienced high growth rates, the Bretton Woods system must be accounted a success. On the other hand the record of the system in the 1950s and 1960s revealed certain quite serious weaknesses, usually categorized as the adjustment, liquidity and confidence problems. The first of these is concerned with the way in which countries eliminate surpluses and deficits on their balance of payments. While the system permitted exchange-rate adjustment in conditions of 'fundamental dis-equilibrium', there was no attempt at any definition of such a situation and therefore no onus on a country with a chronic payments imbalance to act. The way in which exchange-rate adjustments took place over this period revealed a certain reluctance on the part of countries to either revalue or devalue. Devaluation tended to be associated with the failure of a country's economic policies, so that governments tended to devalue only as a policy of last resort. A classic example of this was the saga of the pound sterling between 1964 and 1967, when the UK external payments position was in obvious and substantial disequilibrium. Despite the evidence, the Labour government persistently refused to change the exchange rate for three years, blaming in the meantime the 'gnomes of Zurich' and the lack of patriotism of British consumers as the causes of our ills. After various fiscal and other measures had been introduced which created needless distortions and inefficiency in the economy, the inevitable happened and the pound was devalued in November 1967. Surplus countries frequently found themselves under less pressure to act than deficit countries. Revaluations were also con-sidered undesirable because of their perverse effects on unemploy-ment. In the case of Germany which had a balance of payments surplus throughout most of the post-war years, a major obstacle to revaluation was the not inconsiderable political opposition which came from exporters.

Because of the various factors which create this reluctance to change the exchange rate, most exchange rate changes have taken place under a condition of crisis, which has, of course, tended to exacerbate the underlying problems. The typical pattern of events is that a deteriorating trade balance leads to a loss of confidence in the currency, which in turn produces a speculative outflow of short-term capital which becomes so great that the exchange rate has to be changed. The devaluation of the pound in November 1967, the revaluation of the mark and the devaluation of the franc in March 1968, and the creation of the two-tier market in gold in March 1968 all took place under crisis conditions. The fact that rates tended to be changed under crisis conditions exposed an important weakness of the system. To the extent that, under a regime of fixed exchange rates, countries pursued divergent economic policies, some countries would move into a balance-of-payments deficit and others into a surplus. Short of harmonizing their policies completely, so that those countries with an emerging deficit would pursue a policy of domestic deflation and those with a growing surplus one of reflation, if not inflation, in order that there would be no inconsistency between their external payments, exchange rate adjustment could only take place in conditions of 'fundamental disequilibrium'. A mole-hill had to become a mountain before it could be removed. Although initially designed to create stability, such an adjustment process became an important source of instability.

Another major problem of the system was the way in which the supply of international reserves was to be increased to meet the growing demand for such reserves as a result of the continued growth in world trade over the post-war years – the so-called liquidity problem. In the immediate post-war years the threat to the system came from the shortage of dollars because the United States found itself in a position of substantial balance-of-payments surplus. Because of the IMF quota system for the growth of credit and the fact that the increase in the supply of monetary gold did not keep pace with the demand for gold, the IMF has repeatedly been forced to take action to increase the supply of credit and money in the world. In 1958 countries' credit quotas to the Fund were increased; a little later, the Fund developed the technique of 'stand-by' credit facilities for countries in balance-of-payments difficulties; in 1961–2 the leading countries signed the General Agreements to Borrow and in the late 1960s the IMF as a whole agreed on the creation of Special Drawing Rights, the first genuine world fiat money.

The third problem of the system had to do with confidence. An essential condition for any monetary system to work is that those holding money and using it for transactions have confidence in its future value. Confidence in the Bretton Woods gold-exchange standard involved two quite distinct problems: the confidence of private investors in the future value of a particular currency, and the confidence of both private investors and governments in the 'key currencies' which, along with gold, were used as part of the world's money supply. A crisis of confidence in a particular currency has been a common feature of the working of the system since the 1950s. Each time a currency is considered especially weak or strong because of the underlying trends in that country's balance of payments, a loss or surge of confidence produces an outflow or inflow of short-term capital which itself exacerbates the underlying problem. At the end of the 1960s and in the early 1970s, however, there was a loss of confidence in another sense. Investors and governments lost confidence in the one key currency which was critical to the working of the system – the dollar.

Inflation and the collapse of this system

From an analytical viewpoint, inflation, or, more precisely, an inflation in the United States at a rate in excess of the average of that of other countries, should not be thought of as a separate problem in understanding the behaviour of the Bretton Woods system apart from those already considered. Its major effect was to aggravate the weaknesses already inherent in the system; it made the problem of economic adjustment increasingly difficult without greater flexibility of exchange rates; it created an enormous increase in the supply of dollars in the world economy; and, as a result, it produced a loss of confidence in the dollar which finally undermined the whole system. This is not to say, incidentally, that the changes which it led to, such as greater exchange rate flexibility, were necessarily undesirable; indeed one can make out a good case for saying that this particular aspect of the change was highly beneficial. The only point I wish to emphasize at this stage is the way in which inflation led to the breakdown of the existing system.

We have already seen that one of the great sources of tension between countries within the Bretton Woods system arose from the fact that on the one hand exchange rates were fixed in order to produce a liberal world economic order in which trade could prosper, and that on the other hand countries were unprepared to give up the degree of economic sovereignty which such a system necessarily implied. Different rates of inflation, especially between the United States and the EEC countries throughout the 1960s, highlighted this problem. As a result of their different experiences in the inter-war years, the United States and Germany emerged with a noticeably different set of preferences with respect to the mix of inflation and unemployment which was considered tolerable. The Great Depression left a profound mark on United States society. Real Gross National Product fell by thirty per cent between 1929 and 1933 and unemployment over the same period rose from 3·2 per cent to 25 per cent. As a consequence a reasonably modest rate of inflation was certainly a price worth paying if it meant full employment; something which was reinforced in the 1950s and 1960s when the incidence of unemployment was very high among Blacks and Puerto Ricans and therefore likely to act as a catalyst of racial and social unrest. German history on the other hand was in marked contrast. The hyperinflation of 1923 which impoverished the middle class and so many of their accompanying traditional values and ideals had instilled in the minds of most Germans a profound fear of rising prices. As a result, the electoral appeal of German politicians following the reconstruction of 1948 was to stable prices. Throughout the 1960s the US rate of inflation was significantly higher than that of Germany. Such distinctly different preferences were bound to set up conflicts within the system.

After 1965 the situation became more acute, as we have seen earlier, because of President Johnson's determination to go ahead with his programmes for the Great Society, coupled with the cost of the Vietnam War and the way in which the latter was financed. In 1965 the estimated cost of the war was between $3 and $5 billion. The true cost came out at $8 billion. Similarly, for the fiscal year 1967, McNamara gave three figures: high – $17 billion; medium – $15 billion; low – $11 billion. The actual figure proved to be $21 billion.

Such an escalation in costs had an enormous impact on government spending. Between 1957 and 1965 government spending had only risen at an annual rate of about six per cent per annum. Between 1965 and 1968 it rose by no less than fifteen per cent per annum. Arthur Okun, one of the President's council of economic advisers, recalling this period put it that 'the economists in the administration watched with pain and frustration as fiscal policy veered off course'. Because the President was not prepared to raise taxes, the only avenue left was an excessive creation of money, which is precisely what happened in 1965 and 1967.

The effects of the war and inflation can be seen in the US balance of payments over this period. Between 1945 and 1965, the US trade balance was in surplus – between 1960 and 1964 it averaged over $5 billion. After 1965 there was a steady erosion of this surplus – in 1964 it was $6·8 billion, in 1965 $4·9 billion, in 1966 and 1967 $3·9 billion, in 1968 $600 million and in 1969 $700 million. In 1970 it rose to $2·1 billion, but then, in the crisis year of 1971, it moved into deficit to the order of $2·9 billion, the first time it had been in deficit for over a hundred years. Correspondingly over this period, Europe and Japan were becoming surplus trading areas.

The fact that the US balance of payments was steadily moving into deficit while that of the EEC countries and Japan stubbornly remained in surplus clearly called for some adjustment, either by the US government or by the surplus countries – the latter either reflating their economies or revaluing their exchange rates vis-à-vis the dollar. In 1969 President Nixon embarked on a deflationary policy to try and reduce the rate of inflation and halt the deterioration in the balance of payments. The 1970 balance of payments, as a result, was in substantial surplus. But the cost of achieving this policy in terms of unemployment was judged too great and in 1970 the President embarked on a dramatic reversal of earlier policy. Even though the rate of inflation was still about five per cent, money supply growth nearly doubled. It seemed clear, therefore, that the United States was not tailoring its domestic economic policy to deal with the emerging balance-of-payments deficit and had no intention of devaluing the dollar, by raising the dollar price of gold, as the Europeans were arguing they should. The rationale for the US policy was that it made no sense for the US to reduce domestic demand and so increase unemployment simply to satisfy the whims of European investors and central bankers, and that a rise in the official price of gold which was necessary for a devaluation of the dollar would be a reversal of the trend to demonetize gold which the US government had pursued so vigorously over the post-war years. The alternative method of adjustment, and the one which was the official policy of the US government, required that the Europeans and the Japanese revalue their currencies vis-à-vis the dollar if they did not wish to accumulate dollar balances. Such a revaluation would also tend to eliminate their balance-of-payments current account surpluses.

The strains in the fixed exchange-rate system were all too clear even before August 1971. Germany revalued the mark in the autumn of 1969 after a very long struggle to avoid doing so. In the 'gold rush' of March 1968, the dollar was especially weak and there was speculation against the dollar and in favour of gold. In May 1970 the Canadian government decided to float the Canadian dollar because of the clear divergence between the United States' and its own economic policies. And in the spring of 1971 the Germans found themselves floating the mark once again but this time joined by the Netherlands and by revaluations in Austria and Switzerland. Then, in August 1971, the fixed rate system was finally abandoned.

The uncertainty which is general within the system because of different rates of inflation in different countries can be judged from the fact that subsequent attempts to re-establish fixed rates have failed. An initial agreement was worked out at the Smithsonian museum in Washington in December 1971, in which the dollar was officially devalued by 8 per cent and the band within which currencies were free to move was widened from 1 per cent on either side of this parity to $2\frac{1}{4}$ per cent. The agreement broke down when, in June 1972, the British decided to float the pound. In January 1973 Switzerland floated the franc and later in the same year Italy floated the lira. The dollar was then devalued by a further 10 per cent and then five of the EEC countries decided to fix their exchange rates vis-à-vis each other and float jointly against the dollar. By June 1973, however, Germany had broken the agreement and in January 1974 France floated the franc. By this stage there was a noticeable difference in rates of inflation between all Western countries and general floating was inevitable and desirable.

The liquidity problem during the late sixties and early seventies was very much a concomitant of the adjustment problem. Up until the late 1960s one of the crucial problems of the system was the prospect that the growth of international reserves would fail to keep pace with the demand. But then exactly the opposite problem emerged. Far from there being a shortage of world money, there was a surplus. This was largely the result of a phenomenal increase in Euro-dollars. With exchange rates fixed and excessive money creation by the United States, dollars were being pumped into the international economy. They were held in large amounts by the central banks of those countries which were in surplus; and they were held involuntarily. Because by 1971 the gold liabilities of the United States amounted to over four times its gold holdings, the key currency of the system was clearly inconvertible. And it was this which finally produced the crisis of confidence in the dollar and prompted President Nixon to act.

Gold in an age of inflation

Not many years ago when the world dollar standard was at its height, gold seemed superfluous to the working of the international monetary system and its future comparable to that of any other metal which was demanded for jewellery and industrial uses. Pundits were forecasting that the price of gold on the free market would soon fall well below the official price of thirty-five dollars an ounce.

The basis of the argument was that the decision to create a two-tier market in gold following the 'gold-rush' of March 1968 (in which there was heavy speculation of the dollar because of the United States balance of payments) effectively separated the 'official' from the private use of gold and was tantamount to the abandonment of the gold-exchange standard and the creation of a *de facto* dollar standard. Gold would continue to be bought and sold on the free market at a price which reflected market conditions, but central bankers would not be allowed to trade on this market. Instead, they agreed to keep the official price of gold at thirty-five dollars an ounce and also to a set of rules by which gold could change hands between countries. What it meant in practice was that the gold convertibility of the dollar was severely restricted. Any pretence that the gold-exchange standard might still exist was finally removed, as we have seen, in August 1971, when the dollar was once again under pressure and the United States unilaterally decided to end its commitment to gold convertibility. Only in December of that year, and then rather reluctantly, was the official price raised and then by just twelve per cent.

The rationale behind these decisions, which still represents official United States policy, and which incidentally has been supported by a large body of academic economists, was that it was both irrational and inefficient for the world to carry on using a commodity as money when much cheaper and superior alternatives were available, namely the newly created IMF fiduciary money, Special Drawing Rights. Despite the force of this argument, United States policy has not had the backing of the rest of the world. Common Market countries have pressed for a much greater role to be given to gold in the international monetary system. On the world market, which reflects the decision of countless investors, towards the end of 1974 the price of gold reached the astonishing figure of nearly two hundred dollars an ounce and in the early 1970s, gold shares were one of the most attractive investments. Already one prominent English journalist has written a book calling for the return to the gold standard throughout the whole of the Western world: something which a decade ago would have seemed only possible from the pen of a Frenchman, a crank, or both.

In the face of this growing disquiet, the United States has been forced to modify its policy; the official price of gold was raised by twenty per cent, to $4·43 an ounce, in 1973; in July 1974 Italy was granted a loan from Germany with gold valued at a hundred and fifty dollars an ounce being used as collateral; from the 1 January 1975 United States citizens were allowed to hold gold for the first time since 1933, a decision which reflects the feelings of Congress rather than the administrations; the United States government has decided to sell by auction early in 1976 two million ounces of gold from its Fort Knox holdings and, most recently, the United States has declared that it would be prepared for central banks to buy and sell gold on the free market providing they did not do it as a means of stabilizing the gold price of their currencies and, as a result of the Martinique summit, to value their gold holdings according to the free market price of gold. Ten years ago these changes would have seemed unthinkable.

The only factor which can adequately explain this resurgence of interest in gold is the accelerating rate of inflation which has plagued the whole of the Western world. Because of the uncertainty which it creates and the particularly capricious redistribution of income and wealth which it produces, inflation has posed a serious threat to capitalism as an economic system and in turn to democracy as we now know it. As the rate of inflation has accelerated since the mid-1960s in all capitalist countries, so confidence in all of the leading currencies has been destroyed. The result has been the demise of the dollar-exchange standard and its replacement by a system of floating exchange rates. The increased demand for gold in the private market and the demand for gold convertibility by central bankers is the response to this loss of confidence in currencies. It is not so much a newly found confidence in the intrinsic value of the metal, or a return to a more barbaric form of civilization, but simply a basic loss of confidence in the ability of governments to seriously set about controlling inflation.

Despite the loss of confidence in currencies and the surge of interest in gold, no consensus has yet emerged on the role gold should play in the international monetary system. Indeed it seems doubtful whether it ever will at government level. Nevertheless, in the debate which is currently taking place three broadly different approaches can be distinguished: those who wish to see gold demonetized, those at the other extreme who wish a return to the gold standard, and those who, while wishing to maintain floating exchange rates, nevertheless want controls over the official use of gold abandoned.

The argument for the demonetization of gold is usually limited to the case for greater exchange-rate flexibility (though it should be noted that gold would also be demonetized in a world of fixed exchange rates in which, for example, SDRs were used as fiduciary money). Proponents of this view argue that the system of floating exchange rates is working well, especially in view of the enormous pressures to which the system has been and is subject, largely because of the recycling of petro-dollars, and that a reversion to a system of fixed rates would be impossible because of the substantial differences in countries' rates of inflation.

While recognizing the validity of this point, the present situation nevertheless gives cause for concern on a number of counts; the fact that countries have not agreed on the kind of flexibility which is desirable, that the system was forced to emerge as a result of a substantial rift between the United States and the EEC, and that dirty floating offers possibilities for economic nationalism which could well escalate into controls which restrict the freedom of trade and capital movements.

The cloud hanging over the present international payments mechanism is whether it can continue on a quasi-permanent basis without either producing the sort of economic nationalism which was evident in the 1930s or else permitting a global escalation to hyperinflation. For these reasons it would be preferable if its institutional framework and rules were accepted by countries, even if the system adopted was one of flexible exchange rates. Even a system of free markets would operate more efficiently in an agreed framework because it would then be known that governments were committed to limitations on their intervention in foreign exchange markets.

At the other extreme is a demand for the return to the gold standard, in which the price of currencies would be pegged to gold and in which central banks would have an obligation to exchange gold on demand for their currencies. In an age of inflation, in which there seems no limit to the financial profligacy of governments, the lure of gold is that it imposes discipline on national finances, in that governments would no longer have discretionary power over the creation of money. Money supply creation would be automatically determined by the size of the gold reserve – a balance of payments deficit would produce an outflow of gold which would automatically lead to a reduction in the money supply and the removal of the deficit, while a balance of payments surplus, the result of more-cautious policies, would lead to a gold inflow, an increase in the domestic money stock and an elimination of the surplus. By removing choice over the creation of money from the sphere of government, the gold standard allegedly ensures a world of price stability.

At the theoretical level it seems doubtful whether one can argue that the gold standard provides an automatic and stable system. The evolution of money throughout the period of the gold standard has seen the gradual substitution of credit monies for precious metals. This means that, if the price of gold is fixed, the profitability of gold production will fall secularly, and the rate of inflation will rise. Inflation is therefore possible under a gold standard because of the economic incentives which exist to substitute credit for gold. Just as important is the problem of regulating the world supply of gold, given the potential instability of at least one of the main countries, South Africa, and the fact that the domestic supply would be linked to the vagaries of the balance of payments.

Historically it is true that the gold standard tended to produce price stability; though the degree of such stability is much less than is sometimes suggested. For example, between 1673 and 1675 the price level rose by 15 per cent and from 1707 to 1711 by 54 per cent; from 1711 to 1713 it fell by 28 per cent; from 1739 to 1741 it rose by 18 per cent; from 1840 to 1843 it rose by 22 per cent; and from 1854 to 1856 it rose by 24 per cent. Such periods as these cannot be dismissed as exceptions. There is certainly a case to be made for saying that a gold standard would prevent a drift to hyperinflation; but this in itself does not imply price stability.

In addition to this there is at present the problem, far more pressing now than in the late nineteenth century, of the instability of the supply of gold. At the heyday of the gold standard, gold was produced in a world convinced of the value of private enterprise, and one of – by the subsequent evidence of the twentieth century – remarkable political stability. The supply of gold to the world market was not decided by governments but by the workings of a market economy. At present most gold is mined in South Africa and the USSR. Without wishing to make any judgement on the internal politics of these countries, one would have to make some heroic assumptions about the future of South Africa and the foreign policy of the USSR to believe that the supply of gold coming on the world market would in future always be according to the needs of the world economy. However, the really interesting question to ask before committing ourselves to the gold standard so completely is how much instability it produced in the real, by contrast to the monetary, sector of the economy; and this is something for which hardly any evidence is presented. A return to gold would be a commitment to control inflation, but, if society was convinced of the true cost of inflation, a return to gold would be unnecessary. The German economy has had less inflation over the post-war years than the United Kingdom or the United States, not because the exchange rate was rigidly fixed (it was not), but because the preference of that society, as evidenced through the political system, was to keep inflation within narrow bounds. The adoption of a gold standard is a means to an end and not an end in itself. The crucial point is convincing society of the cost of inflation.

The third alternative is that countries should be allowed much greater freedom than they have had since March 1968 over their official gold holdings. There is no reason why central banks should not be free to buy and sell gold on the world market much as they at present have freedom over buying and selling currencies. This would mean that gold would co-exist along with other leading currencies and SDRs as being part of the world money supply. If a group of countries wished to unilaterally fix the gold price of their currencies they would be free to do so. While their rates would be fixed in terms of each other, as a bloc their currency could float against the dollar. Whatever the particular outcome, the evolving international payments system must incorporate two essential features: greater freedom for the official use of gold and the option for at least some countries to maintain exchange-rate flexibility. At a time when the future of inflation is so uncertain, the rejection of either could prove disastrous.

10   Hyperinflation

'A severe inflation is the worst kind of revolution.'

Thomas Mann, Inflation: The Witches' Sabbath (*1942*)

The devastating consequences of rising prices are most evident during periods of 'hyperinflation' in which the value of money suffers a rapid and substantial depreciation.[1] In 1781 the 'continental money' issued by the American colonies in the War of Independence was only worth a thousandth part of its original value. In November 1795 the Assignats, the paper money issued during the French Revolution, were worth only one per cent of their value in 1790. The most famous of all such episodes is the German experience of 1923. During the two weeks from 24 July to 7 August 1923 the Reichsbank increased the note issue by more than two milliard (a thousand million) marks. The wholesale price index, which stood at 1·0 in January 1913, stood at 2·8 million on 4 September 1923 and 1,374,400 million on 20 November of the same year. At the end of November a kilogram of bread cost 428 milliard marks, a kilogram of butter cost 5,600 milliards, a newspaper cost 200 milliards, a tram ticket cost 150 milliards and the postage stamp for an inland letter, 100 milliards. As a result of the inflation, output slumped, unemployment rose and a whole class of people who depended for their existence on the income from their savings were almost pauperized. The political consequences were disastrous. The massive and capricious re-distribution of wealth which took place from the old middle classes to the speculators and profiteers created bitterness and disaffection, and provided a background against which the Nazi political appeal for order and stability could flourish.

Although fortunately rare, episodes such as these provide an unparalleled opportunity to observe what happens when the money
supply and inflation are completely out of control. While they
doubtless have particular features which are restricted to periods of
hyperinflation, and therefore one has to be very careful in using
them as a basis for generalizing about inflation, they nevertheless
provide an opportunity of seeing in a very clear way the consequences, although certainly on a much more limited scale, which any
inflation must produce. For economics as a science they provide the
next best alternative to the closed experiments of the natural sciences.

The extent of hyperinflations

No strict definition of hyperinflation exists; it simply refers to periods
of rapidly rising prices. In his classic study of money and hyperinflations, P. Cagan defines a hyperinflation as beginning in that
month in which the rise in prices is greater than 50 per cent and as
ending in the month before the monthly rise in prices drops below
that amount and stays below it for at least a year. Using this definition
he analyses those severe inflations which occurred in European
countries after the First World War and during and after the Second
World War. This definition, however, is very much the product of
the particular inflations he analysed and too restrictive for our purposes. In this chapter I should like to broaden the definition so that
it could include the chronic inflations of various Latin American and
Asian countries over the post-war years.

In the present century there have been three major periods of hyper
or chronic inflation: the early 1920s in certain continental European
countries, the period during and immediately following the Second
World War, again mainly in Europe, and the post Second World
War period in certain Latin American and Asian countries.

In the aftermath of the First World War a number of countries
experienced quite severe hyperinflations. Details of some of these for
which monthly data are available are given in Table 4. The most
severe of these inflations was in Germany where both the rate of
inflation and the devaluation of the mark reached astronomical
proportions.

The next period of hyperinflation was towards the end of the

Table 4. Some European hyperinflations of the twentieth century

	Austria	Germany	Greece	Hungary	Hungary	Poland	Russia
Approximate beginning month of hyperinflation	Oct. 1921	Aug. 1922	Nov. 1943	Mar. 1923	Aug. 1945	Jan. 1923	Dec. 1921
Approximate final month of hyperinflation	Aug. 1922	Nov. 1923	Nov. 1944	Feb. 1924	July 1946	Jan. 1924	Jan. 1924
Approximate number of months of hyperinflation	11	16	13	10	12	11	26
Ratio of prices at end of final month to prices at first of beginning month	69.9	1.02×10^{10}	4.70×10^{8}	44.0	3.81×10^{27}	699.0	1.24×10^{5}
Ratio of quantity of hand-to-hand currency at end of final month to quantity at first of beginning month	19.3	7.32×10^{9}	3.62×10^{6}	17.0	1.19×10^{25}†	395.0	3.38×10^{4}
Average rate of rise in prices (percentage per month)‡	47.1	322.0	365.0	46.0	19,800	81.4	57.0
Average rate of rise in quantity of hand-to-hand currency (percentage per month)§	30.9	314.0	220.0	32.7	12,200†	72.2	49.3
Month of maximum rise in prices	Aug. 1922	Oct. 1923	Nov. 1944	July 1923	July 1946	Oct. 1923	Jan. 1924
Maximum monthly rise in prices (percentage per month)	134.0	32.4×10^{3}‖	85.5×10^{6}#	98.0	41.9×10^{15}	275.0	213.0
Change in quantity of hand-to-hand currency in month of maximum change in prices (percentage per month)	72.0	1.30×10^{3}**	73.9×10^{3}#	46.0	1.03×10^{15}	106.0	87.0

† Includes bank deposits.
‡ The value of x that sets $(1+[x/100])^t$ equal to the rise in the index of prices (row 4), where t is the number of months of hyperinflation (row 3).
§ The value of x that sets $(1+[x/100])^t$ equal to the rise in the quantity of hand-to-hand currency (row 5), where t is the number of months of hyperinflation (row 3).
‖ 2 October to 30 October 1923.
The value of x that sets $(1+[x/100])^t$ equal to the rise in prices, at a percentage rate per 30 days.
#31 October to 10 November 1944, at a percentage rate per 30 days.
** 29 September to 31 October 1923, at a percentage rate per 30 days.

Source: P. Cagan, 'The Monetary Dynamics of Hyperinflation' in Milton Friedman (ed.), *Studies in the Quantity Theory of Money*, 1956, University of Chicago Press.

Second World War. The most severe inflation yet recorded was in
Hungary from August 1945 to July 1946 (see Table 5). When the
pengo was finally replaced by the new currency, the forint, on 1 August
1946, one forint was convertible into 400 octillions of pengo (one
octillion = 1,000,000,000³) and because the 1938 exchange rate of
pengo to forints was one pengo to 2·7 forints, the conversion was

Table 5. **The Hungarian Hyperinflation, August 1945–July 1946**

Dates	Price Index Base: 26 August 1939 = 100	Dollar Exchange on the Black Market
1945 July	105	1,320
August	171	1,510
September	379	5,400
October	2,431	23,500
November	12,979	108,000
December	41,478	290,000
1946 January	72,330	795,000
February	435,887	2,850,000
March	1,872,913	17,750,000
April	35,790,361	232,000,000
May	11,267 millions	59,000 millions
1946 First two weeks in June	862,317 millions	7,600,000 millions
Second two weeks in June	954 trillions	42,000 trillions
First two weeks in July	3,066,254 trillions	22,000,000 trillions
Second week in July	11,426 quintillions	481,500 quintillions
Third week in July	36,018,959 quintillions	5,800,000 quintillions
Fourth week in July	399,623 septillions	4,600,000 septillions

Source: Nogaro Bertrand, 'Hungary's Recent Monetary Crisis and
its Theoretical Meaning', *American Economic Review*, September
1948.

828 octillions of depreciated pengo to one pre-war pengo. In the
peak month of this inflation in July 1946 prices more than tripled
daily. The Chinese inflation, though not as great as those of Greece
and Hungary, reached a climax in 1947 and the early part of 1948.
The other hyperinflations of this period were in Poland and Rumania.

Most of the severe inflations of the post-war years have been in
developing countries especially in Latin America and South East
Asia, although none of them have reached the proportions of the
European inflations earlier in the century (see Table 6).

Money and hyperinflation

Hyperinflations can only adequately be analysed in monetary terms. While wage rates rise just as dramatically as prices, and while the exchange rate depreciates (in terms of stable currency) in line with the price rise, these are the consequences of the inflation, not its cause. In explaining hyperinflations, however, by contrast with

Table 6. **Average Rates of Inflation of Less Developed Countries, 1949–65 (per cent per annum)**

1949–65		1949–53		1954–9		1960–5	
Korea	53.8	Korea	134.9	Turkey	14.1	Turkey	58.0
Bolivia	44.0	Bolivia	37.7	Bolivia	87.0	Brazil	32.0
Chile	32.4	Argentina	27.5	Chile	49.9	Uruguay	32.0
Brazil	31.6	Chile	20.2	Argentina	33.3	Chile	25.2
Argentina	28.3	Israel	17.5	Korea	25.6	Argentina	23.9
Uruguay	19.2	Tunisia	11.8	Brazil	22.0	Korea	14.4
		Morocco	11.6	Uruguay	16.6	Colombia	11.6
		Brazil	11.3			Ghana	10.2
		Peru	10.3				

Source: Joseph D. Adekunle, 'Rates of Inflation in Industrial, Other Developed and Less Developed Countries, 1949–65', IMF Staff Papers, November 1968, Vol. XV, No. 3.

inflations of the order of ten per cent or less per annum in monetary terms, it is not just the behaviour of the supply but also of the demand for money which matters. Hyperinflation results not only from an *increase* in the *supply* of money in nominal terms but also from a *decrease* in its *demand* in real terms; on the one hand, central banks pump more money into the economy by setting the printing presses to work and, on the other hand, although people want to increase their holdings of money in absolute terms, they invariably wish to increase their holdings less than proportionately to the rise in prices. Money is such a rapidly depreciating asset that people economize on their holdings as best they can. Put in another way, hyperinflations are characterized by a rapid increase in the money stock and a substantial rise in its income velocity of circulation.

In all the hyperinflations mentioned, the increase in the money stock was phenomenal. As can be seen from Table 4, the ratio of hand-to-hand currency at the end of the final month of the inflation to the quantity at the beginning of the initial month was 395 for Poland, 33,800 for Russia, 3·62 million for Greece, 7,320 million for Germany, and $1·19 \times 10^{25}$ for Hungary. The increase in the volume of bank deposits was equally dramatic (see Table 7).

The enormous increase in the amount of currency meant that printing presses were working to full capacity and still unable to keep up with demand. At the height of hyperinflations there is an apparent

Table 7. **Bank Deposits* during Hyperinflation**

End of Year	Austria	Germany	Hungary	Poland
	(Million Kroner)	(Million Marks)	(Million Kroner)	(Million Marks)
1913	7,423	29,640		
1920	71,371	138,261	18,398	12,094
1921	494,914	197,800	28,496	47,857
1922	9,475,665	272,220	53,038	224,290
1923		1,959 billion	159,958	64,229,000
1924			5,201,805	

* Bank deposits less cash reserves.

Source: Memorandum on Commercial Banks 1913–29 (Publications Department of the League of Nations, Geneva, 1931).

scarcity of money! For example, towards the end of October 1923 in Germany, the special paper used in note production was being produced in no less than thirty paper mills. The printing presses of the government were inadequate for the needs of the Reichsbank and about a hundred private printing firms were also being used by the Reichsbank. At the height of the inflation Dr Rudolf Havenstein, the President of the Reichsbank, described the situation vividly.

The wholly extraordinary depreciation of the mark has naturally created a rapidly increasing demand for additional currency, which the Reichsbank has not always been able fully to satisfy. A simplified production of notes of large denominations enabled us to bring ever greater amounts into circulation. But these enormous sums are barely adequate to cover the vastly increased demand for the means of payment, which has just recently attained an absolutely fantastic level, especially as a result of the extraordinary increases in wages and salaries.

The running of the Reichsbank's note-printing organization, which has become absolutely enormous, is making the most extreme demands on our personnel. The dispatching of cash sums must, for reasons of speed, be made by private transport. Numerous shipments leave Berlin every day for the provinces. The deliveries to several banks can be made . . . only by airplanes.[2]

On 25 October 1923 the Reichsbank issued a memorandum to the effect that although during the day notes worth 120,000 billions (a billion equals a thousand million) of paper marks had been stamped, they had fallen far short of the demand, which had been for about a trillion (a trillion equals a million billion). The Reichsbank regretted that it had been unable to keep up with demand but hoped that by the end of the week daily production would be up to half a trillion!

The scarcity of money also affected the banking system. Because of the shortage of currency, the private banks were unable to cash all of the cheques presented to them and so they were forced to ration such facilities. If their holdings of currency fell to too low a level during a day's trading, as it in fact did at the height of the inflation, they were forced to close their doors. This of course only exacerbated the situation. Payment was demanded in currency in case cheques could not be cashed immediately because banks had to wait a few days before receiving currency, and the value of the cheques would then be virtually worthless. As a result a panic situation arose in business and commerce and new forms of credit were developed. In the summer of 1923 Berlin banks issued new kinds of cheques which were acceptable at their branches and among a good many of their customers, and many private firms and public authorities began to issue their own kind of provisional money.

The other feature of the dramatic increase in currency was the way in which banknotes were denominated in larger units. In the Hungarian inflation the first million pengo note was issued in November 1945, the first milliard note in March 1946 and the first billion note at the end of May and then, at the beginning of June 1946, the first billion note and the first hundred million billion note – the largest denominated banknote ever issued. In January 1946 the government had introduced a new unit of account, the tax pengo, whose value was linked to the price level. Because of the severity of the inflation towards the end of May it also started issuing notes denominated in tax pengo. Despite the new currency the inflation, however, only escalated. The fact that notes and prices were quoted in millions, billions, trillions, quadrillions and quintillions was enough to drive some bank clerks out of their minds and induce others to commit suicide. In general commercial people gave up the practice of quoting precise figures and instead tended to speak about 'one red and two blue' notes.

The behaviour of the velocity of circulation of money during hyperinflation, which reflects changes in the demand rather than the supply of money, shows two characteristics: it rises rapidly as households and companies wish to reduce their money holdings in real terms, and it fluctuates widely from month to month. In other words velocity is not only higher but also more unstable the greater the inflation.

In Austria, Hungary and Poland the maximum rise in velocity (18, 9·5 and 23) was much less than in Russia (258) or Germany (418) and only a fraction of the phenomenal rise in Hungary in 1946 (3,860). If the money supply is increased rapidly and the demand for real balances falls (i.e. the velocity of circulation rises) the price level will increase proportionately more than the money supply increase. In Austria the rise in the price level was about eighteen times as much as the increase in the money stock, in Germany it was just over four hundred and in Hungary after the Second World War prices rose nearly four thousand times as much as the money supply.

The month-to-month fluctuations in the demand for money have been explained by P. Cagan in terms of the cost of holding money. During a hyperinflation the most reliable measure of the opportunity cost of holding money is its expected depreciation. Cagan related expectations of future inflation to a weighted average of past rates and finds that this explains the apparently erratic behaviour of the demand for money quite well.

Hyperinflations usually start with a rapid increase in the money supply, which produces a rapid increase in prices. But the increase in prices raises the expectation of future price rises, and therefore money holders wish to reduce their real balances. Even though they cannot reduce their balances in absolute terms, the aggregate effect of all money holders purchasing more goods and assets is to drive up prices even further. The central bank pumps an increasing amount of money into the system, which in turn produces yet higher prices, raises expectations of further inflation and so on. But even the hyperinflations studied by Cagan, which are by far the most serious recorded, never became self-generating. A self-generating inflation would be one in which, even though the supply of money remained constant, the inflation would continue indefinitely. The reason for this is that prices would rise at an increasing rate, producing an even greater 'flight from money' and so on *ad infinitum*. Two factors which might produce such an outcome are an extremely short time lag between past price rises and a revision of future expectations of inflation and a high elasticity of the demand for money. The nearest to self-generating inflations were the final months of the Russian and German inflations.

The major reason why central banks have increased the money supply during periods of hyperinflation by such gigantic amounts is to obtain revenue for the government. As we saw in the last chapter, inflation is a tax levied on the holders of money balances and collected by governments. Like any other tax it is a way by which the government is able to obtain greater control over real resources than would otherwise be possible. A way, in other words, of financing government expenditures. In the hyperinflations studied by Cagan the tax revenue resulting from money creation averaged less than 10 per cent of 'normal' income from tax: in Austria, it was 8 per cent, in Germany it was 6–7 per cent, in Greece it was 6 per cent, in Hungary (1945) it was 7 per cent, in Poland it was 3 per cent and in Russia it was 5 per cent. Only in the case of Hungary in 1923–4 was it substantially greater, somewhere between 13 per cent and 19 per cent. For the governments concerned, money creation was a substitute for either increasing existing tax rates or establishing new taxes.

After the adoption of the Weimar constitution in Germany, for example, there were numerous plans between 1919 and 1922 for fiscal reforms which would have introduced new taxes, especially on property and capital. M. Erzberger, one of the leaders of the left wing of the Centre Party had successfully introduced fiscal reform in 1919 and 1920 which substantially increased the tax revenue of the central government. As a result he became hated by the more conservative parties and an attempt was made on his life. Despite the increased fiscal revenue government expenditure continued to soar, so that the government found itself with a mounting deficit. In 1921–2 there was a fierce battle in the Reichstag between the socialists, who were in favour of the higher taxes not only to finance the deficit but also to redistribute wealth, and the parties of the right, who were more opposed to the advance of socialism than opponents of deficit spending by the government. In a compromise agreement in 1922 the government was authorized to levy a forced loan of a million gold marks. The fiscal effect of the loan, however, was undermined by a clause which enabled payment to be made at the rate of seventy paper marks to one gold mark. Given the rate of inflation, the revenue obtained from the loan was negligible. At the same time the government expenditure soared, due to unemployment benefits, demobilization payments, the maintenance of law and order, the need to provide food for those living in poverty and burdens imposed by the Treaty of Versailles. Between 1914 and October 1923 total government expenditure totalled approximately 133 milliard marks, of which only fifteen per cent was covered by explicit taxes. With so much political unrest being created by discussion of the tax structure, the government took the line of least resistance and resorted to the imposition of a tax which would not be the subject of debate in the Reichstag and which seemed so easy to administer and collect, at least in the short run – inflation. The same was true in Poland.[3] The government had to undertake extensive programmes for repairing the war damage and the administration of the tax system was unable to cope with collecting the necessary revenue. Until the end of the war, the Polish tax system had been administered by three different governments – Russia, Germany and Austria-Hungary. But at the end of the war the foreign officials who had administered the tax system left. In addition to this the new Polish Republic had the problem of trying to unify the tax system, which meant imposing unfamiliar taxes on a people who up until then had felt it their patriotic duty to evade tax payment because it was collected by foreign governments. In such an unstable political situation an untrained civil service found it impossible to stop the drift to inflation.

The pattern of revenue collection shows a remarkable consistency in all of the hyperinflations. The revenue from any tax, as we have seen, is equal to the tax rate times the tax base. Measured in real terms the revenue from inflation is equal to the rate of inflation (tax rate) times the stock of real money balance (the tax base). In the early stages of hyperinflations revenue increases because the tax rate is increased, while holdings of real money balances are not reduced immediately. Holders of money balances do not immediately revise their expectations of inflation. During the middle phase, revenue tends to fall as investors very rapidly revise their expectations of inflation to experience in the immediate past. Although the tax rate continues to rise the tax base shrinks as a result of the holders of real money balances, wishing to reduce their holdings and succeeding in the aggregate in doing so, driving up the price level. In the final phase of hyperinflation the revenue collection rises again, this time because of the astronomical rise in the tax rate and also because real money balances do not decline as much as they otherwise would in expectation of a monetary reform. Because the banks play such a vital role in the issue of money they also stand to collect part of the revenue from inflation. In a competitive banking system in which the banks were free of all controls on the rates they could pay on deposits and in which no discrepancy arose in the speed with which rates for lending and rates for borrowing were revised because of a change in the expected rate of inflation, the banking system would not collect any revenue from inflation. But in a banking system in which there were ceilings on the rates payable on deposits and banks could charge rates of interest on loans which reflected the inflation but pay rates on deposits which were considerably less, then, as a result of the rapid increases in reserves, the banks could expand and make substantial profits. What tended to happen in practice, however, in most countries that have experienced hyperinflation, was that because of usury laws, the force of habit and so on banks did not charge nominal interest rates which reflected expected rate of inflation, and so bank borrowers gained at the expense of the owners of bank equity and depositors.

Although, as we have seen, hyperinflations can only be understood in monetary terms, a remarkable fact is the reluctance of the monetary authorities to admit that it is of their making. At the height

I—6

of the German inflation the President of the Reichsbank put it that 'It is said . . . that the Reichsbank bears . . . a large part of the blame for the disorganization of the currency and the still increasing inflation. We are unanimously of the opinion that all these reproaches are unjustified. . . .'[4] He claimed that there was not a credit inflation in Germany and that the impulse to monetary depreciation had always come from abroad.

Economic and social consequences

Inflation produces the same *kind* of economic consequences regardless of its rate. The only difference between hyperinflation and lesser inflations is the magnitude of their effects. Trends which are barely discernible during a creeping inflation become glaringly obvious during a hyperinflation. Instead of economizing on holding money by more frequent trips to the bank or the cash dispenser, the economy tends to dispense with money altogether and resort to barter, and in place of the insidious but gradual redistribution of wealth from creditor to debtor, whole classes are impoverished in a matter of months or even weeks. The same underlying forces are at work in all inflations; the only difference is their magnitude and the speed with which they operate.

One important cost of a hyperinflation results from attempts to economize on the holding of money. Because money does not bear interest, inflation is a tax on its holding. At a time of hyperinflation the rate of this tax reaches enormous proportions, so creating an incentive for persons to economize even further on the holding of money. Firms for example tend to pay their workers more frequently; at the height of the inflation in Germany some firms were paying out wages daily or even more frequently. Workers receive wage payments and promptly dash to the nearest food shop to buy goods that can be stored till the next pay out, or exchange domestic for foreign currency, or purchase other assets whose value would rise with the inflation. Shops tend to open and close more than once a day; they open, do business, close and then promptly get rid of the cash which they received as payment to replenish stocks which keep their value with the inflation. Such a process reaches the limit when the rate of inflation is so great that money is dispensed with altogether as the means of payment and the economy resorts to a system of barter. Firms pay their workers in kind rather than cash and consumers swap goods rather than face the prospect of being left holding the depreciating currency. Thomas Mann described the process vividly in Germany in 1923.

But hadn't prices risen correspondingly in the meantime? For the most part, yes, but not necessarily; not if you took your money as fast as your legs would carry you to some innocent grocer or wine dealer or artist. If you were lucky, he had the mark quotation for 9 a.m., but not for 12 noon; the difference – to his disadvantage – could be enormous. On the other hand, if he was a little less innocent he might ring up his bank, sigh, wipe the perspiration from his forehead, and rectify his prices. Yes, the purchaser could also be the loser. For instance, you might drop in at the tobacconist's for a cigar. Alarmed at the price, you'd rush to a competitor, find that his price was still higher, and race back to the first shop, which may have doubled or tripled its price in the meantime. There was no help for it, you had to dig into your pocketbook and take out a huge bundle of millions, or even billions, depending on the date. . . .

On Friday evenings you could see workers coming out of the factories with baskets, sacks, and suitcases full of money. It didn't do them much good, for the frightened and greedy shopkeepers often raised their prices faster than the value of the currency fell. It became necessary to pay wages daily, and in the end the firm of Krupp among others began to print its own bank-notes. The cities, even the smallest of them, also took to printing money; it was up to some high official to decide how much. It goes without saying that for the time being forgery ceased to exist as a trade.[5]

Such a change in the payments system imposes a real cost to society. The extra time taken up by firms in making payments and by consumers in extra shopping is at the expense of output or leisure. In the German hyperinflation, the only one for which statistics were available, real output dropped only at the very end, indicating that the extra cost of transacting was at the expense of leisure. In few instances, however, has the economy dispensed with money altogether and barter been instituted on a wide scale. In most inflations barter seems to have been more prevalent in the country than in the cities and in any case rarely adopted on a large scale. In the Chinese inflation of 1947 the official currencies were given up as a store of value and a unit of account but continued to retain their role, especially in the cities, as a means of carrying out transactions. Business firms usually held their reserves in the form of United States dollars, Chinese silver dollars, gold, short-term notes or commodities such as rice and flour which were easily exchanged. At the height of the Hungarian inflation most transactions involving food were done in barter and most other trade in terms of gold or US dollars. The cost of transacting had risen to such an extent that absenteeism reached fifty per cent of the labour force.

In free China most small shops kept their accounts in United States dollars, while the Communists insisted that all firms should keep their accounts in terms of corn flour or some other commodity. For example the Tientsin *Daily News* published the daily price of corn flour, so that all wages, debts, taxes and other costs could then be computed at the standard rate. Similarly in the Hungarian inflation of 1946 merchants and manufacturers started to compute their costs in terms of dollars. Despite these trends money was still retained as the means of payment.

One interesting innovation in Hungary towards the end of February 1946 was the introduction of what came to be called 'Calory Money'. Because of the inequities created by the inflation the government decided that a percentage of wages and salaries were to be paid in food, depending on the size of the wage-earner's family and their calorific requirements. If the employers were unable to pay in food they could pay in money, but calculated in terms of black market food prices. The experiment, however, had a number of perverse effects. The calory requirements of wage-earners was soon found to be far in excess of the total amount of food, so that workers had to be increasingly paid with newly created money. The experiment also affected incentives. A worker with a large family but low productivity found himself earning more than a bachelor manager. As a result productivity fell. Although introduced to remove inequities the system created one which became important. Workers paid in food found themselves increasingly better off by comparison with those paid in money. After three months the real wages of the former category had risen by nearly a quarter whereas those in the latter had fallen by about fifteen per cent. In the face of such inflations the retention of money as the means of payment suggests that money performs an extremely valuable function in facilitating the complex process of exchange associated with the urban life of twentieth-century economies.

A common feature of all hyperinflations is the frenzied speculation which takes place in goods, securities and foreign exchange. As the internal value of the currency plummets consumers hoard goods and firms accumulate stocks and capital equipment, foreign currencies replace the domestic currency as a temporary store of value, and industrial share prices, especially of those firms which have extensive foreign interests, rocket.

Louis Blanc, writing on the effect of inflation in revolutionary France, put it very succinctly: 'Commerce was dead; betting took its place.' Thomas Mann in a highly personalized reflection on Germany expresses a similar notion.

> Never have those who wanted to make money without working found such favourable conditions as in Germany from 1922 to 1924. All that was needed was a certain degree of ingenuity and unscrupulousness. Honest work, however skilled, brought nothing. Consequently, even ordinarily honest people were infected with the fever of speculation. Peasants filled their houses with sewing machines, pianos, and Persian rugs, and refused to part with their eggs and milk except in exchange for articles of permanent value. Medical students became stock-jobbers. Teachers discussed such topics with their classes as how to convert a little money into a lot of money. The answer: by buying foreign currency, holding it for a while and then reselling it. In that way a million could be turned into five millions and ultimately into a billion.[6]

Gordon Tullock observes how in China in 1947 capital goods were bought by firms, not in order to be used in the process of production but simply as a hedge against inflation, and that whenever firms sold anything they would immediately rush out and purchase stock, even though the commodities purchased bore no relation to their business. Such speculation is costly in that it channels resources away from consumption and investment activity. Bresciani-Turroni observed that in the German inflation:

> The number of middlemen increased continually at a time when the buying and selling of goods, thanks to the very rapid increase of prices, created the possibility of quick profits. Besides legitimate commerce which already comprised a very long chain of middlemen, there grew and blossomed in the hothouse of the currency depreciation clandestine commerce, which was devoted to bargaining in all sorts of foodstuffs, useful articles, artistic objects, gold and silver goods, etc.[7]

Between 1919 and 1925 the number of joint-stock companies in Germany engaged in commerce rose from 933 to 4,226. A substantial number of new banks were started and existing banks increased their branches. In 1923 alone no less than 401 new banks were established. The rapid increase in banks was the result of the increased demand for buying and selling foreign exchange and speculating on the Bourse. Foreign exchange firms also grew rapidly.

It may be argued that because speculation is generally considered desirable from an economic point of view – it enables individuals to hold a preferred collection of assets – the speculation which takes place in hyperinflation far from imposing a cost on society is in fact desirable. This depends on which alternatives are being considered. If we assume a world in which hyperinflation is already taking place, then speculation which is after all the free exchange of goods and finances will be of greater benefit to society in that individuals will be permitted to rearrange their assets in a preferred way. But if we contrast a world of speculation and hyperinflation with a world in which we have no inflation and if we further assume speculation is an inevitable concomitant of hyperinflation, the cost of speculation is the resources which have been diverted from previously productive uses. And the evidence suggests that this cost is substantial.

A further economic cost which was evident in the hyperinflation of the 1920s and 1940s was the increase in 'unproductive' labour, as it was referred to in Germany. Constant price changes meant constant revisions of wage payments, complicated tax assessments, revaluation of stocks, frequent exchange of foreign for domestic currency. In addition to this the rapid price and wage increase produced continuing disputes between workers and management over the real wage. The evidence for this on a national scale is very difficult to adduce; but what is interesting is the record of two sizeable private companies, Borsig and Siemens-Schuckert, which we have no reason to believe were atypical. Borsig claimed that, as a measure of the increase in unproductive labour, they employed in 1913 66 'unproductive' workmen to 100 productive workmen, whereas in 1922 the figure was 120 unproductive workmen to every 100 productive workmen. Siemens-Schuckert shows much the same problem. In 1914 for every productive workman that they employed they also employed 0·537 workmen in the office, whereas in 1923 the figure had increased by 42·6 per cent to 0·766.[8]

These extreme inflations produced great disparities of income and wealth. Workmen who were not organized – such as domestic servants of both sexes and often, professional and academic people such as teachers, writers and artists – were reduced to penury, while a small group who had profited from the inflation became extremely rich. The contrast in Austria was immediately apparent:

> It seems that in Vienna the extravagance and the dissipation of the profiteers knows no limits, and they increase in the same proportion as the currency falls in value. The most striking characteristic of Vienna is the contrast between a small group of people living in luxury (they were those who had been known to defend themselves from the depreciation and to gain advantage for themselves) and a strata of society living in the most abject poverty. The old middle class has completely disappeared.[9]

Exactly the same picture is drawn of Paris in the early 1790s. 'The luxury and extravagance of the currency gamblers and their families form one of the most significant features in any picture of the social condition of that period',[10] notes Andrew Dickson White in an analysis of the period. He goes on to say that:

> The contrast between these gay creatures of the Directory period and the people at large was striking. Indeed much as the vast majority of the wealthy classes suffered from impoverishment, the laboring classes, salaried employees of all sorts, and people of fixed income and of small means, especially in the cities, underwent yet greater distress. These were found, as a rule, to subsist mainly

on daily government rations of bread at the rate of one pound per person. This was frequently unfit for food and was distributed to long lines of people, men, women and children, who were at times obliged to wait their turn even from dawn to dusk. The very rich could, by various means, especially by bribery, obtain better bread, but only at enormous cost.[11]

The facts with regard to Germany in 1923 show a very similar pattern. In 1923, excluding the unemployed, no less than 5,632,000 people were receiving small subsidies or pensions either from national or local government. Meat consumption also shows an interesting pattern between 1922 and 1924. From the last quarter of 1921 to the last quarter of 1922 the number of pigs killed fell from 1,416,051 to 1,131,148, while the number of horses increased from 30,967 to 47,652. Things became so bad in 1923 that the poorest resorted to dog-flesh; 1,090 dogs were killed in the third quarter of 1921, 3,678 in the third quarter of 1922 and 6,430 in the third quarter of 1923! After the stabilization programme was introduced the situation changed dramatically, with only 841 dogs being killed in the third quarter of 1924 and the consumption of pork increasing. Bresciani-Turroni summed up the situation:

It appears that the poverty of the German people was certainly not general, but it was limited to certain classes, in fact to those which had been most severely hit by the inflation. The poverty was revealed by many symptoms, some of which are measurable by statistics: the condition of children (underweight, spread of tuberculosis and rickets); lack of clothing; the lowered feeding standards (fall in the consumption of cereals, meat, butter, milk, eggs, etc., and the substitution of poorer foods, as e.g., the substitution of rye for wheat, margarine and other inferior fats for butter, and all sorts of substitutes for coffee); the very poor condition of houses; the excessive work of women; the appearance of certain maladies formerly almost unknown in Germany, such as acne and scurvy; the rise in the number of suicides due to the lack of means of subsistence; deaths through malnutrition (which were very rare before the war); and the rise in the number of pauper funerals because relatives could not pay the expenses, although a decree by the Minister of the Interior permitted the substitution of pasteboard shells for wooden coffins, which were too dear.[12]

The same general picture also emerges in the Roman Empire in the late second and in the third centuries, during which time the debasement of the currency reached new proportions. Substantial fortunes were made by speculation, while the middle class was almost wiped out and the lower classes sunk into considerable poverty.

One of the most difficult problems in analysing the effects of inflation is to assess the relationship which exists between inflation and the change in the values of a society. While from an *a priori* point of view one can postulate many possibilities, the historical record of many of the great inflations of the past suggests either that inflation led to a deterioration of values or some third factor simultaneously produced both hyperinflation and a deterioration of values. The evidence from the French inflation of the 1790s is quite clear.

Out of the inflation of prices grew a speculating class; and, in the complete uncertainty as to the future, all business became a game of chance, and all business men, gamblers. In city centers came a quick growth of stock-jobbers and speculators; and these set a debasing fashion in business which spread to the remotest parts of the country. Instead of satisfaction with legitimate profits, came a passion for inordinate gains. Then, too, as values became more and more uncertain, there was no longer any motive for care or economy, but every motive for immediate expenditure and present enjoyment. So came upon the nation the obliteration of thrift. In this mania for yielding to present enjoyment rather than providing for future comfort were the seeds of new growths of wretchedness: luxury, senseless and extravagant, set in: this, too, spread as a fashion. To feed it, there came cheatery in the nation at large and corruption among officials and persons holding trusts. While men set such fashions in private and official business, women set fashions of extravagance in dress and living that added to the incentives to corruption. Faith in moral considerations, or even in good impulses, yielded to general distrust. National honor was thought a fiction cherished only by hypocrites. Patriotism was eaten out by cynicism.[13]

In his classic analysis of the German inflation, Bresciani-Turroni refers to 'the profound moral disturbance'[14] which the depreciation of the mark produced and Thomas Mann to the fact that 'an experience of this kind poisons the morale of a nation'.[15]

Stabilization and currency reforms

All of the hyperinflations mentioned in this chapter were brought to an end through the implementation of a stabilization programme, one aspect of which was the reform of the currency. Although currency or monetary reform is sometimes used to refer to any programme which is intended to change the basic features of a nation's monetary and banking system, in the context of the rapid inflations which followed the First and Second World Wars in Europe they refer to the withdrawal of most and sometimes all of the existing currency of a country, and the issue of a new currency and a corresponding revaluation of wages and prices.[16] For example in Austria (1922), Hungary (1924), Poland (1926), Germany (1923) and Russia (1924) – all countries which experienced hyperinflation – a new currency was introduced, while in Albania, Lithuania and Danzig new national currencies were introduced to replace foreign currencies. Between the autumn of 1944 and the middle of 1952 in Europe no less than twenty-four countries introduced currency reforms, some of them, such as Poland (1944, 1950), Rumania (1947, 1952) and Bulgaria (1947, 1952) more than once. Details of these reforms are given in Table 8. For all those countries which had experienced hyperinflation, the major object of the reform was to reduce the money supply and scale down wages and prices. This, however, especially in countries with less inflationary pressure, was not always the primary aim – in some it was to prepare the way for the imposition of capital levies, in others to redistribute wealth among the population and in certain east European countries to destroy one of the remaining vestiges and symbols of capitalism. Type 1 reforms, which were largely a 'mopping-up' of liquid assets, involved the compulsory exchange of old banknotes and 'old' bank deposits for new ones, at exchange rates set by the government which ensured that the supply of money was effectively reduced. Once the reform had been effected however there was no blocking of deposits and individuals and businesses were free to spend their balances as they wished. The exchange rates which were set typically varied between different kinds of assets; for example, in the first Hungarian reform the ratio between old and new banknotes was four-to-one, while bank deposits remained untouched: and in the Russian reform the exchange rates ranged from one-to-one to ten-to-one, mainly to be able to discriminate against peasants having substantial holdings of banknotes. In some cases those holding small amounts of deposits and notes were favoured at the expense of large holders. In the second reform in Rumania the rates became progressive depending on one's holding of liquid assets – for banknotes, from 100-to-one to 400-to-one and for bank deposits from 50-to-one to 200-to-one. In addition certain kinds of asset-owners were granted special treatment. For example, in the third Austrian reform farmers and small depositors were given favourable treatment, while in Bulgaria businesses were hit particularly hard.

The second kind of monetary reform (Type 2 in Table 8) did not reduce the supply of liquid assets by compulsorily applying an unfavourable exchange rate, but exchanged 'old' deposits and banknotes for new, on a one-to-one basis, but then blocked their use by forcing their owners to deposit them in special accounts. Although coin and small denomination notes were exempt, bank deposits and large denomination notes were not. The criteria by which these blocked funds were subsequently immobilized were numerous: per capita, so that consumers would be able to spend until they receive their wage payments; the size of average monthly wage and salary bills of employers, so that wage payments could be made; the date on which the deposit was first opened, 'good' deposits being those opened before the outbreak of war and 'bad' deposits those opened during occupation; the type of liquid asset owned, such as saving deposit being granted preferential treatment over other kinds of asset; and the amount of assets held, with large deposits being discriminated against. In some cases, such as France, almost all of the blocked funds were returned, while in others, such as Belgium, permanently blocked deposits were converted into forced loans to the government which were redeemed through special capital levies. Again, in certain countries funds were released very quickly, while in others they took a long time.

The other kind of monetary reform (Type 3) was a combination of the first two: firstly currency and bank deposits were converted into a new currency and then a portion of the new deposits were blocked. The typical case of such a reform is that of West Germany in 1948.

Table 8. **Classification of European Monetary Reforms**

Country	Month and Year of Reform	One	Two	Three
Belgium	Oct. 1944		x	
Greece	Nov. 1944	x		
Poland I	Dec. 1944		x	
Yugoslavia	Apr. 1945			x
France I	June 1945		x	
Austria I	July 1945		x	
Denmark	July 1945		x	
Norway	Sept. 1945		x	
Netherlands	Sept. 1945		x	
Czechoslovakia	Oct. 1945		x	
Austria II	Nov. 1945		x	
Hungary I	Dec. 1945	x		
Finland	Dec. 1945		x	
Hungary II	Aug. 1946	x		
Bulgaria I	Mar. 1947		x	
Rumania I	Aug. 1947			x
Austria III	Nov. 1947	x		
USSR	Dec. 1947	x		
France II	Jan. 1948		x	
West Germany	June 1948			x
East Germany	June 1948			x
Poland II	Oct. 1950	x		
Rumania II	Jan. 1952	x		
Bulgaria II	May 1952	x		

Source: John G. Gurley, 'Excess Liquidity and Monetary Reforms', *American Economic Review*, March 1953.

Currency reforms in themselves will not cure inflation. This requires a determination on the part of the government not to pursue inflationary policies and in particular to restrain the rate of growth of the money supply. The success of a currency reform must be judged by whether or not it restored the public's confidence in the worth of money as a means of payment and a store of value. In this respect many seem to have been very successful. In those cases, however, such as Finland, Greece, Austria, Poland, Rumania, Bulgaria and Hungary, in which inflation continued to soar even after the reform, it was hardly due to the reform but rather to the absence of an appropriate stabilization policy.

The worst feature of most monetary reforms was their inequity. Various kinds of assets and various individuals were purposely singled out for discriminatory treatment, which was entirely irrelevant to the anti-inflationary objective of such reforms.

Chilean hyperinflation and the fall of Allende, 1973

The most recent and dramatic escalation from inflation to hyper-inflation took place in Chile during the United Popular government (November 1970–September 1973) of Salvador Allende.[17] Even though this experiment in democratic socialism has a number of unique characteristics it is interesting nevertheless as a contemporary example of hyperinflation and also instructive in understanding the nature of the transition from inflation to hyperinflation.

President Allende took office at the end of a period of recession. In the previous four years GNP had grown at an average rate of about three per cent per annum which was lower than the preceding years and unemployment had reached a peak of 8·3 per cent in 1970. Throughout the period the balance of payments had improved noticeably (the net foreign exchange reserves of the banking system had increased from 183 million dollars in 1965 to 343 millions in 1970), the government deficit had been reduced by 1970 to only fifteen per cent of current government revenue, investment in real terms was rising and the rate of inflation averaged between twenty-five and thirty per cent per annum. By the time, however, that President Allende was ousted in September 1973, the situation had been dramatically reversed. Even though the prices of many of the goods which were used in constructing the retail price index were sub-ject to government control, the official consumer price index increased between January 1970 and September 1973 by 119 per cent and, using this same index, the official rate of inflation in the fourth quarter of 1973 was over 500 per cent. In the month of October alone prices rose by 87 per cent. Attempts to estimate the 'true' price rise over the same period suggest an increase in the price level of 2,531 per cent, which also accords with an estimate of the economic department of the University of Chile of a rise in the black market price of the dollar of 3,600 per cent! Over the same period, however, real wages fell by 18·5 per cent, even though in the first year of office real output grew by 8·5 per cent (in 1970 it was estimated by DEPLAN, the government planning agency, that there was 25 per cent excess capacity in the economy), the government deficit increased rapidly until in 1973 it was greater than the revenue of the government, the rate of growth of fixed investment fell dramatically and the balance of payment was in deficit, on both current and capital account, throughout the whole period. On the positive side, the share of wages and salaries in the GNP rose during the government's first year in office (from approximately 55 to 62 per cent). In the next year, however, it fell and to a position below that of 1970. The other major achievement from the government's point of view was the nationalization of areas of industry and agriculture.

In the first instance this inflation was a monetary phenomenon. Between 1964 and 1970 the money supply (M_1) grew at an average rate of 42 per cent a year. In 1971 this rose to 113 per cent; in 1972 to 151 per cent, and the estimated figure for 1973, before the collapse of the government, was between 450 and 500 per cent. The actual rate over the twelve months before the government fell was just over 300 per cent. Corresponding to the dramatic acceleration in the stock of money was an equally dramatic acceleration in the rate of inflation. Over 1971 the rate of inflation was only 22 per cent, over 1972 it was 163 per cent and throughout 1973, 508 per cent.

The major factor making for such an enormous increase in the money supply was the equally dramatic rise in government expenditure and the inability of the government to raise tax revenue by a corresponding amount. In 1970 the actual deficit measured in terms of millions of 1969 escudas was 2,317, in 1971 it was 8,390, in 1972 it was 10,010 and in 1973, 12,348. What is also interesting is that the actual deficits of 1971 and 1972 turned out to be over twice the planned deficits for those years and the actual deficit of 1973 three times the projected deficit for that year. The major stimulus to increase government spending was the financing of the Area of Social Ownership, the publicly owned part of the economy, which grew rapidly during the tenure of the government. Apart from the need for funds to finance more public ownership, by 1972 the current deficits of the public sector were 37 per cent of their total income. The reason for the deficit was not simply the enormous increase in government expenditure but also the inability of the government either to increase the rates of existing taxes or raise new taxes. This was because these changes required the approval of Congress, which was not granted because it was controlled by opposition parties. The economic and political consequences of the Chilean inflation were made worse as a result of the widespread use of controls. One sector in which effects of controls was evident was agriculture. Because of controls over food prices, an enormous food shortage was created, which was then partly alleviated by substantial increases in food imports – in 1972 food imports rose by forty-four per cent. Another consequence of the artificially stimulated excess demand for food was the creation of black markets. In order to reduce the supply of food to these markets the government established buying agencies at a national level and prohibited the transport of agricultural products between different provinces without official authorization. The uncertainty which the food shortage created also led to the hoarding of food by those fortunate enough to be able to purchase it. As a result of controls and the land reforms which the government carried out agricultural output slumped. Cultivated land decreased during 1972–3 by 22·4 per cent – the lowest level for forty years. The government also introduced controls over foreign payment. Severe import controls were introduced and were one of the factors explaining the slump in industrial production in 1973. As a result of the controls it was impossible for certain firms to obtain raw materials and replacements, for which no domestic substitutes were available. This generated bottlenecks and so led to a fall in industrial production. The black markets and the controls also meant that tourists from neighbouring countries had an incentive to enter Chile, sell their hard currencies on the black market, and buy Chilean goods at the official prices. In addition to this Chileans sent their escudos abroad to be sold on the black market for foreign currencies – because such an exchange was outlawed in their own country. In an attempt to break this the government forced tourists to sell so much foreign currency to the government every day.

From a political point of view, the truckers' strike during July and August 1973 was largely motivated by controls – the shortages of spare parts for their trucks, official discrimination against them in favour of state-run firms, and the fact that the charges which they could make were fixed by the government but not adjusted to take into account the rapid rate of inflation. Support was evident from small business people whose firms were bankrupt, housewives who found themselves queueing for the basic necessities and civil servants and skilled workers whose salaries had fallen in real terms as a result of the inflation.

The Chilean example is interesting because it was characterized by two features which were common to the French hyperinflation during the Revolution, Germany under the Weimar Republic and many other hyperinflationary situations – political instability and the inability of the government to raise taxes. The evidence from these periods suggests that a necessary condition for an inflation to become a hyperinflation is the inability of the government to increase taxes to match substantially higher expenditures. If this is so it is surely an important reason why it is *unlikely* that in the immediate future the present British inflation or those of other developed countries will accelerate into hyperinflations of the magnitude of those we have already considered. In all developed countries there is a fairly broad tax base, so that by raising the rates of income and indirect tax governments still have considerable scope for increasing tax revenue. The other characteristic of hyperinflations, political instability, has usually been connected with revolution, war or attempts at radical changes in policy and once again, there is no reason to think that on these grounds the present inflation will develop into a hyper-inflation. Nevertheless one characteristic of the transition to hyper-inflation is the fairly short period of time it took – in France and Germany just five years and in Chile only three. Although it seems certain that because of the present government's deflationary policy the rate of inflation will be reduced, nevertheless, the unsettling effect which this inflation has had on society coupled with the magnitude of the present public sector deficit and the open-ended commitment of this government to take over companies which are bankrupt and extend credit to them on favourable terms is creating a climate in which a future government could easily be forced to use hyperinflation as a method of raising fiscal revenue.

II Capitalism and democracy

'Lenin is said to have declared that the best way to destroy the capitalist system was to debauch the currency . . . Lenin was certainly right. There is no subtler, no surer means of overturning the existing basis of society than to debauch the currency. The process engages all the hidden forces of economic law on the side of destruction and has it in a manner which not one man in a million is able to diagnose.'

J. M. Keynes, The Economic Consequences of the Peace (*1919*)

Inflation is only partially an economic problem. We have already seen that if we are to understand its origins we have to probe beyond the veil of money, because the monetary behaviour of governments is itself the outcome of a political process, concerned with resolving competing claims on the economic system. Precisely the same distinction applies in considering its effect. Although inflation has direct economic consequences, it's impact is not restricted to the production and distribution of wealth; by influencing values and shaping attitudes it sets in motion a number of changes which extend to the political system, and ultimately reverberate throughout the whole of society. In fact, one of the most important and disturbing issues raised by an inflation of the magnitude we are now experiencing in the United Kingdom is its compatibility with our prevailing institutions of capitalism and democracy.

This is the problem which I wish to explore in this chapter. The case to be presented is that inflation is a process which undermines the legitimacy of capitalism as an economic system and of democracy as a political system, and which as a result sets up pressures and conflicts which can only be contained and resolved within a modified or alternative economic and political system, which is dependent on a greater use of coercion and, therefore, less desirable.

In presenting this case it is particularly important to emphasize that inflation can have a damaging effect on the fabric of our society without necessarily destroying it. The attempt to link almost any discussion on the political consequences of inflation to the future of democracy, in the sense of its very survival, is unnecessarily restrictive. What I hope to show in this chapter is that inflation does not have to be of the same magnitude as Germany in 1923 to leave a permanent scar on the life of society.

One particular difficulty in assessing the impact of inflation on society is to separate out its particular effects from those of a number of other changes which take place simultaneously. The post-war years, and in particular the last two decades, have seen noticeable changes in both the structure and values of our society: a sharp decline in the importance of religion, numerous challenges to the institution of the family, the extension of the welfare state and government intervention in industry, a growth in crime and a far greater openness to new ideas and social change. We have to take great care to ensure that we are not mistaking their effects for those of inflation.

Capitalism and legitimacy

As a means of treating the influence which inflation has on society economics proves to be of rather limited value. Although over the past decade economists have turned their attention to such diverse and novel areas as bureaucracy, crime, marriage, education, discrimination, family planning, suicide, drug addiction and crime detection, they remain the prisoner of their own method. The problems are invariably analysed in terms of choice, constraints and maximization; and values are always assumed to be unchanged. For help in analysing the relationship between values and economic structures we have to turn to the work of the German sociologist, Max Weber.[1]

As a result of his detailed study of the history of European and ancient societies, one of the major problems with which Weber became concerned was the way in which authority is accepted within a society and the means by which a social order acquires legitimacy. According to Weber, it is impossible to understand a social order, whether it is slavery, tribalism, feudalism, capitalism or socialism, without acknowledging the importance of authority and the part it plays in binding and holding together a society. However unaware we are of the fact, we are all bound up in a system of interrelated authorities – whether in the family, school, university, factory, trade union, church, bureaucracy or the state; most of us exercise, and are in turn subject to, authority.

Authority may be accepted for a variety of reasons. The dominating force may be economic self-interest; in which case the society is, according to Weber, relatively unstable. Or it may be custom and habit, which makes for rather more stability. The social order is most stable if authority is considered legitimate, a characteristic which every system wishes to acquire. Legitimacy may be established in a number of ways. It may be related to tradition. The systems and the institutions which have existed in the past and which embody the aspirations and experience of previous generations have a certain claim to respect. I behave in a certain way to certain people and institutions almost unquestioningly because that is the way I was taught to behave, the way I saw my family behave and the way in turn which they saw theirs. Tradition is most powerful in legitimizing a social order when bound up with religion. If an existing order has a claim to divine sanction, and if I accept divine authority, then the existing order is something I will to continue. It may also be bound up with the idea of good and bad. If it is to be accepted, authority must be capable of being rationalized in moral terms; it has in some sense either to be considered as good or else to be leading to an outcome which is considered good. Socialism is considered good because it is believed that the distribution of income and wealth which would prevail under such an economic system would exhibit equality, or rather, a greater degree of equality than under capitalism, and that, in addition, the worker would feel less alienated within society. An even clearer example is the belief in natural law: people willingly act or at least desire to act according to a certain set of rules because these have a validity in that they are a part of the natural order of things. Legitimacy is also linked to the idea of efficiency: an existing order is accepted as valid because (according to a certain set of criteria) it works; it provides a material existence for the majority of people which is tolerable; it produces a framework of law and order in which it is possible to work and live without undue harassment and it is relatively peaceful, without disruptions and revolutions.

By these criteria, capitalism and the institutions on which it depends can be considered as having a certain claim to legitimacy. As an economic system it has provided a period of prosperity and offered a degree of personal economic freedom unparalleled in history. The 'invisible hand' of Adam Smith has performed a remarkable function in channelling limited resources to those areas in which they are most valued by society as a whole. The freedom to buy and sell, to save and invest, to borrow and lend, to move from one job and country to another, are in stark contrast both to feudal and contemporary socialist economies. Such economic freedom has also been an important basis for political freedom and the advance of democracy. The decentralization of economic power would appear to be a necessary condition for the decentralization of political power. Although not a sufficient condition, as the examples of Nazi Germany and Mussollini's Italy show only too well, it is difficult to evidence countries which have had a tolerable political freedom without economic freedom. Even the income differences which exist in a market economy and which are crucial in providing incentives for resources to move where they are needed, are not unreasonable. Saving, investment, risk-taking and training all involve particular costs and as a result necessitate higher returns. In a market economy in which freedom of entry into and exit from markets is assured and in which the markets are free of government control, the important point is that these inequalities are reduced to a minimum and in any case remain monetary rather than political. One vital condition, however, for such a capitalist economy to function is the existence of a strong legal system which enforces commercial contracts and ensures property rights.

Yet it is precisely the legitimacy of capitalism as an economic system which is undermined by inflation. Efficiency is a claim which can be made with much less enthusiasm. The over-investment in gold, property, commodities, *objets d'art*, vintage wines and all other hedges against inflation is wasteful, as is the under-investment in productive capital, the basis of future prosperity. Consumption, borrowing and speculation are all encouraged; saving, lending, and investment are all discouraged. Trading becomes considered speculation; investment, gambling; and prudence, a lack of patriotism, for example British multi-national companies moving funds out of sterling. The financial system is transformed into a vast lottery and the City into a casino. This is bad enough even in an economic sense. What makes it even worse is that the process unleashes a spirit of greed and selfishness, which becomes the *modus vivendi* of economic life, and ultimately infects the whole of society.

The inefficiency of the system is only compounded by the intervention of government. Price and wage controls, introduced to cure the problem, only succeed in worsening it; shortages, queues, rationing and black markets appear; the uncertainty leads to hoarding and the shortages become even more acute; and in addition businesses and trade unions have an enormous incentive to evade controls. If price controls are enforced less strictly then wage controls profits rise, which is then produced as evidence of that monopoly spirit which apparently is always lurking just beneath the surface; if wage controls are enforced less strictly than price controls, profits fall, firms go bankrupt, and the system exhibits an inhumanity which is supposedly its mainspring. Public debate thrives on accusation and counter-accusation; but in the public mind it is the market economy itself which is discredited.

More damaging in the longer run than even this inefficiency is the capricious redistribution of income and wealth; something which becomes exceedingly difficult, if not impossible, to justify on a normative basis. Those owning property gain, those renting lose; those borrowing money are subsidized, those lending money are taxed; taxpayers gain at the expense of those holding government debt, but lose to those benefiting from government expenditures. Anyone happening to hold an asset or receive an income fixed in money terms loses, while anyone holding a liability or making a regular payment fixed in money terms gains. This redistribution bears no relation to extra work, greater risk or increased savings; it is totally arbitrary and ultimately no different from that of a lottery.

The arbitrariness of the redistribution itself produces further perverse effects. Because the State taxes those holding money and government debt and effectively levies higher taxes on certain categories of taxpayers, the incentives and the arguments for tax evasion are strengthened. Those who in normal circumstances would not have dreamt of evading income and capital gains tax now feel increasingly justified in doing so. If the government is dishonest enough to levy taxes without even mentioning the fact, let alone seeking Parliamentary approval, the taxpayer resorts to the same tactics. Because of the uneven increase in wages in different sectors, and especially the public sector, the benefits in terms of higher pay from increased militancy and threatened industrial action become clear. Militancy therefore far from being a cause of inflation is one of its most serious consequences; and yet paradoxically enough one that is ignored in the literature of classical economics. In addition to this the whole process effects a debasement in a society in that it forces all of us to become preoccupied with the continually changing real value of our income and its relative status.

As the pace of inflation quickens and the problems are unveiled, the witch hunt begins. Property speculators, Arabs, bankers, estate agents, business tycoons, asset-strippers, trade unionists – all are paraded as the guilty men. Effect becomes totally mistaken for cause: higher rents, higher wages, higher interest rates, higher oil prices and 'gazumping' are seen to be the cause of inflation rather than its inevitable result. So the prescription often concerns itself with symptoms rather than the roots of the problem: rent controls, tougher laws for trade unions, interest-rate ceilings, limits to oil price increases, and tighter controls over banks, building societies, oil companies and multi-national corporations. The most alarming example of double standards in the United Kingdom over the last few years has been the discretionary treatment of property investment. Large property owners have been singled out and charged with speculative development, profiteering and refusing to rent certain properties. The venom which has been poured out on this group seems almost without parallel. Yet throughout the same period exactly the same process has been evident throughout the whole of society. Anyone who bought a house, an equity share, a piece of art or a coin in the hope that this would turn out to be a hedge against inflation is just as much a speculator as a property company. At the same time the major beneficiary of inflation, the government, passes almost unnoticed and certainly uncensored.

The legitimacy of the system is even further undermined by the costs involved in bringing inflation to a halt. A reduction in the rate of growth of the money supply, which we shall argue later is a necessary condition to reduce the rate of inflation, inevitably involves a rise in the level of unemployment. The fact that such a rise is temporary and not permanent is beside the point. To those who assume that the world can only be understood in Marxist terms, it is further evidence of the need for a reserve army of unemployed labour in a capitalist system. The particular paradox of this cost is that the longer the government delays before taking the appropriate steps to get inflation under control, so as to avoid increasing the level of unemployment, the greater the build-up of inflation, the deeper inflationary psychology becomes embedded in society, and the level of unemployment which is then necessary to reduce the inflation is that much greater. Yet because it is the system rather than simply the government which becomes the object of attack, inflation undermines the legitimacy of the existing economic order by rendering it inefficient, inequitable and incapable of moral justification.

Democracy and stability

The fact that Germany experienced a hyperinflation during the 1920s and that the Nazis came to power in the early 1930s is sometimes put forward as conclusive evidence for the fact that inflation is destructive of democracy. By eliminating the wealth and the values of the middle class, as happened in Germany in 1923, inflation creates a vacuum which is readily filled by the sinister appeals of fascist, socialist or other extremist parties. Even in the dramatic case of Germany, however, the Nazis did not come to power directly as a consequence of the hyperinflation. Hitler's attempted Beer Hall *putsch* of November 1923 was a total failure. After the mark had been stabilized in 1924 the economy underwent a considerable recovery, which lasted for the remainder of the decade. Even when Hitler did eventually come to power, democratically, in 1933, it was by a direct appeal to those suffering from unemployment not inflation. The relationship between inflation and political stability needs therefore to be examined rather more closely.

Certain economic effects of inflation have readily identifiable political consequences. In the first place inflation tends to produce greater conflict within a society, largely the outcome of the capricious redistribution of income and wealth. Those who profit by the inflation become the object of envy and hatred; those who lose, resentful and bitter, carefully nursing their grievance and determined to restore what they consider to be their rightful position. In the field of wages this tends to produce stronger trade unions and professional bodies prepared to use more militant methods to protect themselves against a fall in their real wages. This is particularly true of professional bodies within the public sector. A decade ago it would have been unthinkable that nurses, teachers and doctors would have taken industrial action in order to increase their salaries. Yet as a result of the present British inflation all of them have resorted to such tactics. The basis of such action is not that for some mysterious reason they have become consumed with greed, but rather that the reduction in their real income is so acute because of the unexpected magnitude of inflation that they find themselves unable to maintain the standard of living they expected to have by entering certain professions and did in fact have prior to the inflation.

One predictable outcome of such a process is the demand for greater state intervention. It is often believed that if wages were regulated in a more orderly and fair manner and if property prices and the rules relating to occupancy were also controlled, the conflict would cease. In fact the very opposite seems to be true. Some of the bitterest confrontations between labour and management over wage increases have occurred within the framework of a prices and incomes policy. The most dramatic in recent years was the confrontation in late 1973 and early 1974 between the National Coal Board and the National Union of Mineworkers, over the relevance of the Conservative government's norms for wage rises, which resulted in the three-day week being introduced by the government in January 1974 and a general election called the following month. This particular dispute created an atmosphere of bitterness and disunity in society and was itself a challenge to the political system.

It could also be argued that the same process is at work on an international level. One of the most noticeable developments over the past few years has been the way in which producer cartels have been formed by various countries – the OPEC countries in oil; Morocco, the USA and the USSR in phosphate; the seven leading bauxite exporters, including Jamaica which accounts for 75 per cent of world exports since 1974; the four main copper producers since 1974; the union of banana exporting countries, and in January 1975 the eleven major iron ore exporting countries. At the same time the members of the International Tin Council have sought to strengthen their cartel position. Although not formal cartels, the four major tea producers have attempted to co-ordinate marketing and establish a floor for prices, while sugar producers agreed in 1975 to substantial increases in the price of sugar, and in manganese, tungsten, rubber and timber there is the possibility of producers' agreements to restrict competition. It is hardly coincidental that their formation follows a global acceleration of inflation. As a result of the rising commodity prices which accompanied, but were much greater than, the world inflation, primary producing countries found that their real income was increased. In order to protect themselves from falling primary product prices and from the reduction in the real purchasing power of their foreign exchange reserves as a result of the rise in the world price level, and therefore from a fall in their real income, they have behaved in a comparable manner to trade unions and professional associations in this country.

The political conflict produced by inflation is only increased when it comes to the problem of its control. Rather than see a factory or shipyard close down, potentially unemployed workers are prepared to break the law, occupy the premises and so halt the process, demanding in the meantime government subsidies. Once again these acts undermine the legitimacy of government and the rule of law, and expose the fragility of the social order in contemporary Western democracies.

In terms of domestic politics the generation of conflict also tends to polarize the political choice between Right and Left. From a Marxist viewpoint the conflict is the inevitable and predictable result of the private ownership of property and an essential aspect of the liberation of the working classes from centuries of domination. On the other hand, for those who are not members of strong trade unions or are members of professions less powerful than, for example, the doctors, the inequality and the conflict are the result of certain trade unions asserting their power. Hence the political spectrum becomes polarized between those who support industrial action and those who wish to see a stronger legal framework which protects their relatively weak bargaining position. The problem becomes serious when those who support the rule of law believe it to be ineffectual and find themselves unable to trust the government with the task of ensuring political stability and economic justice.

A factor which tends to reinforce both the conflict and the political polarization is the fate of the middle classes, who play such a critical role in the organization of modern society. They occupy the professions, the administration of government and industry and are the proprietors of innumerable small businesses. They tend to have a strong sense of duty and responsibility, which makes for stability and order in society. By temperament they tend to be conventional and ingenuous with a high degree of trust in the social order and the institutions of democracy, the family and the rule of law. As a class they tend to be vulnerable to inflation: they are inexpert and, possibly even worse, slightly disinterested in manipulating money; unlike members of trade unions they are not organized to protect their real income; worse still, if they are members of certain professions they have been brought up to adhere to a code of behaviour which emphasizes discussion and rationality and frowns on militancy and strikes.

Inflation does not affect the middle class evenly. Those who own property, especially farmers, shopkeepers and small businesses, do well because of the increase in its price. Those who own less property but have substantial debts, such as younger members of professions who are buying their own practices and houses, also gain because of the inflation. The people who tend to lose are those with less property, hardly any debt and who are members of professions such as medicine and teaching, whose salaries have not kept pace with the inflation, and those who have retired or are on the verge of retirement and have invested their savings in financial assets. As a result of the inflation all of these groups face a fall in their standard of living. The potential danger to society comes from the way in which they react. If inflation reduces their salaries below those of skilled and semi-skilled workers, then not unnaturally they are prepared to resort to greater militancy. If the inflation is more serious and income and wealth more rapidly redistributed, the ultimate danger is that they lose faith in the existing order and are prepared to use force to overturn it. Already as a result of this present inflation we have seen one organization formed to defend the interests of the middle classes and two retired army officers, Colonel Stirling and General Walker, argue that they would be prepared to use force to establish what they conceive of as economic justice. Symptoms such as these should not be dismissed too lightly; they reflect a genuine disaffection with the results produced by inflation.

But, apart from the threat of militancy, something which has far-reaching consequences is the gradual erosion and ultimately the destruction of the middle-class values of duty, public service and respect for law. The end result of such a process is that the traditional middle class and its values are destroyed and replaced by the *nouveaux riches*, the profiteers of the inflation. Inflation produces therefore a syndrome in society – greater conflict, the polarization of Left and Right and the erosion of middle-class values – which although it may not lead to the overthrow of democracy, nevertheless has very disquieting effects. It makes for a less robust and less stable society, more vulnerable to the appeals of unreason and ultimately of madness.

German hyperinflation and the rise of Hitler

The most dramatic and most discussed historical episode relating inflation to the overthrow of democracy is Weimar Germany. In attempting to interpret the history of Germany from the Treaty of Versailles to the Nazi acquisition of power the two extreme possibilities of the relationship between inflation and democracy – that inflation directly led to the overthrow of democracy or that inflation had no connection with it – must be avoided. One danger is to ignore the other factors at work during the inflation. Even during the period of inflation from 1918 to 1923 Hitler's appeal was primarily based on the attraction of nationalism rather than the evils of inflation and to the extent that he tried to capitalize politically on the economic consequence of the inflation, he singularly failed. Over this same period there were two other forces at work which tended to destroy people's faith in the democratic process and enhance the appeal of fascism – nationalism and the threat of socialism. The fact that Germany lost the First World War was an enormous blow to national pride. The humiliation was deepened by the terms of the

Treaty of Versailles, in particular the heavy burden of reparation repayments, and the fact that the French felt they had to demonstrate their superiority to their European neighbour, which ultimately led to the French and Belgian armies invading the Ruhr in January 1923, ostensibly on the grounds that Germany had defaulted on the payment of reparations. The other major threat to the Weimar Republic was that in the unsettled years following the end of the war, Germany might succumb to the same fate that had struck Russia – communism – and that it might be brought about through the democratic process. The evidence of this period therefore tends to suggest that the roots of fascism are to be found as much in the national humiliation of Germany in the eyes of the world and the threat of a socialist take-over or possible revolution as they are in the inflation.

But the observations that there were other factors at work and that Hitler's actual assumption of power was a decade after the end of the inflation should not lead us to the other extreme – to say that the inflation had no connection with the rise of Nazism which could not be adequately explained by these other factors. The evidence on the redistribution of wealth, the poverty of certain income classes, the fall in real output in 1923 and the uncertainty which the inflation created, is not open to dispute. Equally, almost all writers or critics who lived through the inflation and have written on it have described it as an unmitigated disaster and what they have tended to emphasize most of all is the destruction of traditional values, such as the belief in law, hard work, honesty and duty. The inflation also produced greater conflict and polarization within the political sphere. Some of the bitterest debates of the early twenties in the Reichstag were over taxation and the national finances. The inflation enriched a number of large industrialists, financiers and landowners – Stinnes, Thyssen, Klöckner, Stumm, Wolff, Krupp, Siemen, Marinesman and Herzfeld – who poured money into various right-wing parties opposed to the liberal-republican regime and who were openly contemptuous of democracy, while those who supported the existing democratic order, for example the trade unions, found themselves impoverished by the inflation. By polarizing the political debate between fascism and socialism, they helped to pre-empt the development of a political consensus on appropriate policies. When in the early 1930s another major form of instability – Nazism – threatened

Germany, it did so very much against the background of the previous decade.

Any analysis of the relationship between democracy and inflation over this period must begin therefore by recognizing inflation as only one among several factors which threatened the existing order. But this still begs the question of the role inflation played in the process. The immediate consequence of inflation was economic; it resulted in poverty and the wholesale reshuffling of wealth; the rewards of hard work became as predictable as those of a casino; and it created an atmosphere in which speculation thrived. The capriciousness of the process and the uncertainty of economic life tended to crystallize the political options fairly clearly. Most people simply wanted a return to normality and stability. The 'golden years' of 1924–7, when there was a dramatic recovery gave the impression of a false stability. Then, when the nation faced the prospect of economic instability once again – this time in the form of mass unemployment – and the prospect that this would produce a revolution, there were only two political options, the extremes of fascism and socialism, because the centre, while it was still in existence in a formal sense, had nevertheless lost all credibility because of the inflation. One can therefore see a clear thread woven in the history of Germany from 1923 to 1933, linking the catastrophic effects of inflation to the Nazis' attainment of power.

Doubtless there are some who will wish to argue that this piece of history has very little relevance for contemporary Britain. It is certainly true that those who have benefited from our inflation have been property interests and members of militant trade unions and that we are under no burden of reparations repayments. But to argue the thesis that inflation affects the political system is not to profess 'historical fatalism': it is simply to do justice to the facts. And while one cannot from this unique history draw any inexorable law one can nevertheless see certain tendencies which are at work in all inflations and which point in the same direction, namely political instability and the erosion of democracy.

Part IV

Correction

12 The debate on indexing

'In proposing this remedy I want Government to help business, though not to do business.'

Alfred Marshall (1885)

The apparent failure of the market mechanism to fully reflect inflation, as evidenced by the fact that interest rates, pensions, rents and, at times, wages and salaries have not kept pace with inflation has led to demands for government intervention; not only for the government to control inflation but also to correct the distortions produced by inflation. Such corrective measures are variously referred to as indexation, index-linking, cost-of-living adjustments or the use of escalator clauses.[1] In all cases the object is to ensure that all contracts and commitments which are made in money terms where payment is deferred until a later date are corrected to take account of changes in the purchasing power of money. The argument is that although substantial adjustments are already being made by both the private and public sector of the economy to take account of inflation, such adjustments are nevertheless incomplete. In such a situation the government could encourage the more widespread use of the principle of indexing and in certain important respects could take the lead itself and thus to a large extent deal with the uncertainty and anxiety created by inflation.

A simple example of indexation is a bank loan. Suppose I borrow £100 from the bank at the beginning of the year and agree to repay at the end of the year £100 plus 5 per cent interest. Over the year prices rise by 20 per cent (i.e. the value of money falls by 20 per cent), therefore I am repaying my loan with pounds which are 20 per cent less valuable than those which I borrowed. The £100 which I have to repay is only worth £80 in terms of what it will purchase at the end of the year. At the beginning of the year, I borrowed purchasing power worth £100 but at the end of the year I have given up purchasing power worth £85. Although I 'paid' for the loan at 5 per cent, the change in the value of money was sufficiently large to yield me a 5 per cent return on the transaction. If, on the other hand, the contract had been drawn up to reflect the exact change in the value of money I would have been required to repay purchasing power worth £100 at the end of the year plus a 5 per cent rate of interest. Simply to reflect inflation I would have had to repay £120. If the interest rate were 5 per cent, then with indexation I would repay £125 at the end of the year.

The principle that agreements fixed in money terms should be adjusted for changes in the value of money need not be restricted to the borrowing and lending of money. It is just as relevant to the labour market, so that wages and salaries can be adjusted to take account of changes in the cost of living, or to the property market, so that rents and leases can be corrected for changes in the value of money. It is also relevant to government transfer payments. If the government decides on expenditure programmes to help various sectors of the community at a certain point in time, why should they be eroded by inflation? Students' grants, state pensions, unemployment benefits, child allowances, family income supplements and all other kinds of transfer payments made by the government could be adjusted to take account of changes in the cost of living. The same is true of taxes. To the extent that inflation increases the government's tax revenue, because, for example, with a progressive income tax structure individuals are moved into higher tax brackets even though their real income remains unchanged, taxes could be reduced. On the other hand, fines, payments for licences and any other charges the government makes, could be increased in line with inflation. Another area in which the principle applies is accounting. As inflation changes the value of assets, so depreciation which is based on historic cost will produce a very misleading profits figure. Therefore all asset values could be regularly corrected to take account of this. In principle therefore we could imagine an economy in which all contracts or agreements to pay were related to changes in the value of money so that, regardless of the rate of inflation, inflation would not in itself lead to any income or wealth transfers.

The idea that contracts should be adjusted for changes in the purchasing power of money is far from being a recent innovation. As far back as the sixteenth century in England the payment of tithes was fixed to the average prices of barley, oats and wheat. Various Oxford and Cambridge colleges leased their land in terms of corn rents. As early as 1742 'equity bills' were issued in Massachusetts, followed in 1780 by 'Massachusetts depreciation notes'; in both cases the redemption price of the bills was related to an aggregate price statistic. In 1925 the Rand Kardex Company issued a thirty-year debenture in which both the interest and principal were linked to the wholesale price index.

Indexing has also had the support of many distinguished economists, including, among others, Jevons, Marshall, Fisher and Keynes. Jevons proposed the creation of a 'tabular standard of value', changes of which would be used to adjust the value of contracts fixed in money terms.[2] He suggested that to implement such a proposal a permanent government commission would have to be created and endowed with a kind of judiciary power. The commission would collect current commodity prices 'in all the principal markets of the kingdom' and then compute the average variations in the purchasing power of gold. The decisions of the commission would be published monthly and payments for wages, rents, annuities, etc. would be adjusted in accordance with them; at first the scheme would be entirely voluntary but then, after its undoubted value had been shown, it would be made compulsory for every debt extending over three months.

Alfred Marshall's proposals for establishing a unit of constant general purchasing power were set out in a paper at the Industrial Remuneration Conference in 1885 and was subsequently included in his answers to questions put by the Royal Commission on the Depression of Trade and Industry (1886) and in an article published in the *Contemporary Review* for March 1887, which was included in a memorandum submitted by him to the Royal Commission on the Values of Gold and Silver (1887, 1888).[3] Unlike Jevons' multiple legal standard, the essence of his plan was not to change the form of the currency but to adjust the value of all contracts fixed in money terms to changes in the average price level. He also put forward a proposal for changing the form of the currency so as to make it a true bimetallic standard, but he was very careful to separate the two schemes, and also to warn against the possible dangers of changing the base of the currency.

Recalling Marshall's proposals of the 1880s, J. M. Keynes, one of Marshall's great admirers, recommended to the Royal Commission on National Debt and Taxation (1927) that the government should issue an index-linked bond, claiming that the advantages of such a scheme were even greater than in the 1880s.

> I suggest that there is one further type of bond not yet in issue which might prove popular with particular individuals and so enable the State to raise funds a little more cheaply. I suggest that there should be issued bonds of which the capital and the interest would be paid not in a fixed amount of sterling, but in such amount of sterling as has a fixed commodity value as indicated by an index number. I think that an official index number should be established for such purposes on the lines of the optional tabular standard recommended long ago by Dr. Marshall, and that it should be open to anyone, including particularly the Treasury, to offer loans, the payment of the interest on which and the repayment of the capital of which would be governed by movements of the index number. I can say from knowledge that there are many investors, who, wishing to take no risks would naturally confine themselves to trustee stocks, yet feel a natural anxiety in being compelled to invest their whole resources in terms of legal tender money, the relation of which to real value has been shown by experience to be variable. Throughout almost the whole of Europe investors of the trustee type have been deprived in the past ten years of the greater part of the value of their property. Even here in England all such investors have suffered a very large real loss. We may hope that great instability in the value of the currency may not be one of the things which the future has in store for us. But it is natural that some people should be anxious about it. Unless, therefore, the Treasury hopes to make a profit through the depreciation of legal tender, it would lose nothing, and might gain

something in terms of interest, by issuing such bonds as I have indicated.[4]

The case for indexation

The case for indexation rests on four main arguments: that it would produce a more efficient allocation of resources; that it would produce equity among creditors, debtors, landlords, tenants, taxpayers, the government and so on; that it would lead to a reduction in the cost of controlling inflation and that its widespread use would reduce the fiscal benefits to the government of continuing with inflation.[5]

As we saw in an earlier chapter inflation leads to uncertainty about the future value of money and as a result produces inefficiency. Investors are uncertain about the true rates of return from holding financial assets and so they hedge against inflation by investing in property, coins, rare books, vintage port, commodities, gold and other precious metals – in fact anything whose price is likely to keep pace with inflation. Funds which otherwise might have been used indirectly to support productive investment or to lend to the government have been used to increase consumption. The allocation of savings is similarly diverted into those areas which are not necessarily the most productive from the point of view of society but in which the saver is assured of protecting the value of his savings. In the labour market the failure of wages and salaries in certain sectors to keep pace with inflation creates distortions, produces bad labour relations and leads to strikes. In addition the uncertainty over the future rise in the cost of living is a source of contention in wage negotiations and a possible cause of industrial unrest. One of the major areas in which this has happened in the United Kingdom has been in certain wages and salaries in the public sector, for example those of nurses, teachers, dustmen and miners. If the rate of inflation can rise by as much as ten per cent in a year then workers have a lot to lose from incorrectly anticipating that inflation. In the property market uncertainty over the course of inflation will mean that landlords are unwilling to commit themselves to long leases and in some instances would prefer not to lease at all. Centre Point is just such a case. If the building could have been leased with automatic adjustment of rents for inflation it would be immaterial from an economic point of view whether the building was sold or leased. But if because of inflation the appreciation in the capital value of the building is greater than the discounted value of increased rents, because they are not fully adjusted for inflation, the owner has an incentive to keep the property empty if he wishes to keep open the option of selling the building.

In this context the argument for indexing is that if financial and labour contracts were to be indexed to the rate of inflation, this would reduce the uncertainty over the future value of money so that savers, investors, employers and employees could then make their choices without this additional problem. If, for example, indexed bonds were available for savers, then, instead of buying property, durable consumer goods or foreign exchange, they could hold these bonds in the knowledge that they would not be losing money. Even though the total of saving may be only slightly affected, such a measure would have a considerable impact on the composition of savings in that less funds would be placed in those assets which had previously been hedges against inflation. In addition it would lead to an improvement in the allocation of funds between different investment projects, to the extent that under a system in which loans to companies are not indexed some companies may over-borrow while others may under-borrow, depending on their expectation of the course of inflation. As a result some low-yield projects may be undertaken at the expense of higher-yield projects. Indexation of loans would remove this problem.

Applied in the labour market the widespread use of escalator clauses would take a good deal of tension out of present bargaining and leave employers and employees free to bargain over the real wage, and how it was likely to change through productivity agreements and so on. In addition it would mean that contracts could be for longer terms. If for example the British government were to apply the principle in the public sector and the nationalized industries there can be no doubt that a good deal of the frustration which so many workers in this sector feel would be eliminated.

The second major argument for indexation is based on equity. As we saw in chapter 8 inflation redistributes wealth and income which cannot easily or convincingly be justified either in terms of efficiency or equity. But widespread use of indexing would prevent this taking place and therefore restore greater equity. If interest rates reflected inflation there would be no redistribution from creditor to debtor. If tax allowances and rates were indexed there would be no net redistribution to the government. And if indexation reduced the climate of uncertainty among business then there would be no reason for investing in hedges against inflation.

The third argument for introducing widespread indexation is that it reduces the cost, especially in the labour market, of controlling inflation. If we accept that control of inflation usually requires some tightening of monetary and fiscal policy, the social cost associated with such a policy is the extent to which the growth of real output is checked in the process, or, looked at from another point of view, the extent to which unemployment rises, albeit temporarily, above its normal level. The argument which is being put forward is that with the widespread use of indexing in the labour market the rise in unemployment associated with such a policy will be that much less.

The argument can be best appreciated if we start from a position in which inflation is proceeding at twenty per cent per year, and is expected to continue at that rate, and where the government wishes to reduce it to ten per cent per year and where it takes the appropriate monetary and fiscal actions to achieve this result. If the government is determined and therefore successful in its policy, this means that in the new situation wages will rise by ten per cent less per year. It would therefore be rational in the transitional phase for workers to demand smaller increases in wages. Nevertheless there is a considerable element of uncertainty attached to the whole process and they have no guarantee that the inflation rate will in fact be halved. As a result they continue to demand increases in wages which compensate for the current rate of inflation. One consequence of this will be a sharp rise in short-term unemployment as labour prices itself out of the market. On the other hand if wages were indexed to inflation, then the uncertainty over future price inflation which led trade unions to demand the same increase as previously would be removed, and so the transitional rise in unemployment would be that much less.

Interestingly enough, Marshall used a similar argument in claiming that the severity of depressions would be reduced through indexing. He wrote, however, against the background of the nineteenth-century trade cycle, in which periods of recession were characterized by falling prices. He claimed, in particular, that falling prices led to bankruptcies, which in turn produced a loss of confidence. By producing fewer bankruptcies indexing would reduce the severity of cyclical depressions.

A final argument in favour of indexing is that it would provide the government with a powerful incentive to set about reducing inflation. The government, as we have seen, is a major beneficiary of inflation. By printing more money, being able to pay a rate of interest on its debt which is below the rate of inflation and by increasing the burden of existing taxes, the government collects higher tax revenue as a result of rising prices. If government debt and the tax system were fully indexed this would remove a substantial source of existing revenue and so remove any incentive which the government at present has of continuing with the inflation.

Whenever indexing has been proposed there have always been those who have leaped to the defence of the *status quo*. Jevons' book *Money* drew a sharp attack from Bagehot who claimed that indexing would be wholly unfit for a country with foreign trade because of the increased uncertainty in exchanging currency for gold, that it would make banking impossible because a banker would never know the value of his debts and, in any case, that it was totally impractical because of the difficulties of calculating the index.[6] Similarly Keynes' proposals to the Royal Commission on taxation, that the British government should issue an index-linked bond, were firmly squashed by Sir Otto E. Nieymeyer, Controller of Finance at the Treasury. He did 'not see why it should attract anybody' and although some investors did take such a 'long and elaborate view' for ordinary people 'this would be too clever altogether'.[7] For Sir Otto such a proposal was connected with countries which had experienced great changes in the value of money, such as Germany, and this was not the expectation of the United Kingdom. In any case, when the Treasury had issued five- to fifteen-year bonds, the interest on which varied according to the Treasury Bill rate, which he claimed was similar to Keynes' proposal, they were not a success. He was of the opinion that before the state issued such a bond he would like to see it tried in practice by a private person, such as one of the more enterprising insurance companies.

One problem which indexing involves is the appropriate choice of the index. In the nineteenth century, this debate centred on whether it was possible to construct such an index at all. Today the choice is which among many price indices to use. From the point of view of protecting the interests of savers, workers and property owners, the best index is one that covers a wide range of commodities and services, is readily available, is least subject to government intervention and is most nearly an index of the 'true' price at which transactions take place. On these criteria the most appropriate choice would be either an index of retail prices or else the GNP deflator.

One of the main objections to the widespread use of indexing is that its adoption would provide a powerful stimulus to inflation. Interest rates, wages, rents and social security payments would rise as a result of its implementation and so add further fuel to the flames of inflation. And in addition exogenous shocks to the economy, such as higher import prices or higher indirect taxes, would have a much more inflationary impact in an indexed than in a non-indexed economy. Before accepting this seemingly plausible conclusion we need to distinguish between two quite different arguments.

Firstly there is the argument that under certain conditions the introduction of cost-of-living adjustments could directly raise the price level. If money wages are inflexible in a downward direction and if one objective of government policy is to ensure that unemployment does not rise above a certain level, the introduction of index-linked agreements would put upward pressure on prices. The result of higher costs and prices and an unchanged monetary and fiscal policy would be higher unemployment. If, to offset this, the money supply is expanded the final result will be higher prices and an unchanged level of unemployment. Secondly, and of more interest, it is sometimes suggested that the introduction of indexing throughout the economy would mean an upward revision of the expectation of future inflation by employees and trade unions which would in turn result in higher wage demands and prices, so producing a permanently higher rate of inflation. Both these effects are possible. In one case the introduction of indexing has a once-and-for-all effect in producing a higher price level; in the other it permanently raises the rate of inflation. If, however, the rate of inflation is to accelerate more than just the introduction of indexing is needed. This has to be accompanied by a belief that the government is to pursue a more inflationary policy than in the past and that in introducing indexing it is setting the stage for such a policy change. Imagine that indexing was introduced as part of a government stabilization programme in an attempt to control inflation. In such a situation as this there is no reason whatever for an upward revision of the expected rate of inflation. In fact exactly the opposite would occur – wage rates would rise less rapidly and interest rates would fall, thus bringing in a period of cheaper money.

Another frequently voiced objection follows on from this. This is that if all groups in the community are insulated from the effects of inflation, so that public protest at inflation loses its force, this will weaken the resolve of politicians to bring it under control. In other words, indexation will institutionalize the current rate of inflation and ease the drift to chronic or even hyperinflation. As the Page Committee *Report* remarked, if this were true the converse might also be supposed to be true, namely that where a government did not introduce indexation, inflation would be checked. Exactly the reverse has been the case in the United Kingdom during the past years. In any case, exactly the same argument could be used against paying cash benefits to the unemployed. Does this also weaken the resolve of the government to combat unemployment? Yet it can be said quite unambiguously that when unemployment has risen in the post-war years above levels that were considered intolerable, all governments have shown a great determination to expand demand and reduce unemployment. Furthermore, the introduction of indexation on a widespread scale has not in the past been a prelude to a more rapid inflation. The great hyperinflations of continental Europe earlier in the century were not linked with indexing but with the inability of their governments to raise taxes. In many countries suffering from inflation, such as Finland and France in the fifties or Chile for many decades, indexation was introduced as a consequence of the inflation in order to correct its distortions. And in certain other countries, such as Brazil in 1964, indexation was introduced as part of a stabilization programme.

Although the argument can therefore be discredited without too much difficulty, one nevertheless has the nagging feeling that it contains more than a grain of truth. After all, did not Finland give up indexation in 1968 and France in 1958 as a token that they were serious in implementing stabilization programmes? The existence of indexation might, though not necessarily must, easily become an excuse for reflationary and inflationary policies. In the context of present-day Britain the force of this argument would suggest that indexation would be more convincingly introduced as just one part of a comprehensive stabilization programme.

A third objection to indexing is that it may make the adjustment of relative prices and wages more difficult and possibly more inflationary. Assume for example that the real wage in an economy is too high to provide full employment. In a Keynesian framework in which we assume that money wages are rigid in a downward direction, this could easily be accomplished by an increase in the price level. But if wages were indexed to prices the real wage rate could not change. Similarly, if in an inflationary economy the demand for a particular skill were to fall, this would mean that the basic non-inflationary increase in wages would be that much less and, in an extreme case, negative. If the economy were an open economy, then increases in import prices would be quickly transmitted throughout the economy and it might be impossible to achieve the relative price changes which were necessary following a devaluation.

The evidence on indexing

Some indication of the extent to which indexing has been used by various countries can be seen in Table 9.[8] The four major areas in which indexing has been introduced are the labour market, in which wages are related to changes in the cost of living, the capital market, in which government bonds, bank deposits and mortgages are either revalued according to changes in the price level or are paid interest which is related to inflation, government transfer payments such as pensions, in which the state pension is increased to protect the real income of pensioners, and the tax system, in which various income-tax allowances are increased in line with a rise in the price level.

In some countries indexing has been introduced in only one of these areas; for example in New Zealand only state pensions are indexed, while in Austria only government bonds are indexed. In other countries, and especially in post-war Brazil, Finland and Israel, indexing has been introduced on a very widespread basis.

Indexing, or as it is usually referred to, 'monetary correction', was introduced on a widespread scale in Brazil in 1965 as part of the stabilization programme of the Costello Branco government. By the beginning of 1964 inflation had become rampant in Brazil. In 1963 the cost-of-living index rose by 81·9 per cent and in the first quarter of 1964 it was rising at an annual rate of 144 per cent. The aims of the new government were to combat inflation, raise the rate of economic growth and remove distortions within the economy; the whole approach was based on a 'gradualist' philosophy, by which the government did not plan on reducing the rate of inflation in a sudden and dramatic manner but by steps over a period of time. By 1973 – and several governments later – the rate of inflation had fallen to fifteen per cent. Between 1968 and 1973 real growth averaged more than seven per cent *per capita*. The case of Brazil is frequently cited as an example of a country which successfully implemented indexing.

The details of Brazilian indexing since 1966 are complex, being embodied in more than a hundred laws and decrees. The normal strategy however was fairly straightforward: all nominal values which were to be revalued, such as savings, mortgages, bonds, rentals and the exchange rate, were linked to changes in *past* rates of inflation; but wages were adjusted not only on the basis of past rates but also expected changes in prices and productivity. Because of the absence of a strong trade-union movement, the government revised the legal minimum wage in line with three indicators; the movement of the general price level over the previous two years, the expected rate of inflation in the coming year and the increase in productivity. When the government took office in April 1964 the government deficit was running at about between four and five per cent of GNP. In order to finance its deficit the government introduced Readjustable Treasury Bonds in 1964, in which the redemption price of the bonds was related to the rate of inflation. Other adjustments in the capital market are mentioned in the next chapter. Taxes were

Table 9. The Extent of indexing

	Wages	Social security benefits		Investments					Taxes
		Pensions	Other transfers	Government bonds	Private bonds	Mortgages	Other loans	Rents	
Argentina	1921–53			1972–					
Australia	—								
Austria		—							
Belgium	1948–	1955–	late 50s	1953	1959			—	
Brazil	1964–	1965–	1973–	1964–			1964–	1964–	1946–
Canada	1972–	1952							1974–
Chile	1960s								
Colombia						1972–			
Denmark	1945–	1923–	1923–	1945–67	1953–67				
Finland	1945–67	1957–	1956–67	1952–58	1952–58	—	1952–67	1952–67	
France	1948–58	1948–		1973–					
Iceland	1971–			1955					—
Irish Republic	1941–								
Israel	1945–	1956–	1950s–	1948–	1951–	1950s–			
Italy	1963–	1974–	—						
Netherlands									1972–
New Zealand	1920s–	1967–							
Norway			1967–						
Sweden	1915–22	1975–		1952–	1974				
United Kingdom	1973–74			1975–	1973–				
United States	1917–	1974–	—	1742	1925			—	

(Bar sign means from the date given to the present.)

Source: Summary of different countries' experience of indexing. NIESR *Review*, No. 70, November 1974, p. 47, Table 1.

also adjusted to help live with inflation. Taxes on industrial products, tariffs and taxes on consumer goods were all changed to the *ad valorem* principle and as early as 1961 income tax rates were adjusted according to a sliding scale based on the 'fiscal minimum salary'. Later all tax brackets have been revised every year if prices rise by more than ten per cent in one year or fifteen per cent over a period of three years. Corporate profits tax has also been adjusted to inflation on a similar basis and various measures were introduced to ensure that the accounting profits approached true profits. For example corporations were forced to revalue fixed assets every year on the basis of a formula put out by the government and depreciation was then estimated on the basis of the revaluations. Later the same principle was extended to corporations' working capital including foreign currency accounts. There is also a quarterly monetary correction on tax debts which remain unsettled on a particular date. Since 1968 the foreign exchange rate has been adjusted at irregular but frequent intervals.

Another country which has experimented with indexing on a large scale is Israel. Between 1948 and 1973 consumer prices rose in Israel by approximately six hundred per cent and the Israeli pound has been devalued no less than eight times. Indexing in Israel was developed in the private sector though it subsequently became a part of government policy. Most wages have been tied to a cost-of-living index since the Second World War with automatic and proportional adjustments if the price index rises beyond a given amount over a certain period. The adjustments although not statutory are usually made semi-annually and are the result of special agreements between labour and management and apply to both the public and private sectors. As a result of indexing in the labour market the government has found itself considerably more restricted in the use of devaluation or indirect taxes as a way of influencing total expenditure. Many instruments in the capital market are also adjusted for inflation. Most bond issues have been partially linked to inflation since 1954. Special savings deposits issued by commercial banks have been linked to inflation since 1957 and insurance companies have special schemes which are indexed as well. Bank deposits are not indexed.

Indexing was first introduced in Finland for reasons of equity. In

1945 the government decided to compensate those persons and firms who had lost property as a part of the territories ceded to the USSR. It did so by issuing indemnity bonds equivalent in value to the property loss. The bonds contained a clause which provided for 100 per cent compensation for rises in the wholesale price index. Such a clause was considered necessary in view of the steep rise in prices during the war and the immediate post-war inflation; between 1944 and 1948 the cost of living rose by an average of just over forty per cent and in 1945 it reached over sixty per cent. The inflation produced a serious disruption of the labour market. Because of the imposition of various controls, wage rises lagged behind price rises and by mid-1947, and largely as a protest, there were numerous local strikes. The government faced the choice of either a general strike or else comprehensive indexing in the labour markets. (Incidentally the cost-of-living index used for correction included as one of its components the black market price of butter, as it was estimated that the amount of butter traded at black market prices was forty per cent of national consumption.) Its introduction was followed by a dramatic improvement in labour relations. In 1957 indexing was extended to national pensions and in 1962 all employment pensions were linked to a wage index. Indexed bonds were first issued by the government in 1953 as part of the conversion of the indemnity law of 1945, and indexing spread throughout the whole of the financial sector.

Indexing in Finland was largely abolished in 1968. In March of that year the government introduced a Stabilization Agreement which was signed by trade unionists, industrialists and the government and in the following months the Economic Special Powers Act was passed. The Act specified that all applications of indexing in contracts, whether based on changes in the cost of living, wholesale prices or building costs, were to be stopped. Exceptions were government bonds, insurance contracts, pensions and certain letters of indebtedness which were issued prior to the Act. The reason for the Act was the view that the existence of widespread indexing would have undermined the 23·8 per cent devaluation in November 1967. The devaluation, so it was argued, would have led to higher import prices and export incomes and so given impetus to price inflation. As a result there would have been a substantially higher demand for wages and the effect of the devaluation would have quickly been undone.

Up to the present indexing has not been introduced in the United Kingdom on a widespread basis, mainly because the rate of inflation has not been sufficiently rapid to create serious distortions in the allocation of resources or spectacular redistribution of income. It was, however, introduced in the labour market during the First World War and by 1922 about three million workers were covered by the arrangements. By 1939 this figure had fallen dramatically and in the post-war years declined even further.

One conclusion which emerges from examining the evidence is that the more serious the inflation, the greater is the probability that indexing will take place, either through private or government initiative. In all hyperinflations indexing was introduced on a considerable scale largely at the initiative of the private sector. For example in Germany in 1923 the price of rye was widely used as a standard of value; in Hungary in 1946 the tax pengö, which was a newly created unit of account whose rate was published every day in terms of the regular pengö in order to correct the adverse effects of inflation on income tax revenue, was soon used in business transactions. In the Chinese inflation of 1949 banks were paying interest rates which allowed for the depreciation of the currency. A similar pattern has emerged in the chronic inflations of Latin American countries in the post-war years. During this period Brazil, Chile and Argentina, all countries with high rates of inflation, introduced indexing on a considerable scale. In the early 1970s a number of developed countries have introduced indexing as a response to the higher rates of inflation. For example, in the last few years, Canada, the Irish Republic and the United Kingdom have all attempted some form of indexing in the labour market and in the United States it has been revived so that by 1973 four million workers were covered; from 1974 social security pensions were indexed in the United States and United Kingdom; in 1973 the French government issued index-linked securities and in 1975 some part of National Savings in the United Kingdom should be indexed. Indexing, however, has almost invariably been partial; it has never been extended to all markets and even in those areas in which it has been introduced it has rarely been a complete correction for changes in the price level, even in those countries which have introduced it on a widespread scale such as Brazil and Israel. For example, in Brazil income-tax exemptions and tax brackets would only be revalued if the index rose by more than ten per cent in one year or fifteen per cent over three; the interest paid on government debt is not revalued with inflation; the correction which may be made to all financial assets is made according to an officially approved coefficient whose value is usually less than 0·7; bank deposits for a term less than six months cannot be indexed; and the increase in rent is restricted to two-thirds of the increase in the minimum salary in force. Similarly in those countries which in the 1950s encouraged the use of escalator agreements in the labour market, the increase in the wages was rarely equal to the rise in the cost of living: for example in Australia it was two-thirds, in Chile eighty per cent, in Denmark two-thirds, in Norway seventy-five per cent and in Sweden between fifty and seventy-five per cent. To the extent that wage and interest payments in the public sector as well as government transfer payments and taxes are linked to the rate of inflation, governments have a great incentive to bias the price index which is used as the basis for correction. For example in the United Kingdom in 1974 indirect taxes were cut and subsidies introduced on certain items which featured prominently in the retail price index, thereby artificially underestimating the rate of inflation. An even more blatant example is Brazil. The wholesale price index is the main basis for correction of wages, even though the products on which it is based are not typical of the family expenditure pattern, for example services are totally excluded, and the importance of coffee in the index, which is also subsidised by the government, is out of all proportion to its importance in family budgets. By contrast, house prices and public utility prices are given a very low weighting.

Indexing has been introduced by governments for a variety of reasons. In the case of pensions the main reason has been to protect the real income of a group in the population with very little economic power. In the case of government bonds, it has been to finance the government deficit in a non-inflationary way. For example, after the end of the Second World War, the French government inaugurated a programme of recovery which included nationalization, large-scale deficit financing and rapid growth of the money supply. The result was a rapid inflation and a marked reduction in the flow of savings to the bond market. The Pinay Gold Loan was made in 1952 to attract the resources of private sector savings and was accompanied by severe fiscal measures.

The main reason for introducing escalator clauses in wage agreements has been the desire for equity, the need to reduce tension in the labour market and the belief that control of inflation could be made that much easier as a result of such a policy. The OECD, commenting on indexing in the labour market, stated that 'If indexation clauses are introduced simultaneously with other elements of an effective package of stabilizing measures, the indexation provision may be the means of persuading labour to accept a reduction of wage increases down to non-inflationary levels'. On the other hand indexing was abolished as part of the Finnish stabilization programme of 1968–9 in the belief that such action was a precondition for the programme to be effective. In the case of Brazil indexing was introduced for different reasons in different sectors of the economy: most non-wage adjustments especially in the capital market and foreign exchange market were intended to remove price and interest-rate distortions and so increase resource efficiency; government bonds were indexed to help finance the government deficit; and wages were indexed to reduce the rate of inflation itself and to mitigate the cost of implementing such a policy.

One of the interesting questions connected with indexing is why indexing has been discarded either totally or partially in some countries such as France in 1958 (though it should be noted that it has been brought back in a piecemeal manner in the last few years) and Finland in 1968, but retained in other countries such as Brazil and Israel. The decision to maintain or abandon indexing seems to have little to do with whether the country succeeds in controlling inflation. Brazil has been successful in combating inflation while Israel has not. In both France and Finland inflation has increased since indexing was abandoned. One possible explanation may be the prevailing consensus regarding inflationary expectations at the time the stabilization programme was introduced. In both France and Finland the abolition of indexing was used by the respective governments as a token of their determination to introduce a series of deflationary measures and so induce people to revise their expectations of the future course of inflation and therefore lead to a reduction in interest rates and wage demands. Another explanation may have to do with the capacity of the government to withstand the political pressures attendant on exchange-rate changes. In Finland in 1968 the government clearly felt that if the labour market was indexed the devaluation necessary to correct the balance-of-payments deficit would have been greater than the seventeen per cent which occurred, and would in turn have led to considerable political opposition from exporters and manufacturing workers. A third reason may have to do with the absolute rate of inflation. If the social cost of inflation is greater, the greater the rate of inflation, it is much easier and less inequitable to dispense with indexing if the rate is fairly small, as in France and Finland, than if it is great, as in Brazil and Israel.

A policy for indexing

Indexing is currently being used in the United Kingdom but in a rather piecemeal manner. In 1973, and as part of the policy for controlling inflation, threshold wage agreements were introduced in certain sectors of the economy, whereby wages automatically rose by forty pence for every one per cent rise in the retail price index above six per cent. These agreements were terminated, however, in 1974. The only social security payment which is statutorily indexed is state pensions. As from April 1974 the basic state flat-rate pension will be increased in line with average earnings or the increases in the retail price index, whichever is more advantageous to the pensioner. No taxes are at present indexed for inflation.

Various proposals for the introduction and extension of indexing in the United Kingdom might be considered. The government could pass a law which made it mandatory to index all contracts involving deferred payments both in the private and public sectors. Or such a law might apply only to those contracts in which payment was deferred for a period of time greater than, say, three months. Or it might only apply to contracts in certain kinds of markets and not others, such as the capital but not the labour market. Another suggestion might be that all contracts involving the public sector should employ escalator clauses and in the rest of the economy their introduction should be voluntary, but that all legal barriers which may inhibit their use in the private sector should be removed.

Another problem which arises is the extent to which contracts should be indexed, in particular whether it should be the same percentage as the rise or fall in the price level or some fraction of that figure. The major argument against legislating for the use of escalator clauses for all contracts throughout the economy is that it would be an unnecessary burden on certain parties who preferred to agree on some particular but non-indexed arrangement. The following proposals are particularly relevant to the British economy.

Social Security payments
– All social security payments including, *inter alia*, retirement pensions, guardians' allowances, unemployment compensation and all benefits (such as widows, sickness, maternity, injury, disablement etc.) as well as supplementary pensions, supplement allowances, family allowances and family income supplements, should be increased annually by a factor which fully reflects the rate of inflation. If prices rise by ten per cent in a particular year these payments should be automatically revalued by ten per cent.

Taxes
– All income tax reliefs, such as the personal allowance, income allowance, for wives, children, widows, dependent relatives, blind persons, the elderly and those for life insurance premiums, should be increased annually, by the rate of inflation.
– The various tax brackets of Schedule E income tax should be increased in line with inflation. For example, if prices rose by ten per cent, the present bracket £1,000–£2,500 would be automatically adjusted to £1,100–£2,750.
– All tax arrears should be revalued by the difference between the price level when the tax is finally paid and that when it was first liable.
– The valuation of capital assets on which capital gains tax is levied should be revalued by the percentage rise in prices.
– Corporations should be able to depreciate fixed capital assets and inventories so as to fully reflect the rate of inflation.
– All exemptions from corporation tax which are stated in terms of pounds per year should be revalued to reflect inflation.
– The value of property liable to estate duty should be deflated by the rate of inflation.

Wages and salaries
– All contracts for wages and salaries paid by the central government local authorities, the nationalized industries, the National Health Service and other public bodies should use escalator clauses which would require the employer to raise wages and salaries by the same percentage increase as the price level. Students' grants would also increase in line with the price level.

Rents, rates and fines
– All rents charged by local authorities should be increased annually by the same percentage as the change in the price level.
– The minimum rateable value of all properties subject to local authority rates should be adjusted by a factor which reflects the rate of inflation.
– All fines which are fixed in statutes should be revised in line with inflation.

13 Indexing and savings

'The removal of uncertainty from time contracts would contribute most effectively to the extention of our national industry.'

Joseph Lowe, The Present State of England in Regard to Agriculture, Trade and Finance, with a Comparison of the Prospects of England and France (*1822*)

Savings play an integral part in a modern democratic society; not so much in the sense that the greater the saving, the less the resort the government need have to raise taxes to manage the economy or the more rapid rate of economic growth, but in the sense that it offers individuals greater freedom in arranging their own affairs so that they can be less dependent on government.

Most people feel the need to save for some period of their lives, whether for house purchase or to buy some other expensive asset, to provide for their retirement or to keep something for 'a rainy day'. A basic tenet of our society has been that such saving is desirable and that the more widespread a sense of financial responsibility, the greater the benefit to society.

By destroying the value of savings, inflation undermines the value of saving. Over the post-war years the value of savings has been dramatically reduced by inflation. In March 1972 National Savings totalled £9,546 million; yet (calculated in terms of the purchasing power of money in March 1951) this was worth only £4,269 million. In that same year National Savings Certificates bought in any year from 1951 onward (with the exception of 1957, 1958 and 1959) would have yielded a real annual compound rate of return which was *negative*. In other words, the government far from paying a positive yield for borrowing funds through National Savings Bonds was in fact imposing a tax on those who invested in this government-sponsored form of savings.

Another problem which arises when savings are not indexed is that of mortgage repayments to building societies. For building societies to lend mortgages at, let us say, a real rate of interest of 2–3 per cent at a time when inflation is increasing means that the nominal interest they charge would be 2–3 per cent plus the rate of inflation. If inflation is running at, say, 25 per cent a year, this means that the rate charged in mortgages would be between 27 and 28 per cent. In the early years of repayment, however, because the interest charge is proportionally much greater than capital repayment, monthly repayments would be proportionately greater than the rate of inflation. If mortgage rates were therefore to be market-determined this would provide young people with a substantial disincentive to house purchase. In the United Kingdom over the past two years the effects of this have been that the government has imposed a ceiling on certain short-term interest rates – such as on time deposits at banks for amounts of less than £10,000, which have been kept at $9\frac{1}{2}$ per cent, and National Savings – which if they had been higher would have attracted funds from building societies. The effect, therefore, of inflation in the mortgage market has been that borrowers have been paying interest rates less than inflation and have been subsidised by depositors.

The extent of indexing in capital markets

Numerous governments have applied the principle of indexing in the capital market.[1] One particular area which has received special attention is that of fixed-interest debt. An indexed bond is defined as a security whose redemption value or interest payment or both are related to some index of prices. A fully or integrally indexed bond is one in which the extra monetary payments increase by the same percentage as the interest in the index. For example, if over a particular year the wholesale price index increased by forty per cent and the redemption value of a bond was increased by the same amount, this would be a case of full indexing. This relationship is sometimes termed the 'coefficient of indexation' and in this example is equal to unity. Various devices have been introduced, however, to reduce it below unity. In some cases only the capital repayment has been indexed, while interest has been fixed, such as in the Transit

Indemnity Loan or the Pinay Loans in France. In other cases there has been a partial linkage, in which less than a hundred per cent of the principle is adjusted, such as in various private bond issues in France; in mixed linkage different parts of the loan are related to different indexes; in 'threshold linkages' indexing only comes into effect after the price index has risen by a certain percentage; and in yet other cases the borrower agrees to index either principal or interest, but only up to a certain amount.

France

Between 1952 and 1958 there were various attempts to index bonds both by the government and the public utilities. In 1952 the French government issued gold-linked securities, the Pinay Loan, which were a great success. The bonds bore interest at $3\frac{1}{2}$ per cent free of tax and their redemption value was related to the average price on the free market in Paris of the twenty-franc gold coin. The bonds could and can be used for the payment of certain taxes including death duties. This issue was followed by a number of public utility issues, beginning with that by the Electricité de France in 1952 which related the redemption value of the bond to the selling price of the public utility's output. Details of some of these issues are shown in Table 10. Such issues by the public sector also led to similar offerings by the private sector. In 1953 Pechinly offered a bond issue with a variable interest rate related to the change in earnings and dividends. In 1952 Monod made an issue in which interest payments were a non-linear function of wages, steel and cement prices, in 1955 Michelin made an issue which related interest payment to the increase in company sales and the price of rubber and in 1954 Sidelar had related interest to the increase in dividends. Between 1952 and 1957 it is estimated that indexed bonds made up 30–55 per cent of the total new issues. The Page Committee made an interesting calculation of the behaviour of prices of indexed and non-indexed bonds in the sixties. As can be seen from Table 11, the price of non-indexed bonds fell by 5 per cent between 1961 and 1969 while that of indexed bonds rose by 23 per cent. Indexation was abandoned with the devaluation of the franc in 1958 and the introduction of a stabilization programme.

Indexing was revived in the French capital market in 1973, when

Table 10. **Indexed Linked Issues in France, 1952–8**

Borrower		Index link*	Amounts raised by Government loans Frs billions
1952	Electricité de France	The price to the consumer of Kwh. 100 of electricity.	
1953	Société Nationale de Chemins de Fer	The cost of 2nd Class rail travel (free railway tickets could be taken in lieu of interest).	
1953	Gaz de France	The average price of 25 cubic metres of gas.	
1955	Régie Renault	The increase in companies' sales.	
1956	French Government	The interest payable at 5% p.a. plus 0.05% for every point by which the industrial production level exceeds the 1955 level. Redemption fixed at 105.	81 in 4 weeks
1956	French Government	Fixed interest of 5% tax free but redemption linked to the annual movement in the arithmetical mean of the price indices of fixed and variable interest French securities in relation to 1955.	320 in 3 weeks
1957	French Government	The annual movement in the arithmetical mean of the equity index in relation to 1956.	84
1957	Electricité de France	Fixed interest of 6% but redemption includes a premium related to the growth in electricity production.	
1958	Charbonnages de France	The price of coal.	
1958	Gaz de France	Interest paid at 6% or one-third of the number of milliards of therms of gas sold by Gaz de France the previous year, expressed as a percentage. Redemption price increased by the same proportion as the rise of a therm of gas over Frs 6.	

* Unless stated the link applies to both the interest and the redemption price which is normally capitalized at 20 years' interest.

Source: Committee to Review National Savings, *Report*, June 1973, Cmnd. 5273, Appendix II.

the government issued two new securities, one of which was linked to the price of gold and the other to the EEC unit of account.

Finland

Between 1945 and 1947 Finland introduced a variety of measures to index the rates of return on various financial assets to the rate of inflation. In 1945 the government issued a bond which provided for capital payments being linked to the movement of the wholesale

Table 11. **Prices and Yields of Indexed Bonds in France**

End of year	Price index of bonds issued by public bodies		Yield of private bonds		Share price index
	Indexed	Non-indexed	Indexed	Non-indexed	
1961	100.0	100.0	5.84	6.45	659
1962	107.1	101.7	5.50	6.23	719
1963	112.1	101.4	5.71	6.38	605
1964	112.1	101.7	5.85	6.32	562
1965	110.3	101.3	6.86	7.22	514
1966	107.0	99.8	7.29	7.71	474
1967	111.4	100.3	7.25	7.52	469
1968	121.9	98.5	7.50	7.76	488
1969	122.6	94.2	8.19	8.65	635

Source: *Indexation of Fixed-Interest Securities* (OECD, Paris, 1973).

price index. Then in 1953 the government made the first of a series of bond issues all of which were indexed for inflation, some with a fifty per cent clause and others with a hundred per cent clause. Indexed bonds issued in the private sector were considerably less important; at the end of 1967 they only amounted to just over thirty per cent of total outstanding corporate bonds.

Indexing spread from bonds to national pensions and life insurance policies. In 1946 the National Pension Institution indexed its loans to the wholesale price index, with a factor of fifty per cent. In 1947–8 private insurance companies offered indexed loans. Since 1957 the basic state pensions have been linked one hundred per cent to the cost of living and since 1962 the state has made it mandatory for all private pension schemes to be linked to the general wage, which is calculated by the Minister of Social Affairs. Then in 1955 it was applied in banking. The bank deposit to be indexed had to be for a minimum of twelve months and a minimum amount of $130. The rates paid on indexed deposits were one per cent less than those on other comparable deposits but they carried a five per cent compensation for the increase in the cost of living. From 1963 the compensation was raised to a hundred per cent and most time deposits were indexed.

With the abolition of indexing in 1968, the issue of new indexed bonds and debentures and the 'linking' of bank deposits to the changes in the price level were prohibited because of the prospect that a devaluation would accelerate the domestic rate of inflation. This piece of legislation did not apply however to government bonds.

Israel

Since the early fifties indexation of bonds, both private and public, has been usual. For example, in the latter half of the sixties indexed bonds accounted for between 80 and 97 per cent of total bond issues. By 1970 all bonds quoted on the Tel Aviv stock exchange were index-linked; 4 per cent were linked to the US dollar/Israeli pound exchange rate; 46 per cent were linked to the cost-of-living index; and the remainder gave the holder the option of a lower interest rate with an index-linked principle or a higher rate without any indexing. The use of escalator clauses have also been extended to many kinds of savings deposits, loans and life insurance policies. Although bank deposits are not specifically indexed because they have to compete with indexed bonds they offer a suitably high interest rate. Since the devaluation of 1962, the explicit use of indexation in long-term government bonds has been abandoned, although the government give annual 'inflation provisions'.

Brazil

To implement the idea of monetary correction, which was interpreted as an across-the-board revaluation of assets and liabilities in line with inflation, the government introduced a series of measures. It issued Readjustable Treasury Bonds with maturities of between 3 and 20 years paying an annual interest of 6 per cent, but with the nominal value of the bonds being adjusted quarterly to the purchasing power of the cruzeiro, to finance the government deficit. The adjustment was exempt from tax. By the mid-sixties holders of these

bonds were granted the option of their being indexed either by
domestic prices or the exchange rate for the US dollar. The government also made these bonds more attractive to investors by allowing
them to deduct from their income tax 30 per cent of the total amount
of bonds bought, provided they were taken up within thirty days
of issue. Towards the end of the sixties the government found that
it had to make substantial new issues of these bills simply to honour
commitments arising out of a rate of 30 per cent a year. In addition
to this a law was passed which made it compulsory for companies
to revalue their fixed assets in line with inflation and so make higher
depreciation changes; and which made it optional for the accounts
of paid-up capital, accumulated reserves, profits and losses and
accounts denominated in foreign currency. Measures were also
introduced to remove distortions in the capital market. In 1965 joint-
stock companies were permitted to issue indexed bonds providing
that the maturity period was for a minimum of one year and that
corrections were made at intervals of not less than three months.
Similarly companies are allowed to issue bills of exchange or
promissory notes in which the principal is indexed. At the same time
commercial and investment banks were allowed to index deposits
issued for a minimum of eighteen months: later this time period was
reduced to 180 days. For the commercial banks the holding of such
deposits was restricted to individuals and insurance companies. In
addition such deposits were not to exceed 10 per cent of a bank's
total current accounts and term deposits and a ceiling was also placed
on the interest rates payable.

Other countries

A number of other countries have experimented with the indexation
of certain capital market instruments. In 1952 the Swedish Co-
operative Society issued a 3 per cent loan in which capital repayments
were linked to the cost-of-living index. The revaluation of the capital
was restricted to 50 per cent of its initial value. Denmark introduced
an index-linked savings scheme in 1957 which has been quite
successful. In 1972 the Argentinian government floated a bond issue
in which both the capital and interest payments were linked to the
wholesale price index for non-agricultural goods. The Landsbankin
Islands of Iceland issued an indexed loan in 1955 whereby the loan

was tied to the retail price index and in 1953 the Austrian Electricity
Authority floated a bond in which repayment was linked to the price
of the kilowatt hour. In 1972 the Columbian building societies
introduced a savings deposit which is intended to maintain its value
in terms of purchasing power.

Indexing was also introduced in the banking system by the
Peoples Bank in Mainland China during the rapid inflation of the
later 1940s. Under the Parity Deposit System the value of bank
deposits was calculated in terms of commodity units, where the unit
typically consisted of a set amount of medium-grade rice, peanut oil,
cotton fabric and coal briquettes. At the height of the inflation the
coefficient of indexation was unity. At the same time bank loans
were also related to the commodity unit, so that banks could index
both their assets and liabilities to the rate of inflation.

Problems of indexing savings[2]

As with indexing generally, one particular problem is the appropriate
choice of index. For example, in choosing an index by which to link
the price of bonds one could take the individual selling price of the
enterprise concerned (if it is issuing debt), gold, dollars, the cost-of-
living index, the wholesale price index or the GNP deflator. Many
of the French public utilities which issued indexed bonds in the 1950s
linked them to the selling price of their commodities or services.
While this reduces the risk to the borrower, it does not guarantee
the capital value of the lender's funds if the output price of the
enterprise rises at a different rate from that of the general price level.
In any case because the output prices of different public utilities will
reflect different rates of technological advance, this is not an ideal
index. In addition to this it offers a great incentive to the enterprise
concerned and to the government to keep its prices from rising. If
in Britain the nationalized industries were to issue debt on this basis,
far from simplifying the problems of the lender, they would be compounded. Another possibility which is sometimes discussed is the
price of gold or of a stable foreign currency (if such a phenomenon
exists at present!). The problem with gold is that the official price
since 1945 has been subject to controls while the free market price
has reflected speculative activity, the economic conditions of the gold

mines and the political problems of South Africa. It would hardly be a reliable index. For countries with severe inflation the use of a foreign currency may be better, but once again this price is subject to official intervention.

Apart from the general objections to indexing which were discussed in the last chapter, proposals for indexing various forms of debt instruments have usually met with specific objections. One objection, which was made by the Treasury in both its evidence to the Radcliffe Report on the working of the monetary system (1959) and the Page Report on the future of National Savings (1972), was that if the government introduced an indexed bond or savings instrument, such a security might attract funds from other sources, which could damage certain categories of debt finance and so adversely affect the financing of certain investment projects. If the rate of inflation is sufficiently high, if market interest rates reflect inflationary expectations only very imperfectly, if savers have a very strong preference for a form of savings which is a hedge against inflation or if the private sector does not react at all to the introduction by the government of an index-linked bond, this argument may be true. But these are a remarkably curious set of assumptions to make. If we made similar assumptions in a non-inflationary world, we would get equally catastrophic implications. Fortunately the world does not behave like that. The most likely result would be that if indexing was introduced it would induce private corporations and those deposit-taking institutions which are losing funds to introduce some element of indexing either explicitly or implicitly by offering a higher rate of interest, which would immediately check any possible drain from one market to another.

In the second place there is considerable uncertainty about the impact indexing has on the effectiveness of monetary policy. One way monetary policy affects total spending is by changing the value of wealth. A rise or fall in nominal interest rates will produce an opposite movement in the value of net wealth. Hence a restrictive monetary policy in which interest rates rise in the very short term will lead to a fall in the market value of fixed-interest debt and so a reduction in current spending. If the debt were indexed it is argued that the change in rates, and therefore wealth, would be much less. Against this is the view that monetary policy may be more effective in a market in which indexed and non-indexed debt are traded. For one thing the government could operate on both the real and the nominal rates of interest. By buying and selling indexed bonds they could affect the real cost of borrowing and so directly affect investment expenditures, whereas in a market without indexed bonds they could only affect nominal rates. In addition to this it is claimed that a government can influence inflationary expectations by changing the differential between the rates on indexed and non-indexed bonds. Under such a system the differential between the rates is the increase of inflationary expectations. If the central bank is prepared to deal in both types of securities, then by selling indexed debt and buying non-indexed bonds it can reduce the spread and so change the course in inflation. If only the world were so straightforward! The real problem with the various arguments which have been put forward to show that indexing increases the effectiveness of monetary policy is the assumption common to them all that governments are able to control interest rates. While this is true in the short run, it can only be true in the longer run if it cares nothing for the inflationary consequences of its actions.

Another objection to indexing is that it blurs the 'transparency' of the capital market. The introduction of different degrees of indexing to various bond issues tends to distort the interest rate structure and in particular makes it particularly difficult to calculate the real cost of borrowing. While it would certainly be true that the introduction of various schemes of indexing might introduce changes in the interest rates structure, the argument somehow assumes the structure was ideal in the first place; but the only reason for indexing was that it was not. It is precisely because of the lack of 'transparency' which distorts the real rates of return that indexing is advocated. The introduction of indexing, however partial, is a way of removing, not adding, distortions to the capital market.

In an open economy a further objection to indexing is that it makes the task of monetary policy that much more difficult and that it tends to be destabilizing. The existence of index-linked bonds means that because interest rates rise in line with inflation, there will be an inflow of capital which will offset the adverse trade balance. On the other hand when price expectations are reduced, rates will fall followed by a capital outflow. It is argued that these movements are destabilizing because if the monetary authorities wished to restrict the rate of money supply growth when the rise in prices was accelerating, their actions would be made that much more complicated by the inflow of foreign money. Similarly when they wished to expand the rate of growth of the money supply at a time when the pace of inflation was slackening or even falling, their problems would be multiplied. One factor which this argument, put in this way, leaves out is the offsetting adjustments which would take place in the exchange-rate adjustment. If the exchange rate falls in line with the rising rate of inflation and the deteriorating trade balance, it is by no means obvious that there would be an offsetting inflow of capital funds. The same is true at a time of deflation and an appreciating exchange rate.

Another question raised by the use of escalator clauses in financial markets is the extent to which they should be used; in particular whether they should apply to the liabilities of banks as well as other financial institutions. There is no real difficulty in applying the use of escalator clauses to non-banking institutions. As both the monetary value of their assets and liabilities would change equally with the rate of inflation, their net worth would remain unchanged in real terms. On the other hand it would be disastrous to index the money supply! If any increases in the price level led to a proportional increase in the money supply this would be a sure prescription for hyperinflation! An initial increase in the money supply would lead to a given increase in the price level which would call forth a proportional increase in the price level and so on indefinitely. This means that in order to prevent instability the government has to control the money supply by fixing some nominal magnitude, most usually the stock of high-powered money. While bank deposits could in principle be subject to the use of escalator clauses, and indeed have been in certain countries, this would require the government keeping a firm grip on the rate of increase of high-powered money.

Proposals for indexing savings in the United Kingdom

Up until now there has been no indexing of government or private debt in the United Kingdom. Proposals have been made for limited indexing of National Savings, beginning in 1975. The government plan is to issue a five-year non-negotiable Savings Bond, in minimum units of £10 and with a maximum holding per person of £500, the principle of which is linked to the retail price index. It is to be free of income and capital gains tax, but is only to be offered to people of retirement age. If it is cashed at short notice the benefit from indexing is forfeited but if it is held to maturity it earns a bonus. It also plans to index SAYE up to a maximum monthly investment of £20, which again is free of income and capital gains tax. These savings can be withdrawn after five years, but if they are held for a further two years they offer a bonus. While the introduction of these instruments is a step in the right direction, they are seriously deficient. Nothing so far has been said regarding the frequency of revaluation, the payment of interest or the size of the bonus. In fact they seem little more than a sop to the Page Committee's very strong conclusions on the subject, rather than as any comprehensive attempt to protect the savings of the small investor.

Government bonds

The government should issue short-, medium- and either long-term or irredeemable bonds which are indexed to take account of inflation. The government would fix the maturity value and the coupon rate in nominal terms plus a periodic readjustment by a factor which reflects the rate of inflation. If necessary, because of the uncertainty as to their market rate of interest, the bonds could be issued by auction.

Local Authority debt

Local Authorities should be encouraged to issue new debt instruments which have comparable terms to those above for gilt-edge stock.

National Savings

The capital value of National Savings instruments (National Savings certificates, British Savings Bonds, Defence Bonds, National Development Bonds, Premium Saving Bonds, Save-as-you-Earn, National Savings Bank ordinary and Investment Accounts) should be raised by the same percentage as the rate of inflation, and the fixed nominal interest rate should be paid on the present value of capital. Withdrawals should be calculated in terms of present, rather than some historic, value.

I—8

Part V

Control

14 Prices and incomes policies

'Therefore we who are the protectors of the human race, are agreed, as we view the situation, that decisive legislation is necessary, so that the long-hoped-for solutions which mankind itself could not provide may, by the remedies provided by our foresight, be vouchsafed for the general betterment of all . . . we have decided that maximum price of articles for sale must be established.'

The Edict on Maximum Prices, *A D 301*

Since the end of the Second World War the governments of most Western countries have, at various times, tried to combat inflation by the introduction of incomes policies. The specific names which have been given to these policies have varied from country to country and even, at different times, within the same country – wage and price restraint, national wages policy, wage-price guideposts, guiding lights for wage and non-wage incomes. They have ranged from an appeal for voluntary restraint on the growth of wages and prices to the statutory control of all forms of income, prices, wages, dividends, and rents and the creation of institutions and machinery to administer such controls.

Although the term 'incomes policies' usually refers to post-war measures, price and wage controls are not new. In AD 301 the Emperor Diocletian promulgated an edict for the whole of the Roman Empire which set maximum prices for commodities, freight rates and wages.[1] The scheme covered no less than 900 commodities, 130 different kinds of labour and the freight rates for most commodities in inter-Empire trade; an elementary instructor was able to charge 50 denarii per pupil per month, a teacher of arithmetic or shorthand, 75, a teacher of Greek or Latin literature and geometry, 200 and a teacher of rhetoric or public speaking, 250. The penalties for trading at prices above the maximum were severe. In the thirteenth century Kublai Khan, the able general who conquered China and became the first emperor of the Mongol dynasty, introduced a system of maximum prices. In England the Statute of Labourers in 1357 was an attempt to prevent wages from rising following the Black Death which had reduced the population by approximately one half. In 1563 Elizabeth I passed, in order to deal with inflation, the Statute of Apprentices, which standardized hours of work and provided that wage rates were to be fixed in each county by the justice of the peace. In 1633 after only four years of settlement, one of the colonies, Massachusetts Bay, introduced a programme of comprehensive wage and price controls, with colonial prices being limited to one-third above the English level. Puritan writers of the period classed violators of wage and price laws with 'adulterers and whoremongers'. At the time of the American Revolution many States introduced detailed wage and price ceilings. For example, Massachusetts in 1777 fixed maximum prices on a variety of goods and services; as 7s 6d per bushel of wheat, $4\frac{1}{2}$d a pound for 'fresh pork, well fatted and of a good quality', 3s 10d for a gallon of New England rum, 5d a pound for 'Dunghill fowls and Ducks', 8s for a pair of shoes and 2s per night in Boston for housekeeping with English hay.[2] A similar pattern of detailed wage and price control emerged during the depreciation of the Assignat in France in the early 1790s. On 29 September 1793 the Law of Maximum was passed, which laid down four great rules: the price of an article of necessity was to be fixed at one and one-third of its price in 1790; the prices of all forms of transportation were to be fixed at a certain rate per league; wholesalers were allowed to operate a profit margin of 5 per cent; and retailers were to be allowed a profit margin of 10 per cent. The Criminal Tribunal at Strasburg ordered that anyone selling goods above the maximum price was to have his dwelling destroyed, and one of the charges which appears in the daily list of those condemned to the guillotine is violation of the Maximum Laws.

Despite the fact that prices and incomes policies have been used extensively in the last twenty-five years, a precise definition of what constitutes such policies is much more difficult. As most governments are overtly concerned about inflation and usually urge businessmen to restrain price increases and trade unions, wage increases, it might be argued that all governments operate a *de facto* incomes policy. The term, however, is usually used in a much more restrictive sense than this. The Organization for Economic Co-operation and Development in trying to define the term put it as follows:

> What is meant by an incomes policy . . . is that the authorities should have a view about the kind of evolution of incomes which is consistent with their economic objectives, and in particular with price stability; that they should seek to promote public agreement on the principles which should guide the growth of incomes; and that they should try to induce people voluntarily to follow this guidance.[3]

One feature of incomes policies which emerges very clearly from this definition is that the government must have a carefully worked-out estimate of the desired growth of prices and wages and productivity. More than this, such a view must be consistent with the overall macro-economic behaviour of the economy, fiscal and monetary policy, the balance of payments and the growth rate. If the enunciated 'norms' for price and wage increases are to have any credibility, they must be related to the overall behaviour of the economy, whether the prediction is based on a Keynesian or monetarist analysis.

While the above conditions are *necessary* ones for an incomes policy, they are nowhere near *sufficient* ones. The annual increases in wages and prices must also be broken down by sectors, by industry and by skill in a way which is comprehensive. Particular industries must be given limits within which they can raise their prices and such targets must to some extent take into account the operation of market forces. For example, if it was known that over the foreseeable future coal would be scarce, then the increase in price permitted to the coal industry might be greater than the national average. The same should apply with wages. Certain trade unions might be permitted greater pay increases, even after taking productivity gains into account, simply in order to cope with scarcity. In other words, even within a desired *average* rate of price and wage increases, it would be necessary to accommodate *relative* wage and price changes.

Thirdly, an incomes policy must have some method by which the policy targets are to be made effective. If the policy is voluntary, its implementation may rely on a general sense of public responsibility and on an appeal to patriotism. If the policy is statutory, then it will usually involve the creation of certain institutional bodies able to administer the policy in a fairly detailed manner, with the power to impose penalties on recalcitrant firms and workers.

So far we have interpreted incomes policy as being an essentially anti-inflationary measure. There are some people, however, who see a much wider scope for incomes policies than this; in particular they would like it to be a way of raising the growth of productivity and changing the distribution of income. For example, in a Fabian pamphlet Nicholas Bosanquet introduces the subject by declaring: 'The long-term aims of an incomes policy for socialists must be to raise the level of real wages, to increase the share of wage and salary earnings in national income, and to promote greater justice in relative pay',[4] without any reference at all to controlling inflation. The argument here is that because the share of profits in the gross national product and the relative wage of labour are determined by social and political, as well as economic factors, any attack on inflation must first attempt to change the distribution of income through influencing social and political factors. Incomes policy has also been linked to attempts to raise productivity. In the case of the United Kingdom, the disappointingly slow rise in labour productivity is put down to various rigidities in the labour market, both in management and on the shop floor. In this context, an incomes policy is seen as an attempt to co-ordinate the interests of both groups and reduce rigidities, and in this respect, a good many of the reports of the National Board for Prices and Incomes, set up in 1965, were to do with ways of increasing the efficiency of various industries.

Lastly any incomes policy must be designed so that it is politically acceptable. If business and trade unions are to voluntarily restrict their price rises and wage demands there must be a prior consensus in favour of the adoption of such policies. Similarly, if a government is to impose prices and wages ceilings without facing a threat of non-compliance or a national strike, there must once again be some measure of acceptance of such a policy, at least by the representative bodies of the two sides of industry, the TUC and the CBI. Economists tend to write as if wage and price controls could be imposed or withdrawn in a political vacuum. In most cases there is a price to be paid for the acceptance of such a policy – namely by fulfilling certain other demands of the parties concerned. An example of this is the present 'social contract' in the United Kingdom, in which the government promised to implement certain policies and repeal certain legislation as their part of the bargain.

Incomes policies in the United Kingdom

There have been four major attempts at introducing incomes policies in the United Kingdom in the post-war years: the Stafford Cripps call for restraint in 1948–50; the setting up of the National Incomes Commission in 1961–2 under Selwyn Lloyd; the Wilson government's policy of restraint, 1964–6, and controls, 1966–70; and the Heath government's programme for controlling inflation, 1972–4. There were also three periods when governments made a specific point of calling for restraint, but did not introduce any controls or set up any specific institutions to deal with the problem. Early in 1952 the Conservative Chancellor of the Exchequer attempted to obtain the cooperation of unions and management to ensure that prices did not rise more rapidly than productivity; in 1956, when Macmillan was Chancellor of the Exchequer, trade unions were asked to moderate their wage demands while private firms and nationalized industries were asked to maintain a 'price plateau' for at least a year; and in 1971–2 the Confederation of British Industry proposed to its members a policy of voluntary price increases – throughout 1972 they were to voluntarily accept a 5 per cent ceiling on price rises, with the clear intention that the Trades Union Congress would follow suit.

The first incomes policy was introduced in the aftermath of the Second World War. Reconstruction was a costly business and there was the expectation that the post-war years would turn out to be as recessionary as the early 1930s. In order to maintain full employment and ensure low interest rates to stimulate investment, Dr Dalton pursued a 'cheap money' policy from 1945 to 1947. Full employment was maintained but at the cost of depreciating domestic currency and a mounting balance-of-payments deficit. In February 1948 the government issued the *Statement on Personal Incomes, Costs and Prices*, requesting that money incomes should not grow more rapidly than the growth of real production.[5] The one exception they permitted was those industries which would otherwise be unable to obtain suitable labour. In evaluating the success of this incomes policy two factors are usually mentioned: the personal stature of Stafford Cripps and the trade-union leaders, Deakin, Lawther and Williamson; and the fact that the appeal was made just after the end of the war, when there was considerable sympathy and response to an appeal for restraint made in the interests of the nation as a whole. The policy broke down in 1950, being rejected by the Trade Union Congress at its annual autumn meeting. The end of the policy was followed by a period of rapid price and wage inflation, variously ascribed to the ending of the policy, the effect of the 1949 devaluation in raising food prices and the shortages created by the Korean War.

Although not part of a specific incomes policy, the Conservative government set up in 1957 the Council on Prices, Productivity and Incomes, which consisted of three independent members – who soon came to be known as the 'three wise men'. The object of the Council was 'to keep under review changes in prices, productivity and the level of incomes (including wages, salaries and profits) and to report thereon from time to time', which it did in a series of annual reports from 1958 to 1961. Although at first the Council was highly critical of an incomes policy as a way of solving the problem of inflation, by the time of its final report, and due to a changed membership, it had a different view. It argued for a counter-inflationary policy which tackled the problem on all fronts – by raising productivity, by adjusting the increase in demand and by moderating the rise in money incomes, in particular, pay and profits. With respect to the third of these, it advocated the adoption of a voluntary incomes policy, so that wage rises would be in line with productivity, but also suggested that the government should not hesitate to announce that if such a policy were not adopted it would be forced to take steps to restrain demand directly.

In response to the deterioration in the balance of payments, the Chancellor of the Exchequer, Mr Selwyn Lloyd, took action in the summer of 1961 along the broad lines of the above-mentioned report. He appealed for a 'pay pause', a voluntary restriction on wages, salary and dividend increases, with the government taking the lead by temporarily freezing the wages of the Civil Service. In February 1962 in *Incomes Policy: The Next Step*, he announced the longer-term proposals which he had earlier promised.[6] In the meantime he had established the National Economic Development Council to deal with the problem of long-term planning. The basis of the incomes policy was the announcement by the government of a 'guiding light' of 2–2½ per cent average increase in wages and salaries per annum. Relative wage increases greater than the average were justified only in two circumstances: if there was a shortage of labour or if particular workers were prepared to renounce restrictive practices, accept more exacting work, or work in more onerous conditions. In November 1962 the government set up the National Incomes Commission (NIC) which was to provide an authoritative and impartial view of the more difficult pay questions, which could be referred to it either by employers or trade unions. The establishment of the Commission was opposed by the TUC and its work was also hampered by a lack of research staff.

The third major attempt at an incomes policy came about with George Brown's famous *Joint Statement of Intent on Productivity, Prices and Incomes* which, unlike anything previous, was a joint statement by the TUC, employer organizations and the government on the need to establish machinery to keep the general movement of prices and incomes under review and to examine special cases in order to advise whether wages and price increases were in the public interest.[7] In place of the National Incomes Commission, the government set up in 1965 the National Board for Prices and Incomes which would report on various price and wage rises. The Board had its own staff and was much better equipped to issue reports than was the NIC. The Board itself was made up of trade unionists, businessmen and independent members.

In April 1965, and as part of its attempt at voluntary agreement, the government proposed a whole set of criteria by which individual wage and price changes should be made. The overall objective was to have stable prices and average earnings rising at the same rate as productivity, the norm of which was set at 3–3½ per cent increase per year. Wages and self-employed income were therefore expected to rise at this rate, subject to four exceptions:

Exceptional pay increases should be confined to the following circumstances:

   (i) where the employees concerned, for example by accepting more exacting work or a major change in working practices, make a direct contribution towards increasing productivity in the particular firm or industry. Even in such cases some of the benefit should accrue to the community as a whole in the form of lower prices;

 (ii) where it is essential in the national interest to secure a change in the distribution of manpower (or to prevent a change which would otherwise take place) and a pay increase would be both necessary and effective for this purpose;

(iii) where there is general recognition that existing wage and salary levels are too low to maintain a reasonable standard of living;

(iv) where there is widespread recognition that the pay of a certain group of workers has fallen seriously out of line with the level of remuneration for similar work and needs in the national interest to be improved.[8]

Firms were expected to maintain constant prices except in certain circumstances: if output per employee could not be increased sufficiently so that wages and salaries rose at a rate consistent with the criteria for incomes; if there were 'unavoidable' increases in non-labour costs, such as materials, fuels, services or marketing; if there were 'unavoidable' increases in capital costs per unit of output; and if a firm was unable to secure its necessary capital. On the other hand, if a firm's productivity was rising more rapidly than the national average, if non-labour costs were falling or if profits were based on excessive market power, firms would be expected to reduce their prices.

Because the voluntary system did not appear to be working well, the government proposed in November 1965 an 'early warning system' by which firms were to notify the government of any price change they proposed to make at least four weeks in advance. Similarly, trade unions were required to submit wage claims to the TUC, which would then notify the government. In the case of both price and pay increases the government could refer such increases to the National Board for Prices and Incomes for scrutiny, although it did not have the power to implement the Board's conclusions.

As a result of the deterioration in the overall economic situation, especially in the balance of payments, and also the disappointing record of the attempt at implementing a voluntary incomes policy, the government introduced in July 1966 a standstill for all prices and incomes for six months, followed, in the first half of 1967, by a period of severe restraint, in which exceptions would be permitted only if there were compelling reasons.[9] At the end of this period, wage increases were to be permitted only if they could be justified by increased productivity, improving the relative position of the low-paid, or if they had been agreed before July 1966 but in fact had not been received because of the freeze.[10] In March 1968 the government replaced the 'nil norm' with a $3\frac{1}{2}$ per cent ceiling on annual increases of income, the only exception being increases due to productivity.

When the Conservative government was returned in 1970 it was committed to removing all trace of price and wage controls. The National Board for Prices and Incomes was dismantled and the government were committed to the free play of market forces. Throughout 1972 the Confederation of British Industry called on its members not to raise prices by more than 5 per cent annually. In response to the rising rate of inflation, the government attempted in 1972 but failed to introduce a voluntary prices and incomes policy. Then in November 1972 the government introduced a ninety-day freeze on prices, rents, dividends and pay as the first stage of a programme for controlling inflation.[11] Certain prices, such as those for fruit, vegetables, meat, fish and imported raw materials, which were subject to seasonal fluctuations or determined outside the country, were exempt and any firm which considered that its costs had risen so rapidly that it was impracticable for them not to raise prices was required to submit details to the appropriate government department. The only exception was incomes where productivity had increased.

In the second stage of the policy, the government drew up a code for determining prices and pay, which was to be taken into account by all those concerned with their determination, and established two new agencies to administer it – a Price Commission and a Pay Board.[12] The code set out general principles relating to prices:

(i) to limit the extent to which prices may be increased on account of increased costs, and to secure reductions as a result of reduced costs;

(ii) to reinforce the control of prices by limiting profit margins per unit of sales or turnover, while safeguarding investment;

(iii) in all these respects to reinforce the effects of competition, and to secure its full benefits in the general level of prices.[13]

The exceptions to these principles were the price of exports, imports, auctions, second-hand goods, charges for international freight and passenger traffic, insurance premiums and goods whose prices were subject to international agreement.

Firms could increase prices in the domestic market if these reflected an increase in 'allowable' costs per unit of output, where allowable costs were defined as the costs of labour (subject to not more than 50 per cent of allowable cost increases arising from pay increases), materials, components or fuels, rent of premises or rates, and interest charges. Profit margins were not to exceed the average level of the best two of the last five years; the only exception permitted to this was if its operation would seriously impede investment by depriving the enterprise concerned of essential funds.

The general principles relating to pay were:

(i) to limit the rate of increase in pay in money terms to a level more in line with the growth of national output, so as progressively to reduce the rate of price inflation and improve the prospects of sustained faster growth in real earnings;

(ii) to apply the limit fairly, irrespective of the form of any increase or the method of determining it;

(iii) to facilitate an improvement in the relative position of the low paid;

(iv) to leave to those who normally determine pay decisions on the amount, form and distribution of increases within the limit.[14]

The pay limit proposed by the government was an increase of £1 per week per head plus 4 per cent of the wages and salary bill in the year preceding the freeze, which could be allocated in any way between a firm's employees and, in any case, a maximum increase for any individual of £250 per year. The specific form of these limits were designed to favour the low-paid workers. Dividends were also subject to control – they could not be increased by more than five per cent of the previous year's declaration.

The procedure for ensuring that prices and pay agreements were monitored and implemented according to the code was complicated. Manufacturing companies were divided into three categories: the largest firms would have to give prior notification of proposed price increases to the Price Commission; medium-sized firms would not be required to obtain consent before raising prices, but they would be required to submit regular statements of the behaviour of their prices, costs and profits to the Commission; small firms would not be required to submit information, but they would be subject to spot checks. As far as pay increases were concerned, there was a similar classification: settlements affecting 500 or more employees were to be notified to the Pay Board in advance, while the smallest firms were not required to notify the Board of their decisions. Under Stage III, which started in November 1973, wage and salary increases were restricted to either 7 per cent or £2·25 per week depending on which was larger and they were in any case subject to a maximum of £350 per person per year. Pay increases were permitted annually. A number of exceptions however were permitted in order to help the lower-paid workers and those engaged in dangerous and unpleasant jobs, such as coal-miners. In addition to this, 'threshold' agreements could be freely negotiated between employer (including the public sector) and employee which gave an extra 40p per week for every 1 per cent rise in the retail price index over and above its October 1973 level.

The new Labour government which was elected in February 1974 was committed to settling with the miners on the terms demanded and therefore ending the strike and also abolishing statutory wage controls though not price controls. The government immediately settled with the miners and the statutory wage controls were abolished in July 1974. The statutory policy however was replaced by a voluntary policy usually referred to as the 'social contract'. This was an agreement worked out between the Labour Party and the TUC in 1973 as an alternative to the statutory policy. Prices were to be fixed; the Labour government was to carry out certain policies, such as increased pensions, taxing the rich and the repeal of certain legislation which dealt with industrial relations; and in return the TUC agreed to limit their wage claims – wages would rise only to compensate for price rises, would be twelve months apart, though there would be certain exceptions such as productivity deals, reform of the pay structure, the lower paid (£30 per week and under) and women who were being discriminated against.

As we examine British experience of incomes policy, three features stand out. In the first place the criteria for policies have become increasingly complicated over the post-war years. Stafford Cripps' criterion in 1948 was very simple: incomes must be kept in line with productivity. Contrast this with the Heath policy of 1972–4, in which detailed rules for price and pay increases were laid down, numerous exceptions to the rules were discussed in detail, and the application of the code was discussed separately with respect to most industries. Throughout the post-war years therefore the criteria have become more complex, with each new policy seeking to remedy the loopholes and mistakes of the previous ones. In the second place, and following on from this, the institutional machinery to deal with the implementation of the policy has become more sophisticated. In 1948 no institutional body was created to supervise the policy. The Committee on Prices, Productivity and Employment created in 1957 consisted of just three individuals. The National Incomes Commission consisted of five persons and a modest secretariat. The National Board for Prices and Incomes was an altogether much bigger affair, with a full-time staff and with representatives from industry, trade unions and the government. In 1973 two bodies were created to deal with the administration of the policies and numerous companies were required to file records regarding profits, costs, prices, etc. It is inevitable that as the criteria became more complex, the administration of the policy becomes more cumbersome. The third characteristic of the last two incomes policies is the way in which they resembled those of the United States. George Brown's criteria for earnings and prices were very similar to the US wage-price guideposts of 1962. The overall objective in both cases was price stability, with average earnings rising at the same rate as productivity. The criteria for exceptions was also similar: extra earnings could be justified by the need to move labour, unjustifiable low pay or increased work by workers; while prices could be increased if productivity growth were higher than national averages, there was a need to raise capital and/or due to the movement of non-labour costs. Mr Heath's policy closely resembled that of President Nixon. Both started with an initial freeze, evolved into different phases, were statutory, laid down Codes for wage and price increases and created comparable institutions to administer these codes.

The rationale of incomes policy

The way in which an incomes policy might succeed in reducing the rate of inflation is closely tied up with one's view of the causes of inflation and the nature of the inflationary process. Broadly speaking, incomes policies have been advocated by those who see wages as determined largely by non-economic factors, a view which can conveniently be fitted into the Keynesian model. One way in which an incomes policy can allegedly affect inflation is by influencing the structure of wages and the share of wages in gross national product. If inflation results from the jockeying of various unions to increase their pay relative to each other, then an incomes policy which adopts a definite view of the determination of wage differentials and which is accepted by the parties concerned as fair and is adhered to, will reduce the exogenous element in wage inflation. Similarly, if inflation results from the conflict between workers and wealth owners over the share of wages and profits in the GNP and an incomes policy is able to control these variables, then once again it will reduce inflation by eliminating the source of conflict. To express this argument in terms of the Phillips curve, a prices and incomes policy which successfully affected differentials or the share of wages in the GNP would move the Phillips curve to the left, so that a given level of unemployment was now associated with a lower rate of inflation.

Not unrelated to the above is the observation that in a modern economy with imperfect product and labour markets there are a few key price and wage decisions which set the standard for settlements in other sectors. For example, in the United Kingdom the wage settlements granted in coal, engineering and car production are held to have repercussions throughout the economy. The argument then runs that there is a substantial discretionary element in the wage demands and the bargaining which takes place in these industries, and that if only they could be subjected to pressure, via an incomes policy, this would tend to moderate the wage and price rises which take place. Pressure could successfully be brought to bear because those groups in our society which have market power must be sensitive to public opinion.

A third way in which incomes policy might work is by inducing increases in productivity. For a given increase in money wages, an increase in productivity will mean that the rate of price inflation will be that much lower. Many incomes policies, especially those pursued in the United Kingdom, have attempted to raise productivity by setting down a certain norm for wage increases and then permitting an exception to the rule in those cases where productivity has risen, so providing an incentive to raise productivity. Similarly, a number of the reports of the National Board for Prices and Incomes dealt with ways in which efficiency could be raised in various industries (e.g. banking, building societies). If productivity is raised sufficiently, then wages can be permitted to rise that much more rapidly than prices, which would ease the inflationary pressure created by the pressure of wages.

A rather different process by which an incomes policy might reduce inflation is by influencing expectations. This process is rather different, in that it is not restricted to a labour market in which it is assumed that wages are determined by non-economic factors but applies just as much to labour markets in which wages are the outcome of the laws of supply and demand – which in turn depends on a more rational basis for behaviour by employers and employees. An important factor in determining the speed of inflation is the expectation of the future rate of inflation. If in general it is believed that over the foreseeable *future*, inflation will accelerate, then this will influence *current* behaviour in the labour market through trade unions demanding higher wages, or in the housing market by affecting the terms on which landlords are prepared to draw up leases, or in the capital market by changing current interest rates. Similarly, if inflation is expected to fall, the opposite movements will take place; wages will be raised that much less, rents will be that much lower and current interest rates will fall. If, therefore, an incomes policy can convince people that the government have taken appropriate steps to deal with inflation, so that rates will fall, this becomes self-fulfilling and evident in current economic behaviour.

This was, for example, the rationale of the United States Council of Economic Advisers on the price and wage controls introduced in 1971:

> The basic premise of the price-wage control system is that the inflation of 1970 and 1971 was the result of expectations, contracts, and patterns of behaviour built up during the earlier period, beginning in 1965, when there was an inflationary excess of demand. Since there is no longer an excess of demand, the rate of inflation will subside permanently when this residue of the previous excess is removed. The purpose of the control system is to give the country a period of enforced stability in which expectations, contracts, and behaviour will become adapted to the fact that rapid inflation is no longer the prospective condition of American life. When that happens controls can be eliminated.[15]

An important facet of this argument is the need to specify exactly how and why expectations will be influenced by certain kinds of government action. If expectations can allegedly be influenced simply by the government declaring an incomes policy then the argument assumes as much irrationality on the part of people as earlier. But if, on the other hand, expectations are revised because of the government's monetary and fiscal policies, then it may be asked what use is an incomes policy, for with such a degree of rationality they would have been affected in any case and would have certainly changed their behaviour. The argument is somewhere between these two extremes. An incomes policy coupled with appropriate monetary and fiscal policies will reduce the expectation of inflation more than if there had been no such policy. Once again if we consider the impact of such a policy in terms of the Phillips curve, it moves the curve to the left and so in the short term improves the inflation-unemployment trade-off.

Measuring the success of incomes policy: the evidence from the UK

Before we examine the evidence on how successful incomes policies have been in controlling inflation, it is important that we are clear on what we are attempting to measure and how in principle we would judge them successful or otherwise. In the first place, there is the question of which indicator we should use – retail prices, wholesale prices, weekly wage rates, hourly wage rates or average earnings – particularly as these do not always – in fact rarely – move together over short time periods. For example, in the United States in 1971–2 inflation, measured by the wholesale price index, was rising, while judged by the consumer price index, it was falling. The main criteria in choosing the index are that it should be comprehensive, relatively free of special control by the government and as far as possible responsive to market forces. For the United Kingdom, the retail price index is therefore more suitable than the wholesale price index and in the labour market, an indicator of actual earnings would be better than one of the official rates of pay, preferably on an hourly rather than weekly basis. Secondly, there is the problem to what extent prices can in any case be used as a measure of success in view of quality changes. Assuming firms are restricted in their ability to raise prices, then in order to protect profits they will react by reducing the quality of the goods they produce. For example, cars may sell at the same price, but with less 'extras', or there may be the same price for public transport but a less frequent service. Such an action as this is equivalent to a price increase. But because a change in quality is something for which it is extremely difficult and costly to construct an overall index and measure, this may lead to a false interpretation of official statistics.

Thirdly, there are the differences in incomes policies themselves. So often in empirical work incomes policies are treated as if they were a homogenous instrument of policy such as a tariff or a tax. When the policy is 'on' the world behaves a certain way, and when the policy is 'off' in quite another way. But if our review of the British experience of incomes policy has done nothing else, it must convince us of the heterogeneity of incomes policy; some were voluntary, others statutory, some were concerned with the distribution of income and others not. To put all these together and label them as one policy instrument is a rather crude device.

Yet another problem is the time period over which the policy is to be judged. How short or how long should the period be? If the period chosen is the official duration of the policy as measured by official statements, this may be too short to capture the lagged but important economic effects of the policy. For example, there may be a 'catching-up' process after the policy is officially removed, which reverses the earlier and apparently more successful impact of the policy. On the other hand, if the period chosen is too long, it captures the effect of various other influences which are nothing to do with the policy. In the end, although the matter must be one of judgement, it seems more reasonable to err on the longer rather than shorter side.

One of the most common ways of measuring the effectiveness of incomes policy is to compare the behaviour of prices and wages in two periods, usually just before and just after the inauguration of a policy. If wages and prices grow less rapidly after the introduction of a policy, then this is usually judged a success, while a more rapid growth is usually judged a failure. The problem with this approach is that it takes no account of any other factors which might be relevant to the behaviour of prices and incomes in the two periods – such as the way in which monetary and fiscal policy, indirect taxes or import prices may also have changed from one period to another.

The correct way of trying to assess the impact of incomes policy is therefore to construct a model of the economic behaviour of wages and prices which would predict the movements of these variables in the absence of an incomes policy. And then, after account has been taken of the influence of all other variables, to use the difference between the predicted and the actual rates of inflation as a measure of the policy's effectiveness. Even in this case, it is impossible to say with complete certainty whether the residual difference can be attributed to incomes policy or whether it is the result of some immeasurable or neglected influence.

A good deal of empirical research has been conducted on the effectiveness of post-war United Kingdom incomes policies.[16] The various papers on the subject have not reached identical conclusions and considerable dispute exists over some results, depending on the particular statistical estimating procedure that was used. Nevertheless certain broad conclusions do emerge, which we shall show in the next section are also borne out, interestingly enough, from the experiences of other countries.

(i) Wage increases were lower in the periods 1948–50, 1956 and 1961–2 as a result of incomes policy, but the magnitude involved was trivial. For example, in the Lipsey-Parkin study wage inflation was lowered on average by 0·7790 per cent per annum, while in the Hines study it was significantly less 0·26 per cent per annum. The average effect of incomes policy therefore, was to restrain wage increases by between $\frac{1}{4}$ and $\frac{3}{4}$ of 1 per cent per annum. The only period when wage rises were significantly affected was during the Cripps policy of 1948–50 when wage inflation was reduced by between $1\frac{1}{2}$ and $2\frac{1}{2}$ per cent. Throughout the sixties the effect was negligible

(ii) Price inflation seems to have been affected even less than wage inflation, regardless of whether the retail or the wholesale price index was used. Most studies have found no statistically significant decrease in the rate of price rises, though some tests found a smaller rise in retail prices in 1956 and 1965–6

(iii) No simple conclusions can be deduced about the effectiveness of voluntary by comparison with statutory policies. Measured by their effect on wages, the most effective policies were the Cripps call for restraint in 1948 and the Wilson freeze of 1966–7.

(iv) There is some but not strong evidence to suggest that incomes policies have not so much shifted the Phillips curve to the left but pivoted it about a point of approximately 1·8 per cent unemployment, so that in a 'policy on' period in which unemployment is less than 1·8 per cent the rate of wage inflation is reduced, but that if unemployment is above this rate, wage inflation is higher than otherwise. The explanation for this is that a policy sets norms for wages which tend to be accepted as a minimum throughout the labour market.

(v) All policies have broken down because of their failure in containing inflation. In this respect Table 12 is interesting. The discrepancy between the publicly announced norm and the result is not necessarily an indication of the exact magnitude of failure but it is suggestive.

The general pattern of these conclusions is clear. Incomes policy has had very little effect on prices but rather more on wages. To the extent that it does have an impact on wages this tends to be greatest during a period of freeze, becoming less effective during the thaw

In the long run UK incomes policies have had no permanent effect on either the rate of price or wage rises.

Table 12. **Incomes Policies – the Hopes and the Realities**

Period of policy	Norm for wage increases (%)	Outcome*	
		Change in weekly wage rates (%)	Change in hourly earnings (%)
Stafford Cripps Wage Restraint: September 1948–October 1950	No *general* increase in money incomes	2.2	2.3
Macmillan Price and Wage Plateau: March–December 1956	Unspecific	3.4	3.4
Selwyn Lloyd Pay Pause: August 1961–March 1962	0	2.7	3.6
National Incomes Commission Guiding Light: April 1962–April 1963	2–2½	3.9	3.9
April 1963–October 1964	3–3½	4.1	4.5
March 1965–July 1966	3–3½	5.0	7.1
Wage Freeze: July 1966–June 1967	0	1.9	2.1
Nil Norm: July 1967–March 1968	0 (exceptions permitted)	6.4	6.5
Post-Devaluation: April 1968–December 1969	0 3½ (ceiling)	5.8	6.0
January–July 1970	2½–4½	8.9	9.1
Stage I Freeze: November 1972–March 1973	0	2.9	2.9
Stage II: April–November 1973	4 plus £1 rise per week	13.7	14.0
Stage III: November 1973–June 1974	7	18.5	18.9
'Social Contract': July 1974–April 1975	21 (rate of price inflation)	25.0	25.0

* Adjusted to an annual basis for comparison to the norm.

The foreign experience of incomes policies

As a response to the accelerating inflation of the early 1970s nearly all Western countries have introduced incomes policies in one form or another. Some countries however have operated incomes policies for much longer periods: the Netherlands has had an incomes policy since 1945; throughout most of the post-war years the compulsory arbitration system in Australia was a *de facto* incomes policy; Austria, Norway and Sweden, although not having formal incomes policies, have nevertheless operated a central co-ordination of pay bargaining; and France has had numerous periods of price controls in the 1950s (1952, 1954, 1956, 1957) and subsequently periods of price freezes and guidelines on wages and salaries. Although in the United States there were frequent exhortations in the 1940s and 1950s to unions and management alike to restrain wage and price rises, the first prices and incomes policy to be introduced was the Kennedy administration's Wage-Price Guideposts of 1962. The guidelines were to provide rules for non-inflationary wage and price increases; namely that the increase in wage rates in each industry be equal to the trend rate of overall productivity growth, subject to certain exceptions such as an ability to attract sufficient labour and that prices should be raised only if the industry's rate of productivity increase exceeded the overall rate (if it was less, they should be lowered) subject to the fact that profits were sufficiently high to attract the capital required to finance expansion. They were not strictly enforced and no formal machinery was set up to administer them. By contrast the Nixon administration introduced a three-month freeze of prices, wages and rents in August 1971 and followed it up by creating a Pay Board and Cost-of-Living Council which were to administer subsequent wage and price increases, according to criteria laid down by these institutions. Canada first introduced a prices and incomes policy in 1969 with the establishment of the Prices and Incomes Commission and West Germany moved towards establishing a voluntary incomes policy for the first time in the mid-1960s.

Broadly speaking the policies pursued have been of two kinds – the social contract approach and the guideline approach. The former relies on the government being able to secure the support of all the relevant groups in society – management, trade unions, consumers – in return for the implementation of certain economic and social policies. The policy would typically stipulate allowable increases in wages, salaries, rents, dividends and profit margins and would usually be backed by statutory powers and a process of arbitration. Examples are the Netherlands in the early 1950s and Finland's stabilization programme of 1968–9. One feature of most of the countries in which this kind of policy has been pursued is that they have an element of centrally co-ordinated bargaining. This is not to suggest that the more centralized the wage and price-setting institutions may be, the more successful is an incomes policy likely to be, but only that a minimum of central co-ordination is important. The other approach is for the government to lay down norms, such as the US guideposts of 1962, regardless of whether or not it has the explicit co-operation of various groups. These policies tend to be voluntary and without any arbitration procedures.

Although the literature on the foreign experience of incomes policies is voluminous and impossible to evaluate adequately in a limited space, nevertheless some conclusions can be drawn without injustice being done. In the first place incomes policy as a device for controlling inflation has not been very successful. In a study for the US Council of Economic Advisers of the experience of the United Kingdom, the Netherlands, Sweden, Denmark, France, West Germany and Italy, the conclusion of L. Ulman and R. J. Flanaghan was that 'the accumulation of experience in the countries in this account suggest that in none of the variations so far . . . has incomes policy succeeded in its fundamental objective . . . as stated of making full employment consistent with a reasonable degree of price stability.'[17] In a similar vein a study by the Economic Commission for Europe concludes that 'Western European incomes policies . . . as so far conceived have not proved strikingly effective instruments of economic management. The policies have had achievements to record, but limited and temporary achievements.'[18] The OECD cite the United Kingdom in 1966–7 and Finland in 1968–9 as examples of successful policies.

The US experience of 1971–3, which has been subjected to a good deal of empirical research, is a good example of this general thesis.[19] During Phases I and II non-farm prices rose at an annual rate that was about 2·3 per cent slower than the values predicted from the behaviour of the economy before August 1971; and during Phases III and IV price inflation was still 0·6 per cent less than would otherwise have been predicted. On the other hand although wages rose less rapidly during the control period, this was not the direct effect of the policy on wage behaviour, but mainly the result of an indirect effect via the slowing down of price rises. The success which the policy has achieved therefore was the result of squeezing profit margins. But a policy which operates in this way can only have a temporary success. Over a longer-run period companies will attempt to restore their profit margins, there will be a catching-up process and so the effectiveness of the policy is undone.

One particular way in which policies have failed is through the existence of 'wage-drift' and fringe benefits, so that there is a significant difference between the negotiated wage increases and actual wage increases. For example, in Sweden, where wage bargaining is done through highly centralized institutions, total hourly wage cost, measured in terms of annual average percentage change, rose by 9·4 per cent between 1963 and 1968, while negotiated wage increases rose by only 3·5 per cent. The difference was due to drift (4·1 per cent) and fringe benefits (1·8). Studies which have been done of this discrepancy suggest that it is explained mainly by the pressure of demand. In the Netherlands in 1963 the permissible wage increase laid down was 2·7 per cent. But because of the pressure of demand employers openly stated that they would pay more and the original target had to be raised by 10 per cent. Yet another way in which the effects of controls are undone is in the 'catching-up' process. Immediately controls are lifted there is a change of wage and price increases.

A second conclusion one can draw about incomes policies is that they have led to industrial unrest, unofficial strikes, shop-floor militancy and the development of new unions. For example, towards the end of 1969 Sweden experienced strikes in a number of large enterprises, the first of which was at the LKAB, a large state-owned metal mining complex. In this case the strike was organized by the shop floor contrary to the wishes of the official union. One of the major demands of the strikers was for higher pay, which they claimed was being denied them by the centralized nature of negotiations.

A third conclusion is the difficulty of deciding on and enforcing an equitable pay structure which is different from that which would result from the operation of a system of free markets. A number of companies have introduced rather sophisticated systems of job evaluation. The Netherlands introduced a very rigid system in 1945; all manual workers, for example, were classified as skilled, semi-skilled and unskilled and fixed percentage differentials were set between these different grades and between regions of the country to allow for differences in the cost of living. In the next two years the system was developed and in 1947 a committee was set up which produced a points rating scheme for various jobs. France, Austria and Sweden have also introduced comparable systems. The major problem with these schemes has been to choose an appropriate set of weights and to adjust them over time to reflect market forces. On present experience it would be an enormous gamble to place much reliance on such a system.

Why have incomes policies failed?

Those in the United Kingdom who have argued most strongly in favour of incomes policies tend to explain their rather disappointing performance on the grounds that the kinds of policies which have been implemented up to the present fall far short of the kind which was needed. With the sole exception of the last, the policies have been introduced in times of crisis to deal with the problem of managing cyclical economic fluctuations; there has been no attempt to promote the concept of a policy which would be continuous and embrace long-term objectives; the policies have been conceived in far too narrow terms; cost-of-living indexing should have been built into the policies: there was a lack of co-ordination between the various organizations concerned with implementing the policy; and the implementation procedure has lacked any way of compelling the two sides of industry to change their positions.

While all these objections may be perfectly valid, there are also some additional and more basic problems which have to be faced. One is the method of deducing suitable targets for income increases. In fact until 1962 no quantitative targets for policy were laid down. In order to produce a realistic target for wages and prices, for example, it is not only necessary to be able to predict productivity growth but also the impact of past monetary and fiscal policy on money income and the breakdown of money income between real income and inflation. While economics can give some guidance as to how monetary and fiscal policy affects national income and some explanation of the determination of the short-term Phillips curve, short-term forecasting remains an extremely hazardous business.

In addition to this there is the problem of ensuring compatibility between the overall targets chosen and the current monetary and fiscal policy. If the policy is to be successful in inducing a revision of inflationary expectations, the norms laid down for the growth of incomes over the foreseeable future must be consistent with the likely effect of present monetary and fiscal policy in determining money income over the same period. This was the major weakness of the 1972–4 incomes policy in the United Kingdom. In November 1972, when the wages and prices freeze was introduced, wages were rising at an annual rate of about 16–17 per cent. Phase Two of the policy introduced early in the next year set a ceiling of approximately 8 per cent for wage rises. At the same time the money supply grew throughout 1972 at just over 20 per cent, and continued growing during the first twelve months of the policy at the even higher rate of 23 per cent. On the one hand the government was asking workers and employers to limit wage increases to 8 per cent and yet on the other hand was providing them with the extra money to bid up wages and prices by about *three* times this amount. Such gross and obvious inconsistency was bound to lead to the collapse of such a policy.

It may be asked why, if such an inconsistency is so obvious, governments seem prone to pursue such contradictory policies. The answer seems to be that control of inflation is only one objective of government policy. In addition to this most governments are interested in reducing the level of unemployment and raising the short-term rate of growth. With wage and price controls in force and the expectation by politicians that such policies will succeed on this particular occasion, for a whole variety of special reasons, politicians have an incentive to raise consumption and reduce unemployment.

Another reason for the failure of incomes policies has been their inability to cope with the problem of determining exceptions to the norms laid down for price and wage rises. For example in the criteria set out in the UK government's White Paper of April 1965, the exceptions to the general rule for pay increases included *inter alia* the case 'where there is general recognition that existing wage and salary levels are too low to maintain a reasonable standard of living' and 'where there is widespread recognition that the pay of a certain group of workers has fallen seriously out of line with the level of remuneration for similar work and needs in the national interest to be improved'. Such exceptions are purposely vague. Because it is exceedingly difficult to forecast the precise structure of wages which would emerge as a result of market forces, the criteria for wage rises needs to have exceptions in fairly general terms as a safety valve for the policy. If they did not exist serious resource misallocation might occur. On the other hand the fact that they are vague offers trade unions and corporations a way by which they can circumvent the controls. In a more general sense this problem is exactly the same as that which lies at the heart of the problem of the free market versus planning as a method of allocating resources. If price and wage controls are to work they must be made comprehensive and certain wages and prices must be capable of being adjusted to deal with the problem of shortages in various skills and products. But such a system is equivalent to trying to plan the development of the whole economy and thereby suffers from the usual and well-known defects of any system of economic planning.

Another way in which incomes policies tend to break down is that if they are sufficiently inflexible and if they are in force for more than a few months they create incentives for firms to seek ways to get around them. For example if firms are restricted from raising prices then they can very easily repackage the product so that its 'quality' falls. The costs of production fall but price remains constant, so that effectively firms have been able to raise prices and restore profit margins. The same is true with the labour market. If it is impossible to hire certain skills at the official rate, then the job specification can be slightly changed and firms allowed to pay more. Another example was the shortage of secretarial staff in public-sector employment during 1973–4. For example universities by hiring temporary secretaries from private agencies, ensured that secretaries were in fact being paid a higher rate than that laid down by the Code.

The general conclusion which emerges is that as an anti-inflationary device incomes policies have not been very successful. They have had partial success in particular cases. But it has only been temporary.

They have not succeeded in reducing the rate of inflation while maintaining full employment. The reasons for the breakdown are that the norms on which they are based are frequently inconsistent with monetary and fiscal policy, the difficulties of fixing wage and price differentials, the inefficiencies which they create and the problem of policing the policies. The most successful policies seem to be those which are short in duration, announce some overall freeze with no exceptions, have no specific terminal date and are introduced in conditions of excess supply rather than excess demand.

15 Monetary and fiscal policies

*'There is an old Eastern proverb which says you may stop with a bodkin a
fountain, which if suffered to flow will sweep away whole cities in its
course. An early and timely contraction, upon the very first indication of
excess in the circulation, is the application of the bodkin to the fountain;
commercial convulsion and ruin in consequence of delay is the stream
sweeping away whole cities in its course.'*

Baron Overstone, Tracts and other Publications on Metallic and Paper
Currency (*1846*)

In attempting to curb inflation most governments are usually forced
to implement measures which have a direct impact on aggregate
demand. Typically referred to as monetary and fiscal policies, these
include, *inter alia*, a reduction in the rate of growth of the money
supply and a reduction in the size of the public sector deficit, which in
turn is brought about either by reducing government expenditures
or raising taxes. In the UK economy over the post-war years deflationary 'packages' have also typically included controls on the
creation of credit in the private sector, measures to deal with the
balance of payments (such as import quotas or export subsidies) and
ceilings on interest rates – measures, in other words, which try to
influence the composition of demand as well as its total. Throughout
this chapter we shall focus on control of the money supply and the
reduction in the public sector deficit, though it is as well to remember
that the quantity theory of money focuses attention primarily on the
supply of money, while Keynesian theory concentrates primarily on
fiscal policy and credit controls.

The case for orthodoxy

The purpose of orthodox monetary and fiscal policy when used to
combat inflation is to ease the pressure of demand on existing
resources. If inflation is the result of excess demand brought about

by the creation of money it will only be brought under control by removing that excess demand through a reduction in the money stock; or, if we were to envisage the process in a growing economy, by a reduction in the *rate of growth* of the money supply.

The process by which a reduction in the rate of growth of the money stock leads to a reduction in the growth of prices and wages is important, because it is frequently argued that in a modern economy with large firms and powerful trade unions such a sequence cannot possibly exist. In a world in which the cause of inflation is supposed to be the conflict between monopolistic trade unions over wage differentials, it becomes difficult to envisage either how or why a change in monetary policy will influence wage awards. How is it therefore that the Bank of England, by selling more gilt-edged stock in the market, raising the level of the minimum lending rate and requiring private banks to increase their holding of Special Deposits at the Bank of England, can set in motion a process which ultimately leads to a reduction in wage claims being made by engineering workers in the Midlands, or electricity workers throughout the country as a whole?

When earlier we discussed the cause of inflation we argued that the link between money and prices was indirect rather than direct. Increasing the money supply produces an increase in prices, but only through a prior influence on the behaviour of consumers and firms, which is a process that inevitably takes time. Exactly the same is true of a deflationary policy. The initial impact of a reduction in the rate of growth of the money supply is to drive up the level of short-term interest rates and depress the level of equity prices. Households and companies find that they are short of cash, and that therefore there has to be some reduction in the levels at which they were spending. Firms in particular find a shortening of their order books. Those firms, including banks, which invested in fixed assets, which now can only be sold at much lower prices, discover they have a serious cash flow problem and some therefore may be forced into bankruptcy. Those firms facing a reduced demand for their product will, in the first instance, reduce the overtime working of their labour force, then reduce the length of the working week, and finally, lay off workers. With less firms and less labour employed by existing firms, real output growth will slow down.

As a result of the tightening of money supply growth, the credit squeeze, the recession in real output, and the rise in unemployment, existing employees will revise their expectation of the future increases in the cost of living, which they will add to the basic productivity increase in putting forward wage claims. A wage award, however, depends on the behaviour not only of workers but also employers. As a result of the recession, employers will also find themselves under pressure to limit wage settlements, so that they are not priced out of the market, and bankrupted. To argue that a recession has no dampening effect on wage demands, on employers' offers and on ultimate settlements, is to argue that workers, trade unions and employers act without regard to their own best interest – something which seems highly implausible, once the facts of the matter are obvious. This is not to say that a reduction in money supply growth has an instant impact on wages and prices. The evidence suggests the opposite; the existence of a long and variable lag between the time at which money supply growth is slowed down and the inflation slows down.

The typical sequence in which a reduction in money supply growth leads to a reduction in the rate of inflation is that initially the financial system feels the squeeze, then after some time the growth of real output is checked and then only after a period of two years or so does the rate of inflation begin to slow down. As we saw earlier, the nature of the lag is the result of the many factors which tend to delay cost and price rises in a modern economy. What is particularly important about the process, however, is that even though both prices and costs tend to fall behind changes in demand, cost changes tend to fall behind price changes.

The usual pattern is that during the initial period of the cyclical expansion in the economy prices tend to rise faster than costs, but that during the later phase of the boom and throughout the recession costs rise more rapidly than prices. This latter phase is often interpreted as evidence of cost-push inflation, when in fact it is simply due to the different lags which operate during the inflationary process. The evidence of this for the United States economy over the postwar years can be seen in Figure 6. Because of the different response of prices and costs to changing demand, in the initial phase of each boom prices rise more rapidly than costs, while in each recession

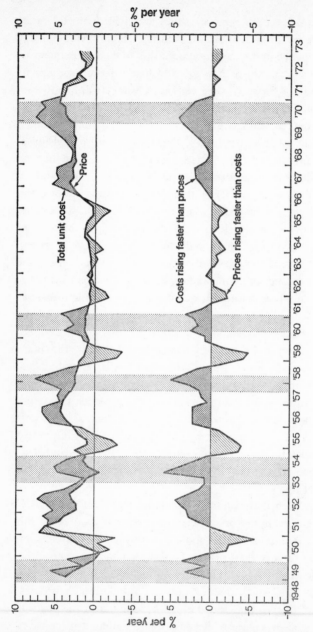

Figure 6. **Rates of change in prices and costs in the United States, 1948–73**
Source: Explorations in Economic Research, vol. 2, No. 1, Winter 1975, p. 13.
Note: Shaded areas show business cycle contractions.

costs rise more rapidly than prices. It is precisely these time lags which give rise to the political problems of carrying through a deflationary policy. During a period in which the economy is in the throes of a recession but in which inflation continues to work itself out through the system, there is invariably mounting pressure for governments to tackle the symptoms of cost inflation by the imposition of direct controls over incomes and at the same time to pursue a more reflationary monetary and fiscal policy to tackle the problem of unemployment and, via low interest rates, to provide a stimulus to recovery.

The magnitude of the recession resulting from monetary tightness will depend on the kind of monetary and fiscal policy the authorities pursue, the extent of index-linking in the labour market, the success of the government in influencing the labour market's expectation of future inflation and the initial pace of the inflation. An abrupt halt to money supply growth is the sure way to bring about a slump. Imagine that the money supply was growing at an annual rate of thirty per cent and the government suddenly decided that there would be no further growth. A policy such as this would put an enormous strain on an economy; a severe credit squeeze would lead to a great number of firms becoming bankrupt and heavy unemployment. The severity of the recession would be reduced if the government reduced the rate of growth of the money supply *gradually* over a period of years. In addition to this, and as we have already seen in the discussion of indexing and incomes policies, the increase in unemployment associated with monetary contraction is made less, the more ready is the labour market to revise its expectations of the future course of the inflation. Indexing achieves this result automatically in that wages will not carry on rising when inflation is past its peak. If at the time the recession starts but the rate of inflation continues to rise, the labour market could be prevailed upon voluntarily to reduce wage demands, then once again the severity of the recession would be eased. At such a time as this there may at least in principle be a case for a statutory prices and incomes policy which prevented the labour market from voluntarily expressing its collective judgement regarding the course of future inflation. Such a policy would be for an unspecified period of time and ideally totally comprehensive. The temptation however for any government which introduced such a policy would be to extend and transform it into a comprehensive prices and incomes policy which became a substitute for, and not an appendage of, a strict monetary policy. And if the government did continue with a tight money policy, the benefits of a freeze would still have to be weighed against the increased inefficiency which such a policy produced.

Any government which pursued such a restrictive monetary policy would be bound, given its international implications, to maintain a floating exchange rate; that is, unless of course other countries simultaneously pursued similar deflationary policies. If a country were successful in reducing its money supply growth and continued to maintain a fixed exchange rate, it would find itself under great pressure to continue with such a policy. Foreign investors would wish to place funds in the country because of the likelihood of an exchange rate appreciation and domestic investors would wish to borrow overseas because of the domestic credit squeeze. Either way the central bank would find itself having to cope with an inflow of funds much greater than was desirable, in that it would inflate the base of the money supply and in turn the money supply itself.

So far we have said nothing specifically of fiscal policy or the size of the public sector deficit. Because fiscal policy has an impact on short-term economic activity it is desirable that fiscal policy should not be expansionary at a time when monetary policy is contradictory. It is also desirable for another reason. If the public sector is in substantial deficit it is that much more difficult for the government to finance its deficit in a non-inflationary way; that is, without it being held by the banks as an additional asset to match a corresponding increase in their deposit liabilities. Most of the occasions on which governments substantially increase the money supply are also times when they find it exceptionally difficult to finance a deficit in a non-monetary manner. The real case however for a deflationary monetary and fiscal policy is not simply that it works, and that a convincing explanation of the process by which it works can be provided, but that, in the final analysis, there is no alternative. Manpower policies, controls, indexing and prices and incomes policies are ultimately no substitute for orthodox monetary policy. Some of these may be useful if carried out in conjunction with monetary policies but in themselves they will never be able to control inflation. The acid test at this point is not theory but evidence. Is there any evidence that inflation has ever been brought to a halt without a reduction in the rate of growth of the stock of money? That, it seems to me, as we consider the case for orthodoxy, is the key question we have to answer. We shall return to it later.

The evidence on deflation

The general relation between money, real income and price changes was discussed in chapter 7. It is still worthwhile, however, to examine those specific periods in the United Kingdom over the post-war years when money supply growth slowed down noticeably. Three stand out especially: the squeeze of 1955–6, the post-devaluation experience of 1969–70 and the 1974–6 deflation.[1]

The only post-war period in which there was a sustained fall in the UK money supply was from early 1955 to mid-1956. In early 1955 there were all the signs of a crisis: the rate of inflation appeared to be rising unchecked and the pound was under great pressure. The government, with Mr Macmillan as Chancellor, decided to fight the inflation primarily by monetary means and hence by controlling the growth of the money stock. At the beginning of 1956 real output fell sharply but gradually recovered when the money supply started to grow again. Money supply growth, however, over the next two years was very gradual and industrial production did not dramatically rise above its level at the end of 1955 until the end of 1958. The remarkable fact about this episode however is that despite the monetary contraction of 1955 prices continued rising until 1958 when they reached a peak at which they stayed until the end of 1960. This episode suggests a long lag between a change in monetary policy and its subsequent impact on the price level; a minimum of two years and more likely three. The fact of the long lag and the puzzle it presented to the government was one of the major reasons why the Radcliffe Committee on the working of the monetary system was set up in 1957.

The second major deflation was in the period 1969–71. Despite the devaluation of sterling in November 1967 the balance of payments was in even greater deficit throughout 1968 and monetary policy in particular very easy. The change in policy was dictated by the IMF and, under the Chancellorship of Mr Roy Jenkins, M_3, which had grown up between 9 and 10 per cent in 1968, in 1969 grew by $2\frac{1}{2}$ per cent. For most of 1969 real money balances were falling, but they rose over the whole of 1970 and the first quarter of 1971 at an annual rate of about 2 per cent, during which period nominal money supply growth rose at about 10 per cent. The initial effect of the monetary slow-down was to halt the growth of real output. From the third quarter of 1969 to the first quarter of 1971 there was hardly any growth in industrial production; and, needless to say, unemployment rose. This period is frequently cited as one which supposedly discredits monetarism. It is true that once again the rate of inflation was not affected for something like two years after money supply growth had reached a peak. Yet inflation reached a peak of just over 10 per cent in mid-1971 and kept falling for the next eleven months to a rate of just under 6 per cent.

The present cycle of deflation is yet another example of a similar pattern. Money supply growth reached a peak towards the end of 1973. Throughout 1974 the rate of growth of M_3 has declined, albeit extremely unevenly: in the first six months of the year the authorities effected a savage deceleration in the growth of M_3 which was partly corrected by an increase in the second half of the year.

Already we have seen the dramatic impact which this credit squeeze has had on asset prices – the equity market slumped to 150, the longer-term interest rate on gilts rose to an unprecedentedly high figure of eighteen per cent, and house and property prices fell sharply from their peak of 1973. And what is true for the UK is true for all advanced countries in the Western world, as money supply growth has over the past two years been successfully halted in various countries. Equity markets have been depressed, interest rates have reached new peaks and the prices of those assets which have been used as hedges against inflation, such as primary products, metals and gold have all fallen dramatically.

Following on from the effect on asset prices in the UK, companies have found themselves caught in a liquidity crisis, and some firms, such as Court Line, and fringe banks like London and County have been forced into liquidation. And lastly, real output growth has also been checked and unemployment is rising gradually. In other words the present cycle is behaving in a comparable manner to others of the post-war years. It would be totally unrealistic to expect any dramatic effect in curbing inflation until the end of 1975. But there is equally no reason why, on the basis of past evidence, the rate of inflation should not fall towards the end of 1975 and throughout 1976, providing money supply policy remains at its current rate of growth.

A similar pattern emerges from these various episodes. A reduction in the rate of growth of the money supply has an initial impact on real output, usually within a period of six months to a year. As a result, unemployment starts to rise and unfilled vacancies to fall. The squeeze has an effect on the rate of inflation but this is usually a process which takes approximately two years. There is no evidence from the behaviour of the UK economy over the post-war years which suggests that inflation can be reduced without a check to real output and a rise in unemployment. But it is important to notice that both the slowdown in the real growth of the economy and the higher unemployment are only temporary phenomena. They are never permanent and when monetary policy is eased it invariably provides a stimulus to real output growth and the level of employment.

It is sometimes suggested that there are ways by which inflation can be controlled without affecting the real growth of the economy. A frequently quoted example is Brazil, which managed to reduce its rate of inflation from over a hundred per cent in 1964 to around fifteen per cent in 1973, supposedly without jeopardizing its high growth rate.[2] However, the four years 1963–6 were years of inflation and relative stagnation. For the previous decade the industrial growth rate had been approximately ten per cent, yet from 1963–6 real output grew by only three per cent per year; and over the same years the price level more than quadrupled. The fact that Brazil had a growth rate of three per cent over these four years may seem high by our standards, but by Brazilian standards it was a clear deviation from a higher long-term rate of growth of the economy. If this particular episode in Brazil suggests anything, it is that a government which tries to control inflation by fits and starts may well produce a worse state of affairs than one which either determines to live with a high but steady rate or one which determines without any caveats and vacillation to bring it down to a more acceptable figure. What happened in Brazil from 1963–6 was that one government would embark on a deflationary monetary policy, realize a reduction in the rate of growth of real output and then reverse the policy because of its consequences, even though, because of the long time-lags with respect to prices, the rate of inflation itself had not been reduced. With a succession of stop-go policies such as this the rate of inflation continues unchecked, the economy stagnates and the economic climate becomes dominated by uncertainty which has an adverse effect on industrial investment.

A question which is sometimes asked is 'How much unemployment do we need in today's world to get rid of present inflation of twenty per cent plus?' Even if the rate of inflation were less, the question would still remain valid and interesting, about this country and elsewhere. The straightforward depressing answer is that no one knows exactly. On the most recent evidence one thing we can say is that when unemployment had risen to between three-quarters of a million and a million in 1970–1 there was a noticeable fall in the rate of inflation. The idea therefore, which is sometimes suggested, that unemployment will have to rise to between two and three million before there will be a noticeable reduction in the rate of inflation is totally without foundation. The Korean War led to an inflation in the United Kingdom in 1951–2 of between 8 and 9 per cent in the growth of wages and unemployment in 1952 of only 1·1 per cent. In 1953 the rate of wage increases fell to between 4 and 5 per cent, but unemployment was 1·6 per cent. The mid-fifties, 1955 and 1956, experienced wage increases of between 7 and 8 per cent, a substantial increase, but unemployment in 1956 was as low as 0·9 per cent. To reduce the rate of inflation to 2·5 per cent in 1958, unemployment rose to 1·5 per cent and continued rising throughout 1959 to 2·3 per cent after which it began to fall. The recent experience of the United Kingdom is no different; the magnitudes are larger than in the 1950s but there is no difference of principle. An escalating inflation in 1967–8 led to the adoption of very cautious monetary and fiscal policies and so unemployment increased in the winter of 1971–2 to 3½ per cent. And the present position is no different.

The problem of unemployment

The major objection to the implementation of monetary and fiscal policies as a way of dealing with inflation is that it invariably leads to higher unemployment, which is considered intolerable from an economic, social and moral viewpoint. From an economic point of view it seems wasteful to have to reduce the growth rate of an economy and have men and machines idle which could be producing real GNP. From a social point of view it is a disruptive force, producing inequality and unrest. If, in addition, it is localized and more widespread among certain groups it tends to produce conflict and possibly violence. From a moral point of view, it is frequently argued that employment is a basic right and something which every state has the responsibility to provide.

In the post-war years the avoidance of unemployment – at least above a certain number, which has tended to grow throughout the period but which has nevertheless always been arbitrary – has been the dominating objective of macro-economic policy. The reason for this was the experience of the 1930s. From 1930 to 1935 unemployment averaged 18·5 per cent and in 1932 it reached 22 per cent. The events of this period had a profound impact not only on those who lived through it but also on the preferences of subsequent generations. What was especially damaging about the unemployment of the period was its involuntary character. Even if people moved from one part of the country to another or from one kind of employment to another, the opportunities for work were severely limited. More than anything else it was this aspect of the 1930s which was so depressing and which formed the basis of Keynes' *General Theory*.

A powerful case can be made for the argument that the kind of unemployment which we have at present is radically different from that of the 1930s and that as a consequence it is misleading to use such a statistic as an indicator of hardship, poverty and economic misery, and consequently as the basis for designing macro-economic policy.[3] In the first place the unemployment of the post-war years is primarily the result of structural factors within the economy and especially the labour market and not a deficiency of aggregate demand. Even though we have had three decades of full-employment, measured unemployment has still never fallen below one per cent. Between 1972–4, in one of the greatest booms ever in our history and certainly the greatest boom of the post-war years, measured unemployment hardly ever fell below ½ million.

In the second place, much of the unemployment of the post-war years has been voluntary rather than involuntary. The idea that unemployment may be voluntary seems a perverse notion against the background of the mass unemployment of the Great Depression. Yet in a fully employed society such as ours, there are numerous reasons why people may choose to be unemployed for certain limited periods of time; they may be in the process of moving from one job to another; those entering the labour force for the first time are hesitant about commiting themselves to a particular kind of work; they may be temporarily laid-off because of a strike either elsewhere in the firm or some industry; those in industries such as tourism and construction may only have seasonal employment; and others such as dockers and actors may only have work at certain periods. For all these kinds of situations, more generous redundancy payments and unemployment compensation will tend to increase the duration of those unemployed and so raise the average level of unemployment.

In this connection the UK experience in 1966 is an interesting piece of suggestive evidence. Before 1966 unemployment compensation was paid as a flat rate, with an additional flat rate allowance for dependents. In September 1966 new legislation came into effect by which, in addition to the flat rate, a fairly generous earnings-related supplement was paid. In the month that the scheme was introduced the number registered as unemployed was 340,000. In October the figure rose to 436,000 and in November 543,000. While it would be wrong to attribute the whole of this dramatic increase to the increased unemployment benefits because of changes in overall demand management, it must surely have played a significant role. It is also interesting to note that unemployment averaged 1·7 per cent between 1956 and 1966, but rose to 2·6 per cent between 1967–71. In addition after this change the inverse relationship between unfilled vacancies and unemployment benefits broke down. Also of interest is the fact that after the change unemployment rose proportionately more among skilled married workers, who would have most to benefit, than among lower paid unskilled workers. In addition, the duration of average unemployment is significantly higher after 1966 than before.

Another feature of the new unemployment is that it has a different duration than the old. In the 1930s the pressure of unemployment was most severe on those families in which the father had been out of work for not just months but years. In *Full Employment in a Free*

Society Beveridge quotes statistics showing that in 1929 only 5 per cent of the unemployed had been out of work longer than one year and 90 per cent for less than six months. By 1932 16 per cent had been unemployed for longer than a year and only 70 per cent for less than six months and by 1936 the figures reached 25 per cent and 65 per cent respectively. This is in marked contrast to the post-war years in which on average between 1948 and 1974 46 per cent have been unemployed for less than eight weeks.

Facing up to unemployment

Although the rise in unemployment associated with combating inflation is temporary and although present unemployment compensation is earnings-related and not ungenerous, we still have to face up to the problem of structural unemployment. A whole range of policies have been advocated to restructure the labour market to improve the short-term Phillips trade-off or over the longer term to reduce the natural rate of unemployment. They are usually referred to as 'manpower' policies and include, *inter alia*, schemes for job retraining, improving the efficiency of employment exchanges, increasing the mobility of the labour force and removing restrictive practices in the labour market.

In considering various anti-inflationary policies which are discussed in this section, namely manpower programmes, prices and incomes policy and the monetary and fiscal policy, an important distinction should be made between those policies which accept the structure of the labour market as given and attempt to change aggregate demand, so that the economy moves from one point to another along the Phillips curve, and those policies which attempt to change the institutions of the labour market and so shift the Phillips curve itself, or, in a Friedmanian framework, reduce the natural rate of unemployment. Manpower policies are part of this latter category. In pursuing an anti-inflationary policy there is of course no reason why a government should be restricted in its choice to using only one of these policies.

The basic theory which underlines the structural approach starts from the premise that what is typically referred to as the labour market is made up of numerous distinct markets which differ from one another because of geography, occupation and the characteristics of workers. Unemployment in the aggregate will change depending on how many workers quit their jobs, the extent to which firms hire and fire labour and the amount of new workers who are seeking work. Therefore total unemployment will be determined by the turnover rate of labour in particular jobs, the speed with which unemployed workers can be matched with job vacancies, the growth of the labour force and the growth of aggregate demand. In addition to this the rate of inflation associated with a particular level of unemployment will depend not only on the aggregate total but also on its dispersion between markets. In such a situation the Phillips curve will be shifted further to the right. The reason is not difficult to see. Because the Phillips curve is a non-linear downward sloping relation, the rate of wage inflation in those markets with low unemployment will be proportionately greater than the lower rate of wage inflation associated with markets with higher unemployment.

Given the existence of these imperfections in the labour market, manpower policies are an attempt (a) to increase the amount of information in and between various markets and to reduce the time which it takes a worker to search for a job and an employer for labour; (b) to improve the quality of the match between job and worker so that the job turnover rate is that much less, by modifying the nature of jobs to fit the available force; (c) to promote the mobility of the labour force between different regions of the country; (d) to remove barriers to entry and exit into and out of particular jobs, such as the need for licences, discrimination and the restrictive practices of trade unions; (e) to reduce labour shortages in certain markets by retraining; and (f) to reduce unemployment in those markets and regions in which it is greatest and so, by the last two measures, to reduce the dispersion of unemployment rates in different markets throughout the economy.

One of the ways in which the UK government has attempted to increase the efficiency with which information is disseminated in the labour market is through the Employment Service. In fact the OECD claimed that 'it should be recognized that the Employment Service is the single most important tool to ensure the proper functioning of the labour market and that it has a crucial role to play in the Government's programme of revitalizing the British economy'.[4] At present the Service has about a thousand offices and is concerned not only with the payment of unemployment benefits but also with the registration of persons for employment, filling vacancies requested by firms, providing information about job opportunities, recruiting people for industrial rehabilitation and vocational training programmes, resettlement of members of the armed forces and occupational guidance for adults, such as wives who wish to enter the labour force. Local authorities also run the Youth Employment Service which attempts to provide information and vocational guidance for school leavers about employment opportunities and which helps to secure openings as well. In the mid-1960s, however, the Employment Exchanges only accounted for a quarter of all placements.

As a consequence of this, plus the fact that labour market bottle-necks continue to persist, the Employment Service has come under a good deal of criticism. Apart from the obvious need of ridding itself of the dole queue image it is claimed that it needs more suitable offices, and more staff – particularly highly specialized staff – especially in those areas of labour surplus. By contrast with other countries the total expenditure devoted to the service is not great. In relation to total government expenditure the resources devoted to this field in Canada, Sweden and Norway are considerably greater. Various American advocates of manpower policies have urged the nation-wide computerization of data concerned with the matching of jobs, workers and services. While this would not be possible for all of the employment service functions, it would noticeably improve those concerned with the supply of information. As a consequence, un-employed workers in depressed regions of the country, would have detailed information about employment opportunities throughout the UK, and similarly firms with unfilled vacancies, would have detailed knowledge of the potential labour force.

Throughout the post-war years imbalances in the labour market, as evidenced by the shortage of certain skills, have continued to persist. Even when unemployment has been high in the aggregate, and especially high in certain regions, there have still been job vacancies which continue to be unfilled because of untrained man-power. One particular reason that is frequently claimed for this is the apprenticeship system, which tends to be rigid in duration regardless of the skills needed for a particular trade, tends to exclude women, supports a rigid structure of wages and permits the development of a narrow set of skills quite unsuited to our rapidly changing economy. The object of subsidized training and retraining programmes is to so improve workers' skills to meet current demand, so that for any given rate of inflation the associated level of unemployment would be that much less; by reducing the amount of structural unemployment the short-run Phillips trade-off is once again displaced to the left. Retraining programmes do involve a cost to society in the form of the foregone output of the worker when he is being retrained. However, from empirical studies which have been undertaken of retraining it appears that the benefits, measured in the form of the worker's increased productivity capacity, far outweigh the costs.

The major government-sponsored retraining which occurs in the UK is provided through the Government Training Centres. Until the early 1960s these were largely concerned with helping workers with special resettlement problems but since that time they have been more concerned with the alleviation of shortages in certain skills. Between 1962 and 1971 the capacity for retraining afforded by these Centres increased five times. By July 1971 there were fifty-two Centres capable of training about 20,000 persons per year. Most of the retraining is to do with skilled workers, for a period of not usually longer than six months. Under the Industrial Training Act of 1964 the government also attempted to improve the efficiency of retraining within the private sector by enabling the cost of retraining to be more evenly spread across firms. Each industry has an Industrial Training Board which assesses the manpower requirements for the industry and then imposes a levy on firms within the industry, which is then given a grant to operate approved courses in certain firms.

Although the retraining system has expanded rapidly in the last decade it can be severely criticized. The capacity for retraining is still small relative to the needs of the labour force; more than one-half of the entrants are already employed prior to retraining, so that it tends to improve on existing skills rather than deal with the problems of the unemployed; the training programmes which are offered are far too narrow, with little opportunity for semi-skilled and operative training; the capacity for retraining is under-utilized, especially in certain areas; the expansion of Government Training Centres since 1962 has been largely in development areas, even though the areas of labour scarcity have been elsewhere; and the extent of co-operation between employment exchanges and the GTCs is poor. As a result there has been a demand for an extension of the service, greater flexibility in the programmes offered, retraining particularly during recessions to reduce cost, extension to areas of labour scarcity as well as supplies, better financial incentives for retraining and the payment of government retraining grants to private industry to assist on-the-job retraining, with the prospect of such grants being varied by industry and by region.

The Industrial Training Act of 1964 has come in for even severer criticism. While the Act has led to an increase in training, raised the technical quality of training and possibly allocated the cost of training more equitably among firms, it does not provide additional funds for training; although economic theory suggests that government subsidies in this field should go to individual workers for general retraining, funds are at present being given to firms rather than workers. In addition to this the Act is criticized because it attempts to improve the overall level of training in firms without subjecting the investment in particular types of training to cost-benefit analysis. Yet another criticism of the Act is that it attempts to replace the market by planning and it is held that the optimal amount of training would be provided if industrial training were left to the decision of the individual firms within the industry. The obvious policy conclusions which emerge are that Industrial Boards should be more concerned with the economic rather than technical aspects of training and that the levy/grant system should be scrapped and replaced by one in which funds are channelled directly to workers.

Apart from lack of information and inadequate training, another reason for an unacceptable inflation-unemployment trade-off is the immobility of workers between different regions of the country. If the regional dispersion of unemployment were reduced the rate of inflation associated with a particular unemployment total would also be reduced. Policy measures have been introduced therefore which attempt to increase geographic mobility by reducing the costs of transport and relocation between regions. At present certain classes of workers are able to obtain free fares, 'settling-in grants', accommodation expenses if they are temporarily settled away from their homes, and small grants for removal under Transfer Schemes. These apply to unemployed workers and those likely to be redundant in a few months, key workers needed to set up new undertakings and unemployed workers from development areas for retraining.

The most important impediment to geographic mobility, however, is the shortage of housing. Although at present the problem is being tackled by attempting to persuade local authorities not to discriminate in favour of local residents, to reduce the cost of house purchase for low-paid workers, and to further subsidize local authority house-building programmes the evidence of success is not very great. Along with housing, the other serious barrier to geographic mobility is the lack of transferability of pension plans.

16 Inflation in Iron Curtain countries

'It is not at all my view that this array of bottlenecks is a cause for gloom or discouragement. On the contrary, the fact that we see so many bottlenecks is evidence that we are expanding our economy.'

Herbert Morrison (1946)

The major conclusion which has clearly emerged from the last two chapters is that in a market economy there is no costless way of controlling inflation. Although prices and incomes policies may conceivably have some effect in reducing inflationary expectations, and manpower policies may be used to improve the efficiency of labour markets, neither are an alternative to deflationary monetary and fiscal policies. From the available evidence it seems that inflation cannot be controlled within the framework of a system of free markets, without both a temporary rise in unemployment and a temporary check to the rate of growth of the economy. Instead of accepting this fact as an inevitable consequence of a market economy and then attempting to devise policies which both reduce the cost and ensure that the burden is borne more equitably, some argue that the only real alternative facing us is to abandon the commitment to a market economy, as the Iron Curtain countries have done, and move to a more centrally planned economy with greater state ownership and greater government intervention in the running of industry. The main appeal of such a change in policy is that it would then be possible to successfully avoid both inflation and unemployment.

The extent of inflation in Iron Curtain countries

In contrast to Western capitalist countries, Iron Curtain countries have experienced remarkably little inflation over the past decade.[1]

On average the rate of inflation has been just one or two per cent a year, though there have been important differences between countries. In one category of countries, the centrally planned Soviet-style economies such as Bulgaria, East Germany, Czechoslovakia, Poland and Russia, the rate of inflation has averaged no more than one per cent a year. In East Germany and Russia the official index of retail prices which stood at 100 in 1961 still remained at 100 in 1973! Over the same period the rate of inflation in Bulgaria and Czechoslovakia was just under one per cent and in Poland and Rumania just over one per cent. Although it has different structural characteristics, the Chinese record of inflation is very similar to this group of countries. A distinction is usually made between these countries and Hungary, which is considered since the reforms of 1968 (the 'New Economic Mechanism') as a model of market socialism. These reforms gave individual enterprises much greater freedom to fix prices independently of the central planning authority, detailed central planning over individual enterprises' outputs and inputs was abandoned, the central bank's detailed control of enterprises' use of cash balances was dispensed with, and certain prices have been freed altogether, though average (but not individual) wages are tightly controlled. Until the reforms the Hungarian rate of inflation was approximately the same as the Soviet group, but since then it has increased to about three per cent a year.

The third kind of Iron Curtain country, and the one we know most about, is Yugoslavia.[2] It also happens to have a far higher rate of inflation and unemployment than any other. It differs from other socialist countries in that the enterprises are owned and managed by the workers and the banking system is more comparable to that of a capitalist country. The objective of the system is that prices should be partly determined by market forces and partly by social contracts between enterprises. Since 1966 the average rate of inflation in Yugoslavia has been 11·6 per cent. In 1971 it was 16 per cent, in 1972 17 per cent and in 1973 20 per cent. This is in spite of the fact that there have been considerable attempts at price controls. For example, an act passed in 1972 gave the federal government responsibility for controlling agricultural produce prices, most industrial prices and rail prices for cargo, and the republics responsibility for the prices of rail and bus passenger services, electricity rates, construction materials, local government rents, utilities and retail food prices. Over the same period the money supply has been expanding rapidly. Between 1968 and 1973 the average percentage increase in the money supply was just over 25 per cent and in 1972 it reached 42·6 per cent.

If we examine the earlier experience of Soviet-style countries we find that their experience of inflation has been far more varied. For example, during the reconstruction period in Poland (1947–9) the average rate of inflation was 7·2 per cent and during the period of intensive industrialization (1950–3) it was 10·3 per cent. In the Soviet Union, for which we have more available data, there was considerable inflation during the pre-Second World War period and during the war itself. Between 1928 and 1940 the prices of consumers' goods sold in state and co-operative stores rose about twelve-fold, the prices of consumer goods in the *kolkhoz* markets (in which collective farms and peasants dispose of their surplus produce) by a factor of more than twenty and the prices of basic industrial products by about two and a half times. According to one of the most carefully constructed indices (the Moorestein-Powell index) consumer prices almost doubled between 1933 and 1936 (from 54·5 to 94·2) and continued rising until the outbreak of war. Both official and unofficial price indices record a considerable inflation during the Second World War despite the existence of substantial controls. Between July 1941 and July 1943 prices of the main products sold in the kolkhoz market increased by a factor of 18·7. According to another calculation, using a weighted index of prices charged in the state and kolkhoz markets, prices increased by 325 per cent between 1940 and 1945. The pent-up inflationary pressure of the war was removed by the currency reform of December 1947, in which old rouble notes were exchanged for new rouble notes at an exchange rate of ten to one. After the reform consumer goods' prices, whether measured by prices in state stores or in kolkhoz markets, declined steadily till 1954, and have remained stable since then.[3]

One major problem about using official price indices from Iron Curtain countries to measure the extent of inflation is their reliability. If prices are fixed by government edict and if they are unresponsive to conditions of excess demand and supply, then using such indices as a measure of inflationary pressure is a meaningless exercise. In an open inflation excess demand manifests itself in rising prices but in a repressed inflation it manifests itself in the form of queues, rationing, shortages and black markets. One of the real problems in interpreting the evidence from these countries is to know to what extent, especially since the mid-fifties, the inflation has in fact been repressed.

Certainly there is *prima facie* evidence which suggests that there is an element of repression. Those countries which register the lowest rate of inflation, such as East Germany and Russia, are also those countries in which most prices are fixed centrally, while in a country such as Yugoslavia, which has a high rate of inflation, pricing decisions are most de-centralized. In addition to this there is a good deal of evidence of shortages, queues and black markets in various commodities and services in all Soviet-style economies over the last two decades. Of necessity much of this is anecdotal and taken from a variety of sources and eye-witness accounts. Again, when Hungary introduced the various economic reforms in 1968 the rate of inflation doubled from 1·5 to 3 per cent over a fairly short period of time and most observers conclude that this was the result of relaxing price controls. Because kolkhoz prices rise sharply in response to excess demand, and over the past decade there have been some bad harvests which would have produced dramatic excess demand, the Soviet Union has suppressed this part of its official price statistics. Apart from the embarrassment of the evidence there seems no conceivable reason why they should have taken such a measure.

In view of the inadequacy of official data, Sovietologists in the West have devoted themselves to devising alternative measures of inflationary pressure. These have included the construction of alternative price indices which more accurately reflect the true transactions price, such as the ratio of prices in the kolkhoz market, which are unregulated, to those in state retail outlets, the overhang of liquid balances and savings deposits which reflects 'forced savings', because of the non-availability of goods which can be purchased, the behaviour of inventories and the relationship between budget surpluses and the expansion of short-term credit. The purpose of this last indicator is that it is an attempt to measure money supply increases; the extension of credit will increase bank deposits while budget surpluses will reduce them, so that the net figure will be a measure of the creation of new money. Estimates of most of these indices suggest that since 1945 there has been continuous excess demand. For example, in the Soviet Union throughout the period the ratio of prices for food in the kolkhoz markets to those in state outlets was always greater than seven, and during the periods 1950–5 and 1960–4 the difference between market and official state prices increased. F. D. Holzman who refined this index to take account of the amounts spent in the kolkhoz market found a similar result – a continuous excess demand since 1945 and an increase in inflationary pressure in the early 1950s. This index was subsequently recomputed and extended to 1971. The evidence suggested that throughout the whole period there was repressed inflation, becoming less in the late fifties, increasing in the early sixties and then remaining fairly constant.

The contention that Iron Curtain countries are characterized by repressed demand inflation has recently been challenged by Richard Portes. He assumes that if these countries were to be characterized by repressed inflation one would expect to observe a rise in the stock of money or liquid assets – the result of forced savings – and a fall in the labour participation ratio because the prices of consumer goods in free markets would become so expensive that they would create a disincentive to work. From the experience of Hungary and Poland, however, over the period 1950–70, he claims that savings were low, the labour force continued to grow, there were surpluses of various goods in state and co-operative shops and that prices on uncontrolled markets did not rise rapidly. As a consequence he concludes that in these countries and possibly in the USSR as well, the explicit rate of inflation was approximately equal to the true rate. As has been pointed out, however, there are a number of weaknesses with this thesis: despite the disincentive effects created by high kolkhoz prices there are still other factors, principally demographic ones, at work increasing the size of the labour force; the possibilities for reducing the hours worked and substituting them by leisure are limited; savings still have a value as a supplement to pensions. The crux of the issue is the extent to which people are able to buy comparable goods and services in the uncontrolled sector of the economy. To the extent that they can and do, the inflation is open, but to the extent that they cannot, it is repressed. This is ultimately an empirical question and there is certainly no reason for thinking that all Iron Curtain countries should be affected similarly. *Prima facie* evidence would suggest, for example, that the extent of repressed inflation is less in Hungary than in the Soviet Union. In all these countries, however, most Sovietologists seem to argue that if present price controls were abolished the rate of inflation would rise, but that it would still be less than in Western countries.

Causes of inflation in Iron Curtain countries

Before examining various theories of the inflationary process in socialist countries it is essential to bear in mind certain institutional features of these countries. In Soviet-style economies the government directs the composition of output in line with the plan, not simply at a national level but also at the level of individual enterprises. As a consequence it also directs inputs of labour and capital and controls the prices of outputs and inputs, including wages and interest rates. Most prices are subject to state control though there are some markets, such as the kolkhoz, which are unregulated. Although trade unions perform certain valuable functions they are not directly concerned with setting wages and in practice they do not strike. As far as the use of money is concerned the economy is divided into a cash and a non-cash sector. Cash is used primarily by the personal sector. Enterprises and collective farms pay workers in cash and most food and consumer goods are bought with cash. Transactions between enterprises rarely involve the use of currency – they usually take place through debits and credits in their accounts at the central bank. The central bank effectively controls the money supply and the total of credit extended by the banking system – which by contrast with Western countries or Yugoslavia is highly restricted and centralized. All transactions of enterprises which involve the use of cash are audited by the central bank.

Because of these institutional characteristics, discussion over the causes of inflation tends to focus on different issues than we have discussed so far in the book. The starting point for most explanations of inflationary pressure (both open and repressed) within Soviet-type economies is the difference between the expected performance of plans and the actual outcome. In many of the plans the targets are rarely achieved, mainly because of over-optimistic assumptions regarding productivity growth and the availability of resources. In fact the term given to their objective was 'overfull employment planning' so that they would ensure there was no involuntary un-employment. But if wages are paid out and the supply of money increased in accordance with the expected performance of the economy, then clearly the difference between the intended and actual output will create excess demand. One evidence of the excess demand which developed in the USSR in the 1930s was the behaviour of wage drift. For example during the first and second Five Year Plans, 1928–37, the planned increase in wages was 40 per cent, whereas the actual increase was 155 per cent. Because of the excess demand managers of enterprises use various means for increasing the effective wage they are able to pay, such as widespread upgrading of jobs, payment of bonus money for regular work etc. The evidence of the excess demand on the consumption side is the different rate of increase of prices in regulated and unregulated markets and the various characteristics of repressed inflation.

It would be difficult to interpret the experience of Soviet-type economies in terms of 'wage-push' inflation. Indeed the basic condition for such a thesis, namely the existence of powerful trade unions, is clearly lacking. At times there has been worker militancy, such as in Novocherkassk in 1962 and the Baltic ports in 1971 when a severe meat shortage led to rapid price increases and resulted in strikes and rioting. Although the authorities responded to these crises by either raising wages or reducing prices it would be difficult on the basis of such evidence to construct a theory of cost-push inflation.

It would also be difficult to argue that there is any evidence, at least up until the present, of imported inflation. Flows of hot money are not permitted because of stringent foreign exchange controls and higher import prices are not allowed to feed through into higher internal prices. If import prices are higher than planned, due to such factors as the oil producers' cartel, then the government subsidizes the commodities concerned so that their internal price is equal to that planned. Even in view of the dramatic increase in world prices in the early seventies, the United Nations World Economy Survey of 1973 commented that 'The price increases, exchange-rate fluctuations and commodity scarcities that characterized the world economy in 1973, though they obviously caused some dislocation, do not appear to have materially affected the internal economies of the socialist countries during the year'. It went on to argue, however, that 'the continued insulation of the domestic markets from outside events seems likely to become increasingly difficult to maintain, in view of the expansion of trade and the deepening economic linkages with the non-socialist world through intensified industrial and technical co-operation and long-term credit financing'.

Many Soviet economists claim a strict proportionality between the money supply and the prices level and therefore advocate a constant annual rate of growth of the money supply for the duration of the plan. There is some evidence, especially from the inter-war years, to suggest that the money supply has not been exogenous but has been adjusted to the 'needs of trade'. Regardless of the extent to which the money supply is autonomous or passive, there certainly was an excessive creation of money in the USSR during the inter-war years which created excess demand and inflation, whereas in the post-war years this has not been so. This improvement could in principle be due either to a stricter control of payroll expenditures by enterprises or a stricter credit policy by the central bank.

Of all Iron Curtain countries the experience of Yugoslavia is the most intriguing. It certainly seems plausible to argue that the present rapid inflation is the lagged result of an equally rapid expansion in the money supply, created because of the lack of control which the central bank exerts over the monetary base. Over the past decade the rate of inflation, money supply growth and the growth of real output have shown a distinctly cyclical pattern which resembles the experience of the United Kingdom and other Western countries. A rapid money supply growth in 1968 and early 1969, which reached a peak of nearly 30 per cent, first made itself felt in a rapid growth of real output in late 1968 and in most of 1969, and then in an increase in the pace of inflation from 8 per cent in 1969 to nearly 15 per cent by the beginning of 1971. However in the second and third quarter of 1969 money supply growth fell dramatically – from nearly 30 to 10 per cent. Real output growth fell sharply in late 1969 and throughout most of 1970 and the acceleration of inflation noticeably slowed down. Then throughout 1970 there was another upturn in money supply growth, to an annual rate of nearly 25 per cent, which resulted once again in a lagged increase in real output from 5 to 10 per cent and, eighteen months to two years later, in an acceleration of inflation. From the last quarter of 1970 money supply growth fell, and continued falling for about a year. Once again real output growth was checked in 1971 and the rate of inflation fell from a peak in the late summer of 18 per cent to less than 15 per cent by the spring of 1972. Since 1971 money supply growth has risen to a rate of nearly 50 per cent, industrial output has responded and not surprisingly the rate of inflation has risen to new levels.

It would be difficult to find more convincing evidence than this for the monetary theory of inflation. Changes in the rate of growth of the money supply have had a clear impact on the growth of real output within the space of a year and on the rate of inflation after eighteen months to two years. Nevertheless apart from analysts in the central bank, the major cause of the inflation is held to be inadequacies in the structure of the Yugoslav economy, and in particular the slow rate of growth of the agricultural sector relative to the industrial sector and the slow growth rate of energy industries relative to those concerned with processing. The particular mechanism by which these factors influence the overall rate of inflation is via rigidities in the pricing system – especially the downward inflexibility of certain prices and the rigidity of relative prices. Because output growth in agriculture lags behind that of industrial output an increased demand for both agricultural and industrial products will lead to higher agricultural than industrial prices. But if industrial enterprises are not prepared to tolerate a relative fall in the prices of the products they produce and if the government wishes to avoid unemployment developing in the industrial sector then they will be forced to expand aggregate demand.

This is clearly one mechanism by which the central bank is forced to expand the money supply. Another is that enterprises and government agencies undertake investment projects and pursue expansionary policies without sufficient attention being paid to their economic viability. The demand for credit by enterprises has been artificially stimulated by a policy of low interest rates – over recent years, for example, discount rates have averaged between three and six per cent. As a result the banking system is put under great pressure, because the alternative would be not to grant credit and so temporarily create unemployment. To the extent that the resultant unemployment would have a specialized and regional bias this could become an important political problem because of the federal nature of the country.

The conclusion we are forced to draw therefore is that inflation in Iron Curtain countries, whether open or repressed is the consequence of excess demand brought about by the difference between intended plans and actual outcome. In Yugoslavia inflation is the consequence of excessive money creation brought about by a policy of artificially low interest rates and the political demands of regional balance.

The siege economy

Over the past decade it is probably true to say that Iron Curtain countries have experienced less inflation, even when account is taken of repressed inflation, than the market economies of Western countries. But inflation is only one aspect of economic performance, and economic performance only one way of judging society. The case against moving towards a Soviet-style situation is that the cost of reducing the explicit rate of inflation would be the erosion of economic freedom and the removal of incentives, in other words the creation of a siege economy.

By a siege economy I mean one in which markets are effectively impeded from working, so that prices are no longer free to reflect conditions of surplus or shortage. In such an economy it would be impossible for individuals, freely and legally, to enter into contracts, the terms of which, including the price, could be fixed by themselves.

A model siege economy would be characterized by widespread wage and price controls, which repressed demand inflation; norms for wage and price increases, derived from principles of natural and social justice; controls over rents, dividend payments and interest rates, and controls on the amounts which all kinds of financial institutions (banks, building societies, insurance companies) could lend to various sectors of the economy; high marginal rates of taxation on income from work, penal marginal rates of tax on the income from savings, and wealth and capital transfer taxes; import controls (in one of their many forms), export subsidies, foreign exchange controls and an effectively managed foreign exchange rate; an emphasis on planning, participation and community involvement rather than the market, as the primary mechanism for deciding what and how much should be produced; and, inevitably, the extension of public ownership, public regulation and government controls.

Many superficially appealing arguments might be advanced by a government which attempted to create a siege economy situation. As it would be introduced at a time of crisis, it would be rationalized mainly on grounds of patriotism and fairness, and even if it was recognized as a second-best situation it would nevertheless be sharply contrasted to a far worse situation, such as a monetarist economy.

A number of features however of the siege economy stand out as particularly important. In the first place the siege economy politicizes the market place. The major defence of a free market economy is that because the operation of markets are the outcome of the decisions of literally millions of workers, savers, investors and producers, it is non-discriminatory and apolitical. The siege economy is the exact opposite. Because, for example, the condition of property ownership, tenancy, and land development as well as the level of rents and the cost of mortgages are all subject to legislation, the housing market has become totally politicized, to be manipulated by politicians not to produce the most efficient market but to maximize the number of votes.

At the stroke of a pen the siege economy not only creates a vast cumbersome system of controls, licences, grants, bodies to decide on exceptional cases, etc., but it simultaneously creates an equally vast system of patronage. Can a certain firm increase their quota of raw material imports? Can another firm raise its price because of 'special factors'? Can someone else increase the rent at which their property is leased? And so on. The possibilities for political favours are enormous.

An inevitable result of such a system is corruption. If individuals cannot transact freely at terms of their own choosing then they will do so illegally. This is an explicit recognition that we are not a society of saints. In such a system the people who are harmed most are those who because of moral scruples refuse to deal at anything other than official prices.

In the second place the siege economy is a vast system of disincentives to efficiency and productivity and a positive inducement to black markets and barter. A market economy can only work because people respond to economic incentives. At higher prices producers are prepared to produce more, at higher wages the labour force is prepared to work extra hours; at higher rents landlords are prepared to lease more property; at higher interest rates savers are prepared to save more. But in a siege economy incentives no longer operate to produce efficiency. There is no point in working harder if there are no goods in the shops or if those that are displayed can only be bought by a system of rationing. There is no point in renting a room to a student in a London suburb, if it might prove impossible to terminate the contract. A siege economy is likely to be characterized by low productivity, inefficiency and low growth.

If prices are not free to respond to market forces a siege economy will also be characterized by shortages. J. R. Hicks writing on the British economy in 1947 described it as 'The Empty Economy'. The very fact that prices are below their market level creates an artificial excess demand and also reduces supply below what it would otherwise be. But the demand and the shortages are a positive inducement to the creation of black markets. If the controls and the rationing are sufficiently stringent, it will become a barter economy, in which money only passes hands through the black markets. The system then becomes a vicious circle. In the interests of justice it is necessary to keep prices 'low'. But 'low' prices are a disincentive to production and 'low' wages to work. Therefore the shortages are made even more severe. This means even stricter rationing and less incentives, which further reduces output. And so the downward spiral continues.

Because a siege economy produces shortages and therefore minimal stocks the system is especially vulnerable to labour disputes and strikes. The consumer is usually protected from the effect of many such disputes by the buffer of stocks. But if these are already low, a siege economy confers much greater power on trade unions and their actions are more readily felt.

In order to illustrate the inefficiency created by a siege economy we shall consider the experience of Britain and West Germany in the immediate post-war years and the more recent experience of Chile. While these examples by themselves cannot be used as conclusive proof against planning, they are nevertheless suggestive.

The experience of West Germany in the immediate post-war years 1945–8 and the contrast with the years after the currency reform and liberalization policies of 1948, is probably the most dramatic example of the effects of controls. The period following the end of the war was a classic repressed inflation. During the war years and earlier substantial sums of liquid balances had been built-up by savers; but they were officially 'blocked' by the authorities. At the end of the war in the American, British and French zones bank accounts were freed so that there was a surplus of purchasing power. (The freeing of these balances was equivalent to an instantaneous increase in the effective money stock.) At the same time, however, the Allied authorities continued to maintain with very little modification the Nazi system of widespread price controls and rationing. One needed a ration card or Certificate of Need (*Bezugschein*) to buy almost anything. Even prices in second-hand markets were fixed. The only uncontrollable markets were in antiques and postage stamps.

The effect of the repressed inflation plus stringent controls was the breakdown of economic incentives. *The incentive to work* fell dramatically because of (a) the physical shortages of most goods which could be bought in the shops, all of which required a ration card and (b) the extraordinarily high price (in terms of wages) of goods traded on the black market – ten cigarettes was equivalent to one week's work, a woollen overcoat to more than a year's work. Therefore the alternatives presented to the worker were absenteeism, cultivating his own small garden or dealing on the black market. Similarly there was no incentive for married women to return to work and in addition there was heavy personal taxation. *The incentive to produce* was removed because a manufacturer could not increase his labour force by paying higher wages, or his output by paying overtime or purchasing additional raw materials by paying higher prices. These could only be got by the use of licences. Taxation was also very high indeed for firms and for certain ranges of income over a hundred per cent. The objectives of the typical businessmen were to keep his business ticking over, maintain raw material stocks and keep the goodwill of his cutomers. *The incentive to save* was totally absent because there was no prospect of being able to increase future consumption through accumulating future spending power.

The creation of a system of disincentives to work, produce and save had an equally dramatic effect on industrial production and output. Despite certain shortcomings, the Index of the Volume of Industrial Production gives a good indication of the order of magnitude involved. Despite hardly any unemployment, industrial production in the Anglo-American Zones during the first quarter of 1947 was only 25 per cent of 1936. During the winter of 1946–7 the output of consumer goods fell almost to zero. Although physical damage to plant because of bombing was considerable its effect is usually overestimated. For example in the French Zone it was officially estimated that only 26 per cent of capacity was out of action for this reason; and that if a few key parts were replaced much of it could be restored. 'It seems certain that the existing industrial equipment would support a level of overall production much higher than the present figure,' commented A. M. Stamp in 1947. One of the major ways by which the tangled system of disincentives choked the economy was by creating bottlenecks resulting from shortages – this was so in the case of steel, coal, timber, transport and certain raw materials.

At the same time one of the major objectives of policy was to avoid explicit inflation. But this only had the effect of making the situation worse. As certain prices were kept down, either their supply diminished or else they were given even greater subsidies. For example, coal which cost thirty Reichmarks per ton to produce was being sold at fifteen Riechmarks per ton.

But the problem of charging higher prices to ease the situation was by no means easy. A change in the price of coal would have ramifications throughout the whole of the economy and would consequently require adjustment of most other prices. Freezing prices is one thing. Constructing an alternative to the market economy is quite another.

Because of the difference between the official and the black market price, producers had a very large incentive to supply goods to the black market. Firms employing twenty-five workers or less were in any case not subject to controls and so produced for the black market while others bartered their output either for raw materials which they could not obtain because of licences or else for consumption goods with which to pay their labour force. As a result the black market flourished and official production and commerce languished; at the same time a system of barter grew up which was comprehensive in coverage and the use of money as a means of payment declined. A German official summed up the situation:

> The switch to barter between individuals and industrial firms is so complete that the German Reichsmark currency in which the German price authorities still continue to fix their prices is practically out of action. The Control Council Law, No. 50, which imposes imprisonment for life for these crimes, in which the majority of people participate, is only regarded as a symptom of the confusion and impotence of the authorities. . . .

What a contrast to the position after the 1948 reforms. By 1951 GNP was 140 per cent of the 1936 figure, and it had more than trebled in three years.

The experience of Britain in the immediate post-war years is yet another example of a siege economy. There were credit controls, import controls, exchange controls, price controls, rationing and inflation created, as we saw earlier, by Dr Dalton's policy of cheap money.

The effects of the system were predictable. There was a clear lack of incentives – a wage structure geared to pre-1939; heavy direct taxation of wages; rationing; subsidies and price-controls. As a result the basic necessities were relatively cheap while the prices of non-essential commodities were out of reach of the majority, except for time-consuming services such as football, entertainment and travel. As a result leisure was very attractive, absenteeism was stimulated and there was little labour mobility either geographically or between skills.

The regulations and restrictions in industry produced bottlenecks and shortages, especially in manpower, coal, electricity, food and gas with certain machinery and raw materials being permanently scarce. Herbert Morrison, who was a member of the Cabinet at the time made a classic defence of the situation. 'It is not at all my view that this array of bottlenecks is a cause for gloom or discouragement.

On the contrary, the fact that we see so many bottlenecks is evidence that we are expanding our economy.'

The most dramatic period of shortage was the fuel crisis of February 1947. Numerous explanations were advanced to explain the crisis – the shortage of coal, the lack of capacity at power stations, bad weather, a shortage of transport, a rejection by the Conservatives in 1942 of a policy of fuel rationing, a confusion over responsibility between three different ministries, low output, poor administration and Dr Dalton's claim that it was 'entirely the responsibility of private enterprise in the mining industry who flitted with stocks of coal lower than ever before in our history' (despite the fact that it was post-nationalization). But the fuel crisis was just one, though the most serious, of many crises which were at heart due to the failure of planning.

The siege economy also gave rise to black markets and barter especially in food, house-repairing and clothing. One writer sums it up by saying that 'there can be little doubt that, by the middle of 1947 a large part of the British population were breaking some of the laws of which they were aware, a greater part were breaking laws of which they were not aware and a still greater part would have been prepared to break the laws if they had had the opportunity'.

The conclusion to which we are drawn therefore is that while the siege economy may suppress inflation, this is an attack on symptoms not causes, and there is no reason to believe that the basic causes of inflation could be removed at less cost than in a market economy. To the extent that it could be achieved by moving to a Soviet-style situation it could only work by undermining institutions such as trade unions, and basic practices such as the freedom to change jobs, which are an essential part of a free society.

17 Freedom in a full-employment society

'Legislatures are as powerless to abrogate moral and economic laws as they are to abrogate physical laws. They cannot convert wrong into right nor divorce effect from cause, either by parliamentary majorities, or by unity of supporting public opinion. The penalties of such legislative folly will always be enacted by inexorable time.'

John Mackay (1914)

It is now time to draw the various strands of the argument together. Our starting point has been the conviction that an inflation of the magnitude we have experienced in the United Kingdom over the last few years is a serious economic and social problem. Not only does it create inefficiency in the classical economic sense, but it also results in an arbitrary and provocative transfer of wealth, leading to greater militancy by wage earners, ratepayers and the recipients of government grants which ultimately has an unsettling effect on the whole of a society, whose claims to legitimacy are gradually (and over the last few years not so gradually) but surely destroyed. It would be serious enough if the process took place in a stable society, sure of itself and its values; the gravity of the present inflation however is that it is taking place in a society which has already thrown overboard many of those traditional values which make for restraint and decency, and which as a consequence is more vulnerable to attack from philosophies, which however superficially appealing, are fundamentally alien to it. To the extent that the change in values has taken place independently of the inflation (and I for one believe they have), the inflation has unmasked the face of a secular society come of age; and the sight is deeply disturbing.

The fact that the ultimate roots and consequences of inflation lie outside the realm of economics and the expertise of the economist should not blind us to the fact that in a proximate sense inflation is a monetary phenomenon. It is caused by governments undertaking commitments, such as arbitrarily fixing interest rates or pegging the level of unemployment, which are fundamentally inconsistent with their being able to control the rate of growth of the money stock. It can be brought under control only by reducing the rate of growth of the money stock. Although there is no logical and necessary relation between money supply growth and the size of the government deficit, there usually tends to be a strong relationship in practice. It is no accident that the unprecedentedly high money supply growth in the UK during this decade has been matched by equally unprecedented deficits on the government accounts. But it is not simply the size of the government deficit which is important. What in the long run may turn out to be of even greater importance is the size of the government sector itself. The larger the size of the government sector, the more unwieldy is government expenditure, the greater is the burden of taxation, the more likely it is that public sector prices are set by political rather than economic criteria, the easier it is for trade unions to control an industry, and the greater is the proportion of the electorate either employed by, or receiving benefits from, the government. By purposely seeking, or unwillingly acquiescing in, a greater public sector, we are stacking the cards against our being able to readily control the public sector deficit and the future growth of the money supply.

Because inflation is a monetary process it can be controlled only if the rate of growth of the stock of money is brought under control. But such a process is painful and takes at a minimum eighteen months to two years before its effects are apparent. While the cost may be reduced and the length of time shortened if money supply growth is reduced gradually rather than either abruptly, or in fits and starts, nevertheless one of the major conclusions which emerges from the monetarist approach to controlling inflation is that no painless or instant remedy exists. For this reason the control of inflation inevitably becomes a political and not simply an economic problem. If unemployment is to rise even temporarily, the electorate has to be convinced of the need to bear such a cost and have confidence that such a strategy will succeed. If in addition, the expectation of future inflation can be influenced by price and wage controls, this becomes an avenue to be exploited by those concerned with the execution of the policy. But on this issue there must still be doubts about whether or not it can have any significant effect in controlling inflation.

The crucial question then with which we conclude is whether we shall be able to successfully control the current inflation.

One possibility, and one which is frequently talked about, is a take-off to hyperinflation, such as happened in Weimar Germany or Allende's Chile. It is as well to remember that the time it took in both these countries for a moderate inflation to escalate into a hyperinflation was not long: in Germany about four years and in Chile less than three. The two conditions which appear to be necessary for such a transition – the inability of the government to raise taxes to cover its expenditure programmes and a political instability – are both absent in this country (and for that matter in many other western countries) at present. Through income tax (and more especially the fact that it is paid on a PAYE basis), value added tax, customs and excise tax rates and national insurance contributions, the government still has a viable tax base so that unless tax evasion rises on such a dramatic scale, it seems it will for some time to come. The same holds for political stability. Despite the small majorities of the present and recent governments and the increasing importance of smaller and sectional political parties, political instability is not a feature of this country at present. Although therefore the likelihood of a fairly rapid transition to hyperinflation must be rather small, there are nevertheless some disquieting features. Most important of these is the growing size of the public sector financial deficit and borrowing requirement since 1970, the public sector expenditure commitments of the present Labour government over the next four years and the refusal of the government to consider ways other than inflation and tax increases by which such programmes can be financed and the deficit reduced.

Another possibility is that we ostensibly take some action to control inflation, but that because of political pressure the policy is reversed before it has time to take effect and that we end up with the worst of both worlds, a stagnant economy accompanied by a rising rate of inflation which the government then attempts to suppress by creating a siege economy situation. One can imagine a government embarking on a deflationary monetary policy, but because of the time which it takes and the intolerable rise in unemployment which ensues in the short run, reversing its policy and reflating the economy. Inflation carries on unchecked but the real growth rate has fallen. As the inflation rises, so the government finds itself under increasing pressure to do something to cut the inflation and so it imposes price and wage controls, import controls, credit controls and controls over capital movements, so that the inflationary pressure reveals itself in ways other than increases in prices. This is in fact a clear path to a *dirigiste* economy. But if either this or rapid inflation lead to that government being defeated and unable to carry through its programmes we shall have succeeded in producing the political instability which is necessary for a take-off to hyperinflation.

The third and most hopeful prospect is a permanent reduction in the rate of inflation. A rising rate of inflation is not some inevitable law which contemporary Western democracies are compelled to observe. Inflation in this country can be mastered, providing that we have the political will to do so. One necessary condition however is that the Bank of England reduce money supply growth to approximately between five and eight per cent a year. While the control of money supply growth is essential if inflation is to be reduced, it is virtually impossible for this to be achieved at present without undertaking certain fundamental changes in economic policy. Three in particular are important.

In the first place it is vital that we revise our idea of full employment. If we persist in using Beveridge's definition – a condition of permanent excess demand in the labour market, so that there are always more jobs than can be filled by the existing labour force – then we shall never succeed in bringing inflation under control. The rejection of Beveridge's particular definition is not a rejection of full employment but of over-full employment. One of the great fallacies of post-Keynesian thought over the past three decades has been to identify full employment with some arbitrary number and then make its attainment the major objective of macro-economic policy. The paradox is that although over the post-war years full employment has been the overriding objective of policy, unemployment has risen with each succeeding recession to ever higher levels. Until there is a political commitment to stable prices and a stable economy we shall have to put up with intolerable levels of unemployment.

In the second place it will be impossible to control money supply growth unless the public sector is forced to abide by the principle of balanced budgets. Unbalanced budgets are invariably a source of inflation. The immediate priority in returning to financial discipline in the public sector must be to cut the planned growth of public expenditure, because the long-term control of inflation is inconsistent with present government policy. Next there must be a more efficient method of controlling public expenditure. In the financial year 1974–5 the planned deficit was £2·3 billion. The actual was nearly £8 billion! The present method of control which is carried out – in terms of the planned growth of public spending at constant prices – is clearly unsuited to an era of inflation because the outcome is so sensitive to errors in forecasting the rate of inflation. More important than either of these questions in the longer term is the need to restore a proper system of pricing within all areas of the public sector – the nationalized industries, housing, medicine and education. Non-economic pricing, creating as it does inefficiency and excess demand, is a sure prescription for public sector deficits and inflationary finance.

Lastly there must be a commitment to reduce the size of government itself. Earlier we argued that, in a free economy, the greater the size of government the greater the inflationary pressure to which an economy is subject. If government expenditure and involvement in the economy continues growing in Britain at the same rate and in the same manner at which it has grown over the last ten years, the government will in the not too distant future find itself forced to pursue inflationary policies, as an alternative to increased taxation, to finance its growing expenditure. If Western capitalist economies are to avoid drifting into corporatist and socialist states as the alternatives to hyperinflation, there is no long-term alternative but for the frontiers of government to be rolled back.

The road along which we as a nation are travelling at present is highly uncertain and dangerous and its destination unknown. As a result of the recent rapid acceleration of inflation we have been taken to the brink and allowed to peer over the edge. But from the incessant demands for reflation it is doubtful how many have taken advantage of the opportunity. Controlling the present inflation is a responsibility which no political leaders can shirk, because the failure to do so could prove an unmitigated disaster.

Notes and References

Chapter 1

1 Details of the extent and character of the unemployment during the 1930s are given in W. H. Beveridge, *Full Employment in a Free Society* (Allen and Unwin, 1944).
2 J. M. Keynes, *The General Theory of Interest, Employment and Money* (Macmillan, London, 1936).
3 *Report of the Committee on the Working of the Monetary System* (Her Majesty's Stationery Office, London, 1959).
4 See Axel Leijonhufvud, *On Keynesian Economies and the Economics of Keynes* (Oxford University Press, 1968).
5 Aubrey Jones, *The New Inflation* (Penguin Books, 1973). E. J. Mishan, 'The New Inflation', *Encounter*, May 1974.

Chapter 2

1 Jacques Rueff, *The Age of Inflation* (Regnery, 1964).
2 Greater detail on the UK price statistics can be found in Joan M. Harvey, *Sources of Statistics* (Clive Bingley, London, 1969).
3 *The Price Statistics of the Federal Government* (Stigler Committee) (National Bureau of Economic Research, 1961).

Chapter 3

1 A most useful analysis of secular inflation is to be found in Anna J. Schwartz, 'Secular Price Change in Historical Perspective', *Journal of Money, Credit and Banking*, February 1973, vol. V, number 1, Part II.
2 John Porteous, *Coins in History* (Weidenfeld and Nicolson, 1969), p. 13.

Chapter 4

1 See David Hume, *Of Money*, reprinted in Eugene Rotwein (ed.), *David Hume: Writings on Economics* (Nelson, 1955); Adam Smith,

An Enquiry Into the Nature and Causes of the Wealth of Nations (1776); Sir William Petty, *Quantulum cunque Concerning Money*, 1682; Irving Fisher, *The Purchasing Power of Money* (Macmillan, New York, 1920).

2 David Hume, *Of Money*, reprinted in *David Hume: Writings on Economics*, pp. 37–8.

3 David Ricardo, *On the Principles of Political Economy and Taxation*, vol. 1 (edited by Piero Sraffa) (Cambridge University Press, 1951), p. 298.

4 See R. G. Hawtrey, *Currency and Credit* (Longmans, 3rd edn. 1934); F. Lavington, *The English Capital Market* (Methuen, 3rd edn. 1934) and *The Trade Cycle* (London, 1922); Alfred Marshall, *Money, Credit and Commerce* (Macmillan, London, 1923) and *Official Papers* (Macmillan, London, 1926); D. H. Robertson, *Money* (Nisbet, London, 1922) and *Essays in Monetary Theory* (King, London, 1940).

5 Some of the earliest studies in this tradition, as well as an excellent restatement of the quantity theory, are to be found in Milton Friedman (ed.), *Studies in the Quantity Theory of Money* (Chicago University Press, 1956). Also of interest is Milton Friedman, *The Counter-Revolution in Monetary Theory*, Occasional Paper 33 (Institute of Economic Affairs, London, 1970).

6 The situation in the United Kingdom is slightly more complicated because of the definition of reserve assets. For an elaboration of this see 'Resource Efficiency, Monetary Policy and the Reform of the UK Banking System', *Journal of Money, Credit and Banking*, February 1973, Part I.

7 If we take the logs of equation (1), differentiate with respect to time, and rearrange terms, we have

$$\frac{d \log P}{dt} = \frac{d \log M}{dt} + \frac{d \log V}{dt} - \frac{d \log T}{dt}$$

that is, the rate of growth of prices equals the rates of growth of money plus the rate of growth of velocity less the rate of growth of fiscal transactions.

If we use the Cambridge form of the basic quantity equation $M = kPY$, in which k is the proportion of income demanded as money, P the price level and Y the flow of real income, we get

$$\frac{d \log P}{df} = \frac{d \log M}{df} - \left[\frac{d \log k}{dt} + \frac{d \log Y}{dt} \right]$$

that is, the rate of inflation is equal to the growth in the supply of money less the growth in the demand for money.

8 It should be noted that in *The General Theory* Keynes argued that change in interest rates would affect consumption expenditure. Nevertheless Keynesians have concentrated on investment spending.

9 International Monetary Fund *Annual Report* (Washington DC, 1970).

10 *Report of the Committee on the Working of the Monetary System* (HMSO, London, 1959), Cmnd. 827, para. 981.

11 *Ibid.*, para. 391.

12 A detailed analysis and documentation of the real-bills doctrine is to be found in B. A. Corry, *Money, Saving and Investment in English Economics 1800–1850* (Macmillan, London, 1962), chapter 5.

13 N. Kaldor, 'The New Monetarism', *Lloyds Bank Review*, July 1970.

14 A more detailed account of the empirical evidence is to be found in A. A. Walters, *Money in Boom and Slump* (Hobart Paper 44, Institute of Economic Affairs, 3rd edn. 1971); C. R. Barrett and A. A. Walters ,'The Relative Stability of Monetary and Keynesian Multipliers in the U.K.', *Review of Economics and Statistics*, 1966, and A. A. Walters, 'Money Multipliers in the U.K.', *Oxford Economic Papers*, November 1966.

Chapter 5

1 Aubrey Jones, *The New Inflation* (Penguin Books, 1973), p. 12.

2 'The Maudling Memorandum on Incomes', *The Times*, 12 September 1972.

3 *Federal Reserve Bulletin*, August 1971, p. 656.

4 Joseph Grunwald, 'The "Structuralist" School on Price Stabilization and Economic Development: The Chilean Case', in Albert O. Hirschman (ed.), *Latin American Issues: Essays and Comments* (The Twentieth Century Fund, New York, 1961), p. 96.

5 A. C. Harberger, 'The Dynamics of Inflation in Chile', in A. C.

Harberger (ed.), *Measurement in Economics: Studies in Mathematical Economics and Econometrics in Memory of Yehuda Grunfeld*, 1963; A. C. Diz, 'Money and Prices in Argentina 1935–1962', in D. Meiselman (ed.), *Varieties of Monetary Experience* (Chicago University Press, 1970); C. F. Diaz-Alejhandrino, *Exchange-Rate Revaluation in a Semi-Industrial Country: The Experience of Argentina 1955–1961*, 1965; R. C. Vogel, 'The Dynamics of Inflation in Latin America 1950–69', *American Economic Review*, March 1974.

6 F. W. Paish, *Rise and Fall of Incomes Policy* (Hobart Paper 47, Institute of Economic Affairs, London, 2nd edn. 1971).

7 E. H. Phelps-Brown, 'Labour Policies: Productivity, Industrial Relations, Cost Inflation', Sir A. Cairncross (ed.), *Britain's Economic Prospects Reconsidered* (Allen and Unwin, 1970), p. 138.

8 Aubrey Jones, *The New Inflation*, p. 30.

9 A. G. Hines, 'Trade Unions and Wage Inflation in the United Kingdom, 1893–1967', *Review of Economic Statistics*, vol. 31, October 1964, pp. 221–52.

10 D. L. Purdy and G. Zis, 'Trade Unions and Wage Inflation in the U.K.: A Re-Appraisal', in M. Parkin (ed.), *Essays in Modern Economics* (Longmans, 1973).

Chapter 6

1 A. W. Phillips, 'The Relation between Unemployment and the Rate of Change of Money Wages in the United Kingdom 1861–1957', *Economica*, November 1958, pp. 283–99. An extension and elaboration of the evidence can be found in R. G. Lipsey, 'The Relation between Unemployment and the Rate of Change of Money wages in the United Kingdom 1862–1957; a Further Analysis', *Economica*, February 1960, pp. 1–31.

2 For a rigorous presentation of this particular thesis see 'The Role of Monetary Policy', *American Economic Review*, March 1968, pp. 1–17 and David Laidler, 'The Phillips Curve, Expectations and Incomes Policy' in Harry G. Johnson and A. R. Nobay (eds), *The Current Inflation* (Macmillan, London, 1971).

3 The natural rate of unemployment is defined as that equilibrium rate which results in a Walrasian general equilibrium system.

4 This section draws heavily on Donald F. Gordon, 'A Neo-

Classical Theory of Keynesian Unemployment', *Economic Inquiry*, December 1974.

5 Michael Parkin, Michael Sumner and Robert Ward, 'The Effects of Excess Demand, Generalized Expectations and Wage–Price Controls on Wage Inflation in the UK', (University of Manchester, Inflation Workshop, Discussion Paper 7402).

Chapter 7

1 W. H. Beveridge, *Full Employment in a Free Society*, p. 18, paras. 4–5.

2 One of the best discussions of the role that trade unions play in the inflationary process is Peter Jay, 'Do Trade Unions Matter?' and the discussion following in *Inflation: Causes, Consequences, Cures* (Readings 14, Institute of Economic Affairs, London, 1974).

Chapter 8

1 D. Nichols, 'Some Principles of Inflationary Finance', *Journal of Political Economy*, 1974.

2 R. I. G. Allen and D. Savage, 'Inflation and the Personal Income Tax', National Institute of Economic and Social Research *Review*, no. 70, November 1974.

3 An excellent theoretical analysis of the impact of inflation can be found in Rueben A. Kessel and Armen A. Alchian, 'Effects of Inflation', *Journal of Political Economy*, December 1962.

4 James Tobin, 'Inflation and Unemployment', *American Economic Review*, March 1972, p. 15.

5 Harold Wolozin, 'Inflation and the Price Mechanism', *Journal of Political Economy*, October 1959.

6 Tom E. Davis, 'Eight Decades of Inflation in Chile 1879–1959: A Political Interpretation', *Journal of Political Economy*, August 1963.

7 A. A. Alchian and R. A. Kessel, 'Redistribution of Wealth through Inflation', *Science*, vol. 130, no. 3375, 4 September 1959; A. Alchian and W. R. Allen, *University Economics* (Wadsworth, California, 3rd edn. 1972), chapter 33.

8 G. L. Bach and James B. Stephenson, 'Inflation and the Redistribution of Wealth', *Review of Economics and Statistics*, vol. LVI, no. 1, February 1974.

9 *Ibid.*, p. 13.

10 E. J. Hamilton, 'Profit Inflation and the Industrial Revolution 1751–1800', *Quarterly Journal of Economics*, February 1942; W. C. Mitchell, *Gold Prices and Wages under the Greenback Standard* (California University Press, 1908); A. H. Hansen, 'Factors Affecting Trend of Real Wages', *American Economic Review*, 1925; and C. Bresciani-Turroni, *The Economics of Inflation* (Allen and Unwin, 1937).

11 See R. A. Kessel and A. A. Alchian, 'The Meaning and Validity of the Inflation-induced Lag of Wages behind Prices', *American Economic Review*, March 1960.

12 See Graeme S. Dorrance, 'Inflation and Growth: The Statistical Evidence', IMF Staff Papers, vol. XIII, 1966.

Chapter 10

1 A number of good studies of hyperinflation exist: Bresciani-Turroni, *The Economics of Inflation* (Allen and Unwin, 1937); Seymour Harris, *The Assignats* (Harvard University Press, 1930); Frank D. Graham, *Exchange, Prices and Production in Hyperinflation: Germany 1920–23* (Princeton University Press, 1930); Bertrand Nogaro, 'Hungary's Recent Monetary Crisis and Its Theoretical Meaning', *American Economic Review*, September 1948; A. J. Brown, *The Great Inflation 1939–51* (Oxford University Press, 1955); J. van Walre de Bordes, *The Austrian Crown* (London, 1924); Philip Cagan, 'The Monetary Dynamics of Hyperinflation' in Milton Friedman (ed.), *Studies in the Quantity Theory of Money* (Chicago University Press, 1956); Colin D. Campbell and Gordon C. Tullock, 'Hyper-Inflation in China 1937–49', *Journal of Political Economy*, June 1954.

2 F. K. Ringer (ed.), *The German Inflation of 1923* (Oxford University Press, 1969), p. 96.

3 Details of the Polish experience can be found in *Memorandum on Currency and Central Banks 1913–1925* (League of Nations, Geneva, 1926).

4 Ringer, *op. cit.*, p. 93.

5 Thomas Mann, 'Inflation: The Witches Sabbath', reprinted in *Encounter*, February 1975, pp. 61–2.

6 *Ibid.*, p. 61.

7 Bresciani-Turroni, *op. cit.*, p. 215.

8 Bresciani-Turroni, *op. cit.*, p. 217.

9 *Bergswerkszeitung*, 1 January 1922, quoted in Bresciani-Turroni, *op. cit.*

10 A. D. White, *Fiat Money Inflation in France* (Toronto, 1914), p. 55.

11 A. D. White, *op. cit.*, p. 56.

12 Bresciani-Turroni, *op. cit.*, p. 329.

13 A. D. White, *op. cit.*, pp. 69–70.

14 Bresciani-Turroni, *op. cit.*, p. 332.

15 Thomas Mann, *op. cit.*, p. 63.

16 See J. G. Gurley, 'Excess Liquidity and Monetary Reforms', *American Economic Review*, March 1953, pp. 76–100; and Boris P. Pesek, 'Monetary Reform and Monetary Equilibrium', *Journal of Political Economy*, October 1958, pp. 375–88.

17 This account of the Allende experience draws heavily on an unpublished paper by Carlos Rodriguez of Columbia University.

Chapter 11

1 Max Weber, *Economy and Society* (Bedminster Press, New York, 1968). An excellent and extremely readable introduction to the Weber work is to be found in Donald G. Macrae, *Weber* (Collins, 1974).

Chapter 12

1 See D. Finch, 'Purchasing power guarantees for deferred payments', IMF Staff Papers, 1956, pp. 1–22.

2 W. S. Jevons, 'A Tabular Standard of Value', Ch. XXV of *Money and the Mechanism of Exchange* (London, 1875), pp. 318–26.

3 Alfred Marshall, 'Reply to the Royal Commission on the Depression of Trade and Industry' (1886), reproduced in *Official Papers by Alfred Marshall* (Macmillan, London, 1926), pp. 9–12; Alfred Marshall, article in *Contemporary Review*, March 1887, reproduced in A. C. Pigou (ed.), *Memorials of Alfred Marshall* (Macmillan, London, 1925), pp. 188–211; Alfred Marshall, letter (1911) to Irving Fisher, reproduced in *Memorials of Alfred Marshall*, p. 476.

4 J. M. Keynes, 'Evidence Presented to the Committee on National Debt and Taxation' (1927), in *Minutes of Evidence* (Colwyn Committee) (HMSO, London, 1927), vol. I, pp. 278, 287.

5 The most powerful contemporary case for indexation is Milton Friedman's *Monetary Correction* (Occasional Paper 41, Institute of Economic Affairs, London, 1974).

6 Walter Bagehot, 'A New Standard of Value', *The Economist*, 20 November 1875, reprinted in *Economic Journal*, vol. II, 1892, pp. 472–7.

7 Sir Otto Niemeyer, dismissal of Keynes' proposal, *Minutes of Evidence, op. cit.*, vol. II, p. 633.

8 A useful survey of indexing can be found in S. A. B. Page and Sandra Trollope, 'An International Survey of Indexing and the Effects', *National Institute Economic Review*, no. 70, November 1974.

Chapter 13

1 Useful surveys of indexation in capital markets can be found in: Committee for Invisible Transactions, Capital Markets Study, *Formation of Savings*, vol. II (OECD, Paris, 1968), pp. 39–41, 97–105, 139–40, 176, 194; Committee to Review National Savings (Page Committee), *Report* (HMSO, London, 1973), Cmnd. 5273, pp. 190–8, 309–14; Committee on Financial Markets, *Indexation of Fixed-Interest Securities* (OECD, Paris, 1974); B. I. Cohen, 'The Use of indexed debts in underdeveloped countries', *Public Finance*, 1966, no. 4, pp. 441–57.

2 Some of the problems associated with indexing debt are discussed in more detail in: G. Arvidsson, 'Should we have indexed loans?' in D. C. Hague (ed.), *Inflation* (Macmillan, London, 1962), pp. 112–26; 'Reflections on Index Loans', *Skandinaviska Banken Quarterly Review*, 40–1, 1959–60, pp. 1–14; Robert Eagly, 'An Interpretation of Palander's Twin Securities Markets Proposal', *Southern Economic Journal*, July 1960, pp. 51–4, and 'On Government Issuance of an Index Bond', *Public Finance*, 1967, no. 3, pp. 268–84; G. L. Bach and R. A. Musgrave, 'A Stable Purchasing Power Bond', *American Economic Review*, December 1941, pp. 823–5; Richard Goode, 'A Constant Purchasing-Power Savings Bond', *National Tax Journal*, IV, 1951, pp. 332–40;

Peter Robson, 'Index-Linked Bonds', *Review of Economic Studies*, no. 75, October 1960, pp. 57–68 and 'Inflation-Proof Loans', *National Westminster Bank Quarterly Review*, May 1974, pp. 48–60.

Chapter 14

1 Naphtali Lewis and Meyer Rheinhold (eds), *Roman Civilization* (Columbia University Press, 1955), vol. II (*The Empire*), pp. 463–73.

2 *Acts and Resolves of Massachusetts Bay*, V, pp. 583–9; *Boston Gazette*, 3 February 1777; (Boston) *Continental Journal and Weekly Advertiser*, 6 February 1777. The wage-price relationship revealed by the Massachusetts law throws light on the question of real wages. Adam Smith in *The Wealth of Nations* observed on the eve of the Revolution that 'wages . . . are much higher in North America than in any part of England'. A rough calculation shows that in Massachusetts it took about a day's work to buy five pounds of butter, and two days' work to pay for a pair of shoes. Real wages in Revolutionary Massachusetts, though princely remuneration when compared with wages of European workers, were pitifully low by modern standards.

3 *Policies for Price Stability* (OECD, Paris, 1962), p. 23.

4 Nicholas F. G. Bosanquet, *Pay Prices and Labour in Power*, Young Fabian Pamphlet No. 20.

5 *Statement on Personal Incomes, Costs and Prices*, Cmnd. 7321 (HMSO, London, 1948).

6 *Incomes Policy: The Next Step*, Cmnd. 1626 (HMSO, London, 1962).

7 *Prices and Incomes Policy*, Cmnd. 2639 (HMSO, London, 1965).

8 *Ibid.*, p. 7.

9 See *Prices and Incomes Standstill*, Cmnd. 3073 (HMSO, London, 1966), and *Prices and Incomes Standstill: Period of Severe Restraint*, Cmnd. 3150 (HMSO, London, 1966).

10 See *Prices and Incomes Policy After 30th June, 1967*, Cmnd. 3235 (HMSO, London, 1967).

11 *A Programme for Controlling Inflation: The First Stage*, Cmnd. 5125 (HMSO, London, 1972).

12 *The Programme for Controlling Inflation: The Second Stage*,

Cmnd. 5205 (HMSO, London, 1973). *The Price and Pay Code – A Consultative Document*, Cmnd. 5247 (HMSO, London, 1973).

13 Cmnd. 5247, *op. cit.*

14 *Ibid.*

15 *Economic Report of the President*, Council of Economic Advisers, January 1971.

16 See David Smith, 'Incomes Policy', in R. E. Caves and Associates (eds), *Britain's Economic Prospects* (Allen and Unwin, 1968), chapter 3; R. G. Lipsey and J. M. Parkin, 'Incomes Policy: A Reappraisal', *Economica*, May 1970, pp. 115–38; J. M. Parkin, 'Incomes Policy: Some Further Results on the Determination of the Rate of Change of Money Wages', *Economica*, November 1970, pp. 386–401; L. Godfrey, 'The Phillips Curve: Incomes Policy and Trade Union Effects', in H. G. Johnson and A. R. Nobay (eds), *The Current Inflation*, chapter 6; K. Wallis, 'Wages, Prices and Incomes Policy: Some Comments', *Economica*, August 1971, pp. 304–10; M. Parkin, M. T. Sumner and R. A. Jones, 'A Survey of the Econometric Evidence of the Effects of Incomes Policies on the Rate of Inflation', in M. Parkin and M. T. Sumner (eds), *Incomes Policy and Deflation* (Manchester University Press, 1972).

17 L. Ulman and R. J. Flanagan, *Wage Restraint: A Study of Incomes Policies in Western Europe* (University of California Press, 1971), p. 216.

18 Frank Blackaby (ed.), *An Incomes Policy for Britain* (Heinemann, 1972), p. 362.

19 A large literature is emerging on the Nixon policy post-August 1971. It includes, *inter alia*: Barry Bosworth, 'Phase II: The US Experiment with an Incomes Policy', *Brookings Papers on Economic Activity*, 2, 1972; Robert J. Gordon, 'Wage-Price Controls and the Shifting Phillips Curve', *Brookings Papers on Economic Activity*, 2, 1972; Gottfried Haberler, 'Incomes Policy and Inflation: Some Further Reflections', *American Economic Review*, May 1972; Lloyd Ulman, 'Cost-Push and Some Policy Alternatives', *American Economic Review*, May 1972; Arnold R. Webber, 'A Wage-Price Freeze or an Instrument of Incomes Policy; or the Blizzard of 1971', *American Economic Review*, May 1972; Arthur M. Okun, 'Have Fiscal and/or Monetary

Policies Failed?', *American Economic Review*, May 1972; *Economic Report of the President*, 1972 and 1973; G. Ackley, 'An Incomes Policy for the 1970's'; H. S. Houtakker, 'Are Controls the Answer', *Review of Economics and Statistics*, August 1972.

Chapter 15

1 Greater details of these three episodes and the period from 1880 to 1960 are to be found in A. A. Walters, *Boom and Slump*, Hobart Paper 44, Third Edition.

2 See Samuel A. Morley, 'Inflation and Stagnation in Brazil', *Economic Development and Cultural Change*, vol. 19, no. 2, January 1971, and comments by J. Bowen and E. Hinshaw, J. P. Wogart and S. A. Morley in vol. 21, no. 3, April 1973; Alexandre Kafta, 'The Brazilian Stabilization Programme', *Journal of Political Economy*, 75 (August 1967).

3 See John B. Wood, 'How Much Unemployment?', Research Monograph 28 (Institute of Economic Affairs, London, 1972); Martin Feldstein, 'The Economics of the New Unemployment' in *The Public Interest*, no. 33, Fall 1973 (New York); *Lowering the Permanent Rate of Unemployment*, Study prepared for the use of the Joint Economic Committee, US Congress, 93rd Congress, 1st Session, Joint Committee Print (Government Printing Office, Washington DC, 1973).

4 *Manpower Policy in the United Kingdom 1970*, (OECD, Paris, 1970).

Chapter 16

1 Official statistics on inflation in Iron Curtain countries can be found in *The European Economy in 1973*, Economic Commission for Europe (United Nations, New York, 1974).

2 A useful source of information on contemporary features of the Yugoslav economy is the annual *OECD Economic Survey*.

3 F. D. Holzman, 'Soviet Inflationary Pressures 1928–1957: Causes and Cures', *Quarterly Journal of Economics*, LXXIV, May 1960.

Select bibliography

Ball, R. J., *Inflation* (Allen and Unwin, 1964) and *Inflation: Causes, Consequences, Cures* (Readings 14, Institute of Economic Affairs, London, 1974).

Bresciani-Turroni, C., *The Economics of Inflation* (Allen and Unwin, 1937).

Brown, A. J., *The Great Inflation 1939–1951* (Oxford University Press, 1955).

Friedman, M., *Studies in the Quantity Theory of Money* (University of Chicago Press, 1956).

Hutton, G., *Inflation and Society* (Allen and Unwin, 1960).

Johnson, H. G. and Nobay, A. R. (eds), *The Current Inflation* (Macmillan, London, 1971).

Johnson, H. G., *Inflation and the Monetarist Controversy* (De Vries Lectures, Amsterdam, 1972).

Jones, A., *The New Inflation* (Penguin Books, 1973).

Keynes, J. M., *A Tract on Monetary Reform* (Macmillan, London, 1923).

Keynes, J. M., *The Economic Consequences of the Peace* (Macmillan, London, 1920).

White, A. D., *Fiat Money Inflation in France* (Toronto, 1914).

Index